Bill 'Swampy' Marsh is an award-winning writer/performer of stories, songs and plays. He spent most of his youth in rural south-western New South Wales. Bill was forced to give up any idea he had of a 'career' as a cricketer when a stint at agricultural college was curtailed because of illness, and so began his hobby of writing. After backpacking through three continents and working in the wine industry, his writing hobby blossomed into a career.

His first collection of short stories, *Beckom (Pop. 64)*, was published in 1988; his second, *Old Yanconian Daze*, in 1995; and his third, *Looking for Dad*, in 1998. During 1999, Bill released *Australia*, a CD of his songs and stories. That was followed in 2002 by *A Drover's Wife* and *Glory, Glory — A Tribute to the Royal Flying Doctor Service* in 2008. He has written soundtrack songs and music for the television documentaries *The Last Mail from Birdsville — The Story of Tom Kruse, Source to Sea — The Story of the Murray Riverboats* and the German travel documentaries *Traumzeit auf dem Stuart Highway, RFDS Clinic Flights (Tilpa & Marble Bar)* plus *RFDS Clinic Flights (Einsatz von Port Hedland nach Marble Bar)*.

Bill runs writing workshops in schools and communities and is a teacher of short story writing within the Adelaide Institute of TAFE's Professional Writing Unit. He has won and judged many nationwide short story writing and songwriting competitions and short film awards.

Bill is the author of the very successful series of 'Great Australian' stories, including: *Great Australian CWA Stories* (2011), *New Great Australian Flying Doctor Stories* (2010), *The ABC Book of Great Aussie Stories for Young People* (2010), *Great Australian Stories — Outback Towns and Pubs* (2009), *More Great Australian Flying Doctor Stories* (2007), *Great Australian Railway Stories* (2005), *Great Australian Droving Stories* (2003), *Great Australian Shearing Stories* (2001) and *Great Australian Flying Doctor Stories* (1999). Bill's story of *Goldie* was published in 2008. *Swampy*, a revised edition of Bill's first three story collections, was published in 2012 and the compilation *The Complete Book of Australian Flying Doctor Stories* was published in 2013.

More information about the author can be found at
www.billswampymarsh.com

Great Australian
OUTBACK
SCHOOL
STORIES

Great Australian
OUTBACK
SCHOOL
STORIES

Bill 'Swampy' Marsh

ABC
Books

The story 'Five-Star Welcome' was first published in *Old Yanconian Daze* (1999) then in *Swampy — Tall Tales and True from Childhood and Beyond* (2012); 'There's a Redback on the ...' was first published in *Great Australian Flying Doctor Stories* (1999) and as a part of *The Complete Australian Flying Doctor Stories* (2012)

First published in Australia in 2013
by HarperCollins*Publishers* Australia Pty Limited
ABN 36 009 913 517
harpercollins.com.au

HarperCollins*Publishers*
Level 13, 201 Elizabeth Street, Sydney NSW 2000, Australia
31 View Road, Glenfield, Auckland 0627, New Zealand
1–A Hamilton House, Connaught Place, New Delhi — 110 001, India
77–85 Fulham Palace Road, London W6 8JB, United Kingdom
2 Bloor Street East, 20th floor, Toronto, Ontario M4W 1A8, Canada
10 East 53rd Street, New York NY 10022, USA

National Library of Australia Cataloguing-in-Publication data:

Marsh, Bill, 1950– author.
  Great Australian outback school stories / Bill 'Swampy' Marsh.
  978 0 7333 2549 6 (pbk.)
  978 1 7430 9862 2 (ebook)
  Series: Great Australian stories.
  Rural schools—Australia—Anecdotes.
  Education, Rural—Australia—Anecdotes.
  Australia—Social life and customs.
371.100994

Cover design by Christa Moffitt, Christabella Designs
Cover image by Robin Smith/Getty Images
Author photo by Elizabeth Allnut
Typeset in 10/15pt ITC Bookman by Kirby Jones
Printed and bound in Australia by Griffin Press
The papers used by HarperCollins in the manufacture of this book are a natural, recyclable product made from wood grown in sustainable plantation forests. The fibre source and manufacturing processes meet recognised international environmental standards, and carry certification.

5 4 3 2 1   13 14 15 16

Dedicated to all those amazing teachers who ventured out into small rural and outback schools throughout Australia, only to run up against little ratbags like myself.

Special thanks to — Brigitta Doyle and the editing and promotions staff at ABC Books without whose support these stories may never have seen the light of day. To the Summer All Over team of Trevor Chappell, Michael Pavlich and Angie Trivisonno-Nelson; Ian and Sheryl Parkes, The Steadman family, and my precious support crew of Kath Beauchamp, Fran Callen, Craig Langley, Margaret Loveday, Joel Shayer and Margaret Worth.

Thanks also to Great Southern Rail, especially Jessica Playford and Robyn Williamson, for allowing me the privilege to perform my stories and songs on The Ghan's ANZAC Tribute journey 2011 and 2012. Without that support I would not have been able to travel as far and as wide as I have been able to in the writing of this book.

To all those wonderful people who willingly gave of their time and shared a part of their lives with me.

Contents

Contributors

Larry Adams

Bernard Arrantash

Kathleen Beauchamp

Ross Beckhouse

Paquita Boston

Barbara Brozek

Bill Burnside

Fran Callen

Roddy Calvert

Ray Campbell

Kit Clancy

Bill Cole

Graham Cowell

John and Nancy Cox

Bob Daly

Les and Norma Davey

Joyce and Doris Davidson

Maude Ellis

Rev Bruce Gallacher

Nola & Mick Gallagher

Margaret Gibbons

James Giddings

Padre Colin Gordon

John Hammond

David Harris

Tony Hayes

Anne Hindle

John Howard

Pauline Jensen

George Joyce

Allen Kleinig

Roman Kulkewycz

Craig Langley

Margaret Lamke

George A Lee

Norrie Lochhead

Margaret Loveday

Tom Maywald

Courtney McCarthy

Bev Mezzen

Kalyna Micenko

Marny Micenko

Graeme Osborn

Frank Partington

Covey Penney

Ethel Priestly

Garry Purcell

Emily Pyman

Ray Roberts

Ray Rushby

Warren Schulz

Edwina Shallcross

Joel Shayer

Peter Simpfendorfer

Justin Steadman

Trish Steadman

Yvonne Stokes

Les Sullivan

Mary Wake

Gloria Wright ...

... and many, many more

A Blessed Childhood

Right, well I was born in Port Pirie, which is on Spencer Gulf in South Australia, and we lived in a kind of suburb of Port Pirie known as Solomontown. My father was an electrical engineer on the railways and my mum was a schoolteacher. Actually I was born on the day Darwin was bombed — February 19th 1942 — and the story goes that, upon his first sight of me, my dad went out and bought a hand pistol to protect us all from the fiendish Japanese invasion.

Another event that may be of interest was that, at about that same time, an English passenger ship had been quarantined out in the bay of Port Pirie, due to an outbreak of yellow fever. The ship's doctor just happened to be a young bloke called Gordon Stanley Ostlere and he said, 'Well, while I'm stuck out here on the ship I may as well spend my spare time writing a book.' So under the pseudonym of Richard Gordon he started writing and that was the beginning of the famous comic doctor series, with titles like *Doctor in the House* and *Doctor at Sea* which went from book form to radio, then on to film and television. They were very affectionate, charming and human stories, much like the veterinary books that James Herriot wrote.

Port Pirie was at that time, and still is, a mining town so I began my adventures in life crawling around in the dirt of our backyard. In fact, my first meals most probably consisted of mercury and cadmium and all sorts of other strange metals. Then when I was a little older, Dad was shifted within the railways from Port Pirie to Port Augusta and that's where I started my education.

Now I don't remember this but, family folklore has it that, when we first moved to Port Augusta, the railways people hadn't yet organised our housing so we lived for a while in a cave under somebody's house. That was on Hospital Road. And when we did shift into the railway house Mum did her removal bit by placing me in the pram, topping it up with pots and pans and curtains and so forth and walking her load around to our new place on the corner of Moyse Street and Spencer Terrace. That place is still there actually. It was a grand old house that I remember as having a passageway the exact same length of a cricket pitch — twenty-two yards — and there were curtains that you could pull across to separate the living areas from the bedrooms. To us, it was 'posh-oh'. It even had stuff called 'veltex' on the floors and there were strange slatted things on the windows which had the exotic name of 'Venetian blinds'.

Then because my mum was a teacher, she started working at Port Augusta Primary School. I was one of her Grade 1 students and she made me sit in the front row, upright and cross-legged, perhaps to be a shining example of just how a good pupil should behave. So I sat there, legs aching, while Mum held up pictures of all sorts of weird and wonderful animals like a cat and we'd chant 'C—A—T'. But for some reason I mustn't have proven to be the model student my mother had hoped I'd be because before long I was shifted to Mrs Brown's class.

Oh, and that's right, I remember there was a huge pepper tree in the schoolyard. The pepper tree was perfect for us kids; when you crushed its leaves they gave forth a full-blown aroma that could disguise the most incriminating of smells. It was also wonderful for climbing and, more importantly, you could take the little berries off the tree and fire them through a drinking straw. 'Wham', as straight as a die, they went for miles. Straws were readily available because back then they delivered milk in tiny bottles and the milk had a fair-dinkum layer of yellow cream on the top. The only trouble was, by the time we got to taste the milk — especially in the summer months — it was more often than not on the turn and the cream was a bit off. But we still drank it because the teachers said it was good for us and, in those days, you didn't argue with the teachers. And, of course, the milk was free and the bottles themselves had little silver caps that, when you flicked them, they'd spin through the air like little mini space ships. Of course, later generations pinched the idea from us Port Augusta kids and they called it a Frisbee, and they made a fortune.

Though, no doubt the highlight of Grade 1 was the day of the Great Night Cart Disaster. The night cart was a huge cart on wheels. It carried lots of drums and it was drawn along by a team of docile draughthorses. For those who aren't familiar: back in those days the toilets were down the bottom of the backyard, backing onto a small lane. The dunnies we used were a can and, because toilet paper hadn't yet arrived in Port Augusta, we'd wipe ourselves with newspaper. So we'd do our business in the can and then once a week the night cart would arrive to take the can away.

Accompanying the night cart would be a couple of ragged men, draped in hessian bags. They'd open a flap at the back of the toilet and remove the odoriferous can, which was, by now, swarmed by flies and inundated by redback spiders. These men would then lift the can up onto their shoulder and run up a plank and dump the doings into the drum-collection of accumulated poo and wee. And these men were strong, and they were agile. They had to be; as a child I imagined them to be a slightly desperate and mad lot who'd be found after working hours in a hotel down near the wharf, trying to numb themselves from the reality of their occupation.

But to forget their occupation would've been impossible on that fateful day — the day of the Great Night Cart Disaster — because that morning as we Protestant children gathered at Port Augusta Primary School, we looked up and saw the night cart edging its way down the hill, seemingly to be under the complete control of the docile draughthorses. Then something went awry. Something upset the long-suffering horses and they panicked, and took off, heading in our direction, and as they got to the bottom of the hill they must've thought better of galloping headlong into our Port Augusta Primary School so they did a sharp left and the cart, not understanding Newton's laws of motion, kept heading toward us under its own inertia. Then, right at the critical moment, the cart flipped over and, in doing so, the cans and their contents were flung in all directions. And us kids stood agape as we witnessed half of Port Augusta's collected doings splatter out across the road before us. It was wonderful. It was a catastrophic calamity, and all us Protestant kids, we were screaming and we were cheering and we were laughing as the men, adorned in their hessian garb, struggled, sloshed and slipped amid the muck, mayhem and now-empty drums, trying to restrain the horses. It was absolute toilet Armageddon. The most perfect start to a school day, ever.

Those were the days, just after the Second World War, when refugees from far-off places like Poland and Italy came to settle in the likes of Port Augusta and Whyalla. And many of them were Catholic. I clearly remember the first Italian I saw. It was a woman. She was out on the front beach of Port Augusta, and she had a bikini on. It was outrageous. Scandalous. Port Augusta was in a state of catalepsy at such a sight. So was I, but in a different way. To me she was the most beautiful woman I'd ever seen; her brownish skin, her dark mysterious eyes, the cigarette that hung from her plump lips, and whatever was hidden beneath that skimpy bikini caused my imagination to flip into its first hormonal cartwheel.

I believe that the arrival of the refugees also had an effect upon my mother. In many ways she was my inspiration. Our mother collected the family history: a passing parade of preachers and drunkards and insane people like artists and writers and layabouts. After Dad had passed, the dear, dear lady continued as a teacher until she was seventy, not only at Port Augusta but at various other country schools. She also wrote. Mum loved writing, and I've still got a collection of her poems, penned in the stye of Milton; wonderful odes that were part of her secret and imaginative life.

She never read any of these to me and I didn't even see them until much later, shortly before she died. It was around the same time that I caught her attempting to burn a stack of old family letters that were full of scandals and treacherous incriminations and all those things every family has. So perhaps with the realisation of her own fate, she'd decided to ditch the evidence. Oh my gosh, I would've been in my mid-forties by then, and that's when she gave me a few of her other precious treasures plus some of her poetry. Then long after she'd passed, I just happened to open one of her books of poetry and out fell an old black-and-white photograph; it was of a gorgeous Italian man and I thought, Perhaps, just perhaps, there might've been a wonderful romance there.

During my primary school years in Port Augusta many things were changing. It was the time when world-famous actors started coming to South Australia to make films up in the wilds of the Flinders Ranges; stars like the beautiful Maureen O'Hara, and the dimple-chinned Robert Mitchum, and a tall lanky bloke called Chips Rafferty who kept forgetting his lines.

They were also the days when it was such a thrill to be given the job of Ink Monitor, which allowed you the privilege of mixing the black powder in with some water, then taking it to the double wooden, iron-framed desks and filling the tiny white ceramic ink wells. It was a huge honour to be Ink Monitor. Huge.

And it was also a time where you'd sit beside your best friend, the friend you'd sat beside right from when you'd both started writing on slates. In Grade 1 and 2 we had slates and you'd wipe off your writing with rags, which were sodden and stinking of old spit. Then after you could form letters such as C—A—T you graduated to a lead pencil and you'd scrub out your mistakes with what was called a 'rubber' which, most probably due to the influx of Catholics, was later named an 'eraser'. Then once you'd mastered the vagaries of the pencil you graduated to an ink pen, with its nib so fragile that if you pressed down too hard, the nib points would cross and flick ink everywhere. And we had thick blotting paper to absorb the blotches and splotches.

My best friend's dad was a bank manager, and one day we saw a stack of blotting paper in his house so, being the enterprising sorts we were, we took it to school and started selling it. We were well on our way to making our first fortune until someone discovered that when you reused the blotting paper or scraped pencil over it, there, in mirror image, was the indented private financial statistical lives of most of the residents of Port Augusta. It was an absolute catastrophe. Almost on the scale of the day of the Great Night Cart Disaster, except this time we were at the epicentre of the mayhem. But we survived.

In a sense I had a blessed childhood — a childhood with this amazing space all around me — of being able to look up into an enormous sky that stretched forever; of the unpredictable Spencer Gulf to one side and the rugged Flinders Ranges to the other; and I'd lie in bed at night and I'd listen to the sounds of the trains leaving Port Augusta and heading west, and those trains would take my imagination by the hand and they'd lead me out across a vast continent where I'd discover the most wonderful places and experience cultures that were filled to overflowing with the most exciting, tantalising and exotic people. Little did I know of course that, in those days, the first major train stop was at a little, dusty, wind-blown, one-horse town called Kimba.

A Good News Story

My husband and I live on a station property next to the Shark Bay World Heritage Site of Western Australia. We have four children: one girl and three boys. For their primary education, apart from a short spell, I taught them all through School of the Air. Following that they completed three years of boarding at Geraldton before we sent them to Perth for their last three years. We did that just to give them a bit more 'life' exposure. And it's worked out well because, since then, they've all gone on to lead successful lives. The eldest is now a midwife. The second eldest is an Agricultural Science/Commerce graduate from the University of Western Australia. He spent two years in Port Lincoln, South Australia, as a grain merchant for a co-operative of farmers who have a joint venture with a larger grain company. He's now based in Geraldton.

Our third child, he's now twenty-three and he's an electrician supervisor for a large German-run mining company who build big reclaimers and stackers. If they show any mining footage on the television you'll usually see those big machines with a bucket-wheel that stretches out and scoops up the ore. That's a reclaimer and then the stacker stacks the ore. Well he does the wiring on them. He's a fly in–fly out worker and he's been doing four weeks on and one week off ever since he left school. Of course, apart from his natural ability, one of the other reasons the company was so keen for him to have the job was that they were of the mind that, if you came from a farming background and you went to a boarding school, you'd be able to handle just about any sort of work and conditions they required.

Our youngest son is an electrician as well. His name is Stuart and he's also a fly in–fly out worker. He's currently working on a mine near the Capricorn Roadhouse. While our second son's job is in the construction area, Stuart's is more in the maintenance area. He could be doing anything from replacing the electric motors that drive the conveyor belts to just simply changing a light globe, or he might be rewiring the internet connections or replacing and rewiring a fuse box that's burnt out.

Stuart's is an interesting story. He's dyslexic, and if he'd been taught in a conventional school I feel that he might well have fallen through the cracks. Reading and writing don't come easily to him. But because School of the Air was sympathetic to his needs and I was able to teach him for his first seven years, he did learn to manage his schoolwork, even though it was a laborious task. One way we managed was that after he'd written his original draft of schoolwork, I'd then do a proofread copy of it and we'd send both copies in to School of the Air for marking. And that worked well. Then after he completed his primary schooling he went to Geraldton where he boarded for the first three years of high school and, I must say, he had such fantastic support there. He had two support lessons a week and if he did an important exam he had a scribe with him. A scribe was a volunteer who sat with Stuart and wrote down what he dictated.

But after those three years in Geraldton it was then a real case of, well, what do we do now? The other boys had done their final two years at a fabulous school in Perth — Aquinas College — and so should we send him there, like we did with the others, or should he stay in Geraldton where he had such great support? Anyway I got in touch with Aquinas and when I explained the situation they said, 'Look we'll make an appointment for you to come and talk to some people.'

I was quite apprehensive about it all because I had the feeling that Aquinas didn't really want kids like Stuart. They were after kids who were more academically inclined, while in Geraldton the teachers were saying, 'What do you want him to go there for? We want him to stay here.' They even intimated that if he stayed on in Geraldton he had the qualities to become a school prefect. So it was a very difficult decision to make. Very difficult. But I knew how much our other boys had enjoyed Aquinas and, in particular, how beneficial it was for them to have had the experience of being a little fish in a big pond rather than, at Geraldton, being a big fish in a little pond. And they needed that sort of a challenge. It broadened their horizons.

Well I turned up at Aquinas and there I was sitting around a table with the deputy principal and the dean of students and somebody else, and it was me who virtually interviewed them. I said, 'Well, what can you do for my son?'

After our chat my husband and I, along with Stuart, decided that he should attend Aquinas, despite there being virtually no support for his learning difficulty. So, what I started doing was exactly what we'd done with School of the Air, where he wrote his original copy of schoolwork then I did an edited copy. So he'd email his work and I'd save the original copy. I'd then edit what he'd done and when he submitted his work at school, he'd submit both his original copy and the edited copy. And believe me, his original copy was quite a challenge. But the teachers were happy with that and nobody complained.

So that's what we did for most subjects and then at the end of Year 12 he won the Curriculum Council Award for Metalwork in Western Australia. That's the top prize for metalwork in the state, and it was fantastic. Yes, so I think our sending Stuart away to Perth was probably the hardest decision we've ever had to make, especially taking into consideration how his dyslexia could well have affected his high school education, and thankfully it turned out to be the right decision.

My feeling is that, even though he was given less support, it was Stuart's strength of character that made him rise to another level. In doing so he was better prepared for life after school. It was a good news story. A very good news story, and more was to follow because when he went off to do his apprenticeship he was judged 'Rookie of the Year' for his company. That was fantastic too, and it just goes to show how, in many cases, the kids who struggle at school do so because the system's not geared to their particular needs.

A Smile on their Face

This story goes back to the early 1990s when I was doing a bit of part-time teaching at a small community school just outside of Bellingen, on the New South Wales north coast. It was a pretty free and easy sort of existence which suited my 'hippie' lifestyle. At that stage I was living with some people and so, when we decided to pitch in and buy a property together, I needed to get a decent-paying job.

I also think, at that time in my life, I was really wanting to get to know some Aboriginal people and to get a closer understanding of their culture. Then one day I saw an advertisement for a teaching job, at a predominantly Aboriginal Catholic school, in the far north of Western Australia. So I applied for the position and I was then interviewed over the phone by the nun who was the school's principal. I got the feeling that they must've been quite desperate because when I asked what her expectations would be, as far as I can now recall, she said that my main objective would be to teach the children how to write their names and how to say their prayers. That didn't seem to be too much of a problem, or so I thought at the time.

'Anything else?' I asked, and I was told that, as a female member of her staff, I'd be expected to live a good clean kind of Christian Catholic life. I wasn't Catholic, but I didn't drink, so I said, 'Yes, I'll certainly be able to do that.' Mind you, that proved to be quite ironical too because, as it turned out, there were a few of the Catholic teachers who'd be out half the night drinking and carrying on. Enough said.

Anyhow I got the job and I went up there in the April and even though it was after the wet season, I'd never known such heat. Yes, it got warm in Bellingen but this was like a slow motion sort of heat. It was draining. To start with I had to share a house with a woman who worked in the mining industry. With me being a hippie, that was philosophically difficult as I was very much against the, you know, raping of the earth and all of that. But the clash of ideologies didn't come to much because for the first couple of months I'd come home from school, dead tired, and I'd fall asleep, partly due to the heat and partly from the exhaustion of teaching.

And the teaching was exhausting. Much tougher than I'd thought. At the school there would've been six or seven different classes, from Kindergarten upwards, with a staff of maybe ten, plus there were the Aboriginal teachers' aides. I had about twenty kids on my roll, though I'd be lucky if half of them turned up on any one given day. Most of the kids lived on the reserve just outside of town; then there were those from outer communities who would occasionally visit town with their families. So they'd come and go.

Initially there were a few cultural things I struggled with, like how there was a volatility about the kids. It wasn't only until later did I realise that there was a lot of subtle things going on. Just a wrong look and a fight would break out, or perhaps there was some sort of a family feud going on outside of school, or even difficulties at home with domestic problems and all that. And also, with me having come from a pretty free and easy community school, I now found myself in a restrictive Catholic school environment.

But being the creative person I am, I adapted to the situation the best I could and after a while I was given more freedom. And that's when I began to tune in more closely as to what the kids enjoyed doing. Like I didn't really have to follow any kind of curriculum or anything, so we did a lot of art. We started a garden. We grew pawpaws, we grew veggies and, because eating appealed to the kids, I decided to do cooking lessons.

With the cooking lessons and with me being a vegetarian, I avoided cooking meat. So I'd write the recipes up on the blackboard and the kids would copy them down in their books. We'd then work out what ingredients we needed and estimate how much they'd cost. We'd pool our money. I'd put some in and the kids added in whatever they could, then we'd go down to the supermarket to get whatever we required. When they got to the till they'd have to work out how much they had to pay for their items and how much change they'd get. After that we'd come back to the school where we'd write up our real costs. Then we'd go to the cooking room where they'd have to sort out who was going to do what job in the kitchen, and we'd start preparing the meal. When the meal had been cooked, before we ate, we'd all sit around a big table and give our thanks to everyone who'd been involved in producing the food. Then we'd get stuck in.

The whole process was a fun way of learning maths and the English language. By saying 'the English language', I mean they generally spoke in Kriol, which is a kind of Aboriginal English. Anyhow, the cooking project was a very communal thing to do and it was also culturally significant and appropriate.

Another technique I used was for the children to learn through playing games. I had noticed how their parents would sit around the park and play cards during the day. I thought, Okay, I'll make up cards relating to maths and literacy topics, where the kids had to match pictures to sounds or to words. I then got the kids to sit in circles and we'd play the card games, just like their parents did — and they'd be learning.

Also, when I first went up there I found that, if the Aboriginal children wrote something wrong on a piece of paper, they'd get very upset and angry about it. They'd break the pencil and they'd screw up the piece of paper and throw it in the bin and run out of the classroom. That was because they felt like a failure. It was useless giving them rubbers —

erasers. They disappeared in a flash, never to be seen again. Okay, I thought, so then what's the best way around this? So I got one of those huge wooden reel things — you know the ones they roll telephone cable and the like up in — and I slapped blackboard paint on that and they'd sit around this table and write things down with chalk. If they made a mistake, it didn't matter. They just rubbed it out with an old piece of rag. And they didn't get upset and angry any more. They didn't feel like a failure, which, mind you, is a really big thing with the Aboriginal people. It's a shame-based culture. That's why they don't take risks, and so you have to remove that element of failure for them to be able to succeed.

Then with me being a yoga teacher, we also did some yoga. As well as that I'd go out and record local Aboriginal stories. We'd sit and listen to those and write them down. After they were written down I'd then play some relevant music and ask one of the children to narrate the story in English — rather than Kriol. What I was doing may not have been totally culturally appropriate but, by using their own stories, I found that they would relate to them more easily. In doing so, they were more prepared to join in and, when that happened, I'd encourage them to dance the story, as they saw fit.

I not only wanted them to be able to write their own names and be able to say their prayers. I wanted them to go beyond that and start to enjoy the actual learning process. I really wanted them to feel that school was an okay place to come to; a place that could be fun and that had some sort of significance and relevance to their lives. To that end, we'd go on lots of excursions and they'd write up the experience in their story books. They'd do a drawing and they'd read their story out. We might have lit a fire and done some cooking, or I'd taken them down to the dam for a swim after school.

For a more cultural-based experience I would organise camps and I'd take the kids and their grandparents out to one of their outstations for a few days. The old ladies once caught a turtle and they cooked it and we ate it. We'd go for walks and, as we walked through the country, the old women would say things like, 'I was born over there, under that tree,' or they'd recall their days of running away from the police when they'd come to round them up and take them away. Back when all that 'stolen generation' business was happening, the church had provided a safe haven for these people, and they remained grateful for that. That's why they were so keen for their grandchildren to attend the church school.

Yes, things got tough at times but, in the main, they were beautiful kids. And we were getting somewhere; somewhere far greater than them just being able to write their names and say their prayers. That said, at the same time I was also starting to have difficulties with the school. Things like the principal wanting the children to come along in a clean uniform every day. I really thought the emphasis on that was wrong. Totally. I mean, it was a huge battle for them to even buy a uniform let alone wear a clean one every day.

There were also other things, like how their grandparents always carried a stick to fight off any stray dogs or to fight off the drunks or whatever. So, of course, the kids would come to school with sticks. And that wasn't allowed, and you weren't allowed to climb trees. You weren't allowed to do this, you weren't allowed to do that, and I just could not reconcile all that Aboriginal cultural stuff within the restrictive Catholic school system.

An example was: they were putting the kids away in the detention room for running away from school. To my mind, the only reason they'd want to run away from school was because they were having some sort of problem at the school. Yet if they ran away, they'd be placed in a classroom, in detention. I didn't agree with that, so one day I decided to let them play musical instruments while they were in detention. And that was frowned upon. I was accused of allowing the kids to have fun when they were supposed to be being punished. Playing music wasn't what detention was all about. I was defying the authority of the principal.

Another time I took the children outside while they were in detention and a teacher came along and said, 'You shouldn't be doing that, it's too stimulating for the kids,' and I said to him, I said, 'So, what are you saying? That the classroom can't be a stimulating place, can it?'

Oh look, I ended up stirring everyone up the wrong way, and that's what led to me being pushed out of the school. So yes, it wasn't always easy, that's for sure, but it was sad that I had to leave. Very sad, but at least I'd got across to the children that learning can be fun and that it can be relevant to them and their culture. But the greater success for me as their teacher was that, even though a lot of the kids had extremely difficult home lives, those who did come along to school did so with a smile on their face.

About George

Yes, so about George; George Craker. He's no longer with us unfortunately, but both George and I attended teachers' college in Sydney between 1958 and 1960. George came from Broken Hill. He was the son of a miner. He'd been the vice-captain of Broken Hill High School and he came down to Sydney to go to teachers' college and he was boarding in a house in Bondi. I was also at Bondi, living with my family. Initially I think George was fairly lonely. As you may be able to imagine, the Sydney lifestyle was very different from that of Broken Hill. But he was a gregarious man and once he got to know a few people, he started to enjoy the place. What also helped, of course, was that he was very active in sport. If we weren't at teachers' college we'd be kicking a football around the oval or hanging out around Bondi Beach, surfing or whatever. George and I became good mates. In fact my parents came to embrace him as, virtually, another son.

So we went to teachers' college together for those couple of years. In each intake there were six groups of thirty young men and women. Two of the groups — and these were men only — were specifically trained to work in one-teacher schools. The other four groups trained as general primary schoolteachers. George specialised in one-teacher schooling, which means of course, you're the only teacher at the school and so you have to teach all the various grades and know everything.

George's first appointment was to an amazing little place called Rufus River. Rufus River is down in the south-western corner of New South Wales. Now just a little of its historical background: back in the 1840s Rufus River was the place where a number of Aborigines were killed in retribution for the attacks they'd made on white drovers and their stock, and that infamous event came to be known as the Rufus River Massacre. Anyhow, the actual river itself is only about five or ten kilometres long and the township is set among a network of creeks and anabranches that lead into Lake Victoria. The closest place to Rufus River of any note is the town of Wentworth, which is at the junction of both the Murray and Darling rivers. From recollection, back in those days Wentworth would've been at least a good two or three hours' drive away, and along a rough dirt road. So it was quite an isolated place.

When George arrived to take up his teaching job, Rufus River was little more than a rabbitoh community. By that I mean, the families somehow survived on the money they made from killing rabbits. So it was a very poor community, and very small. I don't know what the exact population was but it couldn't have been too many because I remember George telling me about one incident. It was during an election and, as what usually happens, the school building doubled as the polling booth. At that stage George was still only about eighteen. He was too young to be a returning officer so he volunteered to be a polling clerk. Anyhow on this election day at Rufus River, when the polls closed and they started counting the votes, the local bloke, who was the returning officer, recognised every single one of the ballot papers, either by the handwriting or the cross or the order in which they'd placed their votes. So he knew exactly how everyone had voted and George reckoned that, on a few occasions, when the returning officer took a look at a ballot paper he'd burst out with, 'I told that bloody so-and-so not to vote for that particular party.' That might give you some idea as to just how small the community was: this returning officer knew everyone, and he knew everything. Well, he thought he did.

Then I can't actually remember George saying too much about the school itself other than it was within walking distance from where he lived. From what I can gather it was only tiny, say with a maximum of around ten students, and it had very limited resources. Being a primary school, the pupils' ages ranged from five to about twelve or fourteen and those few who did go on to high school had to go into Wentworth. Still, I believe George had a moderately enjoyable time with the children and he seemed to have got on quite well with the parents too.

But I do recall him describing his living conditions as 'absolutely appalling'.

The place he rented had been long-abandoned by the Main Roads Department. It wasn't much more than an old bark hut. Stuck on top of the dirt floor was built a very basic wooden pole frame structure with galvanised iron tacked on as walls and a roof. Searing hot in summer. Freezing in winter. As for his furniture, he'd been provided with a well-worn, wire-strung single bed, a dilapidated table and one wonky chair. For his cooking there was one of those old wooden stoves, which might've helped warm the shack in winter, but made the place unbearable to live in, in summer. There must've been a shower or a washroom somewhere in the place, but the loo — the toilet — was one of those long-drop types which was outdoors, and down the track a bit. And that was all he had. That was his sole residence; just this old shack with a dirt floor and a few sticks of furniture. But that was okay. At least he had a roof over his head, even if it did leak.

Though what proved to make matters worse was that, once the school day had finished at three-thirty, there were no social activities whatsoever at Rufus River so he just went back to his little shack and sat there and read. I don't even think there was a wireless in the place that he could listen to and, when I think about it, I'm now wondering if the only lighting he had was an old kerosene lamp.

But as George was soon to find out, Rufus River had a history of young men arriving there, straight out of teachers' college, and suffering mental breakdowns due to having to live such an isolated existence, and in such terrible conditions. To that end the Inspector of Schools was sent out once or twice a year to make sure George was still alive and coping. Mind you, the inspector would also perform a similar role in many of the other remote communities throughout New South Wales — but this was especially the case in Rufus River.

Anyhow George had been there at Rufus River for some months and the loneliness really started to get to him. To make matters worse, with Rufus River being set among this network of creeks and anabranches that led into Lake Victoria, the mosquitoes were eating him alive. They were making a real meal of poor old George and, if the mozzies weren't enough to try and cope with, then came the frog-mating season. Hundreds of frogs. Thousands of frogs. And with it being mating season all these frogs became extremely active, particularly at night.

George said that when all these frogs got together, they croaked so loud he couldn't even hear himself think, let alone catch a wink of sleep. And this catastrophic cacophony of noise went on night after night after night until one night, George found himself running around outside his hut like a crazed man, armed with a shovel, trying to kill every frog he could. Of course, it was an impossible exercise because there were just too many of them. Far too many. Plus it was pitch dark. Plus he was being eaten alive by the mozzies. So he just stood out there, a sole figure in the deep darkness and he thought, What am I doing? This's just insane behaviour. I'm going mad. It was at that point he became aware that he was going through the early stages of breaking down, mentally.

Anyhow, he somehow managed to last out the school year there. In those days, the inducement from the Department of Education was that if you'd survived a year or two in a remote area, they'd appoint you to a more favourable location. And that's what happened. Fairly soon after Rufus River, George was appointed to Frederickton, on the north coast of New South Wales, near Kempsey. By then he'd met a woman and they'd married. So George and his new wife headed off to Frederickton.

When they arrived they were shown to the little house that was kept especially for the new teacher. That was a relief. It looked great. Yes, the grass and garden needed work because no one had lived there for some time. That wasn't a problem. A bit of gardening would be enjoyable. So all looked good; that's until they opened the place up and discovered that the snakes, rats, spiders, mice, cockroaches, plus a variety of bats and birds and all other sorts of vermin had taken up residence inside the house. And so they then had to spend their first couple of weeks at Frederickton cleaning the place up, in an attempt to try and make it habitable. Though as George said, 'At least the place had a wooden floor.'

Amazing

My name is Bruce Gallacher. I'm a patrol minister with an organisation known as Frontier Services and I currently work out of Kununurra, in the far north-east of Western Australia. I wasn't born up here though. I'm from Malcolm Fraser's blue-blood country of Hamilton, Victoria. Malcolm Fraser being one of our past Liberal Party Prime Ministers. My early education was at Grey Street Primary. I also went to Sunday School though that didn't last too long because I was kicked out for reasons I would like not to discuss here. I always joke that I am now paying for my sins.

After I finished primary school I went to Hamilton High, but me and the school didn't get on too well so I left when I was sixteen and I got a job in a shoe store. It was around about that time my mother came to the conclusion that I was going off the rails and she suggested it might be a good idea if I joined the Presbyterian Fellowship Association, or PFA as it's known. That was an excellent move. It's why I'm here today, really. It was the start of the journey. But of course, having left school when I was in Form 3 there was a whole long process I had to go through to eventually become a minister, and at times that process was a nightmare. But I'll leave that part of my story for your book on Bush Priests.

So then we leap forward to Hughenden, in the central-north of Queensland. Hughenden's about four hundred kilometres inland from Townsville and approximately five hundred kilometres from Mount Isa. I really loved my time there. The station properties were few and far between and initially the people who lived out on those places were quite shy and wary of me. It took time. And it took work. Wherever people gathered that's where I went, and that's where I still go. I'm not a rodeo person but I went to all the rodeos and people soon learnt that I liked a chat and a beer, and that was a foot in the door.

As a patrol minister I'm ecumenical in my dealings. It's got nothing to do with 'Bible bashing' or trying to convert a person to this belief or that. I don't even plug the Uniting Church. If I do a wedding or a baptism, yes, it's within the Uniting Church, and that's fine. But my main role these days tends to be more pastoral, which means there's a lot of counselling. It's all about getting to know people and gaining their trust and being an ear to their concerns. That's what I'm about. If someone dies I always make myself available, plus there's still isolation issues. Some of the women in particular still have a hard time of it out on a few of these more remote properties. What's more, quite often their husbands don't even realise they're struggling. Take an event like the annual local bush race meeting for example. Out there, gatherings like that are not just about horses. They're about people. It's a great social event. So I went to one of these annual race meetings this time but I didn't get to see one horse race because I spent the whole day being a pastor to women who just needed to talk.

I go everywhere. Another time I did a baptism out at the Prairie Hotel. Prairie's on the highway between Hughenden and Townsville. There's only the pub and a hall there and they wanted me to come and baptise nine of their kids.

'Sure,' I said.

They then found some of the old Anglican church pews and a lectern under the hall and so they polished them up and we held the baptism in the beer garden of the pub. Do you remember the poem 'A Bush Christening' by Banjo Paterson?

On the outer Barcoo where the churches are few,
And the men of religion are scanty,
On a road never cross'd, 'cept by folk that are lost,
One Michael Magee had a shanty.

Well I went through that and I got the kids to act it out, and it was huge fun. Nine kids on the trot, and I got all their names right. But typical of me, I couldn't leave it at that, could I? Then I had this flash of inspiration about how great it'd be to take a photo of these kids all lined up along the bar. So that's what we did. We got these nine kids sitting up along the bar, with the dads kneeling down behind them, holding them up. It looked good, but no, it still just didn't seem quite right, so I said, 'How about we put a stubby in between the kids' legs?'

So they did that and we took a photograph and the photo made it onto the front page of the Townsville newspaper and, I tell you, didn't the North Queensland Presbytery make a meal of that. Oh, they were up in arms. Oh, I like creating trouble. But it was a fantastic day and by doing things like that you get accepted into other arenas as well.

Another thing I did, and this was at both Prairie and Cameron Downs schools, was take them for their fortnightly Religious Education. Prairie tended to be more like your usual school but Cameron Downs was different. It was a great little community, stuck out in the middle of nowhere. The school itself was actually started by the owners of Cameron Downs Station who wanted to have a governess come and help their kids and their workers' kids with their education. So they built their own classroom. Once that was up and running they invited the surrounding station people to be part of it, and eventually the state government recognised it as a school and they supplied a qualified teacher. That was a long time ago now, and these days they have it set up with the internet and all that so they can get School of the Air and whatever.

I actually remember the first time I went out to Cameron Downs. It was just at the end of the wet season and the road was still pretty slippery, and when I arrived I said to this bloke, 'Gee,' I said, 'I thought I was going to get bogged out there on a few occasions.'

'Well,' he said, 'if you do get bogged, we'll be happy to come and get you out the first time. The second time we'll tell you that you're a bloody idiot and the third time we'll just leave you out there.'

And even though I did have a few close calls, I never had to be left out there. I never even had to be pulled out. Though many were the times, as I ploughed along the muddy road, slipping and sliding this way and that, that the guy's message was ringing loud and clear in my mind.

Anyhow when I was going out to Cameron Downs the numbers were dangerously low. I think they only had about nine children and so, to keep their levels up to where they could still qualify to have a teacher, a few extra kids came along to help boost the numbers. I think there were a couple of Kindergarten children in there somewhere, plus they'd formed some sort of a daycare thing. So while the teacher was teaching the primary-aged kids, a much younger lot might've been asleep over in the corner, in the crèche.

But I loved it, and when I came to visit I did whatever I could, just to give the teacher a bit of time off, so that she could go and do all the other stuff she still had to do. Because, as you may well know, in the current society we live in, with all the computers and all the other things that were supposed to make life easier, it's become an absolute nightmare of paperwork in these one-teacher schools. These teachers do it tough. They really do. They still have to do all of the administration work that's required of them as well as prepare and deliver seven lots of schoolwork to the seven different grades of kids.

So my role out at Cameron Downs soon ended up extending far beyond Religious Education. I didn't take on any of the actual teaching of their schoolwork of course, but I read stories to the kids. I enjoy acting and so we did a bit of drama. I could play the recorder so I helped the kids with their recorder playing. Then at the end-of-year break-up I joined in their concert. All the parents came into town. They had a big barbecue at the school, then the recorder group played and the choir sang and, with it being near Christmas, I helped the kids put on a modern-style Nativity play. It was a great night. An excellent time was had by all, and I was accepted by both the adults and the kids, and that was a really special thing. It was another step along the way.

But it's just such a different life out in some of those more remote places. People don't realise that even to get their kids to school, some of the mums have to drive miles and miles. Then of course, they have to turn around and come back in the afternoon to take their kids back home again. And at Cameron Downs school, like in many other places, there was also a horse paddock where the kids who rode to school could leave their horses. And they were all good riders. I tell you, they had to be. Out in places like that it's all hands on deck when it comes to doing jobs like the muster. Not only do the kids get involved — I've even heard of little babies having been strapped on behind their mothers when they rode out to take part in the muster.

Something else that amazed me was that, one of those kids who went to Cameron Downs, she used to drive an old ute to school. She was only about nine or ten and her dad had chocked up the accelerator, the clutch and the brake pedals so she could work them, and away she'd go. Her parents would ring the school when she left home and the school would ring back after she'd arrived. Of course she couldn't go out on the open road so she drove along the fence-line track of their property. It was amazing: there'd be this old ute coming along — a cloud of dust trailing behind — and right up there in front, all you'd see was this tiny little head bobbing up and down as she looked out through the steering wheel.

Ambidextrous

After the Second World War my father bought an uncleared housing block up at Ettalong, on the central coast of New South Wales. Then after he'd built a timber–fibro garage on the block, we moved up from Sydney to live in that. I was about eight at the time and we continued living in the garage until he'd finished building our house. And that took many years because he was still employed at the Goodyear's tyre factory in Camellia, in Sydney. So every weekday he'd either bus or drive from Ettalong to Woy Woy. From Woy Woy he'd catch the steam train down to Hornsby where he'd change onto one of the old electric red-rattlers. He'd then red-rattle it to Strathfield where he'd change trains again and go to Granville, where he'd change trains yet again to get to Camellia. And he did that for years and years.

The central coast was just being opened up back then and there were a lot of people like us up there who were building their own places. For many families it was the only way they could afford a house. But basically it was still all just dirt tracks, with a bit of a road base, that ran through the sandy scrub and so we'd just wander around in our bare feet. I don't know, it might've been because we were kids, but for some reason we didn't seem to worry about snakes or spiders or anything like that. And there were a quite few spiders there too, particularly funnel-webs. One night my mother pulled the bedspread back and there was a funnel-web curled up on the sheets.

Ettalong Primary School was a couple of miles from our place, perhaps a bit more. It was built in 1923, wooden, with the high ceilings. There were about six classrooms, with a teacher for every class. Some of the classrooms had open fires, though you rarely needed them on the central coast. It was quite a large school but it also served other towns such as Umina, which was then known as Ocean Beach. Then there was Patonga, Pearl Beach, Booker Bay. Actually the school's still standing. It's not that far from the beach and when we got a bit older we'd go down for a dip during lunchtime. We didn't worry about sharks either.

To be honest I didn't particularly like school and I blame my hang-up with maths, on the fact that, from day one, I was never taught properly. But typical of teachers back then, they just read everything straight out of the textbook and never actually taught you how to work things out.

I recall one maths teacher who I very much doubt was even capable of showing us how to work an answer out. That particular teacher was also the local Cub Master. I'd been in Cubs in Sydney and I followed it through at Ettalong, going on to became a scout leader. Cubs and Scouts were big back then. Lord Baden-Powell started the movement and I enjoyed it. And also, seeing that my father used to bring five hundred second-hand bricks at a time, on an old truck up from Sydney, my going to Cubs and Scouts was one way of escaping from the horrible job of having to clean bricks. I might've been poor at maths but I do remember that twenty-eight thousand bricks went into our house and I cleaned about twenty-six thousand of them.

The local fishing industry was also quite big back then and, next to the school, there was a sawmill that supplied wood to the local boat builders so they could build their old clinker boats. A clinker boat's the one with the overlapping wooden panelling along the sides, which was packed with cork so it wouldn't leak. The wood they used was called turpentine wood and it was perfect for boats because, if you looked after it, it was very long-lasting. Then when the school expanded, they took over the land that the sawmill was on and they gave us kids the okay to go in there to clear it. So during recess and lunch, away we went. Oh we built bonfires and cubby houses, you name it. We were the perfect demolition team. As keen as mustard, and all for nicks.

Actually, now I'm thinking about it, Simon Townsend, the feller who used to present the television programme *Simon Townsend's Wonder World*, he married the daughter of one of the local boat builders. They met when he was a cadet reporter on the *Woy Woy Herald*, then later on he took my photo after I became the top sheet-metal apprentice in New South Wales. And I did it without excelling in maths, though I did have to push myself. Oh, and Eric Worrell, the naturalist and reptile collector, he started the Australian Reptile Park up there and, as kids, we'd collect bluetongues and frill-neckeds for him and he'd pay us sixpence or a shilling per lizard, depending upon supply and demand.

Then after I finished at Ettalong Primary I went to Gosford High School. To get to Gosford, it was about a half-hour bus ride from Ettalong to Woy Woy. Then there was a three-quarter of an hour train trip up to Gosford, followed by a walk up the hill to the school. It was still all steam trains back then; you know, the old 32 Class Loco with the dog-box carriages. But there's one thing from Gosford High School that's always stuck in my mind. Back then you used to be able to buy paddle pops that were wrapped in like small greaseproof paper bags. The thing was that, if you kept these small greaseproof bags in one piece, they made fantastic water bombs. You'd just fill one up with water, twist the top, toss it and when it hit, it'd explode. Great. The ideal water bomb. Anyhow on this particular summer's day all us boys were out on the playground having a big water-bomb fight and during this fight the manual arts teacher just happened to walk around the corner and 'Splat!' — he copped one. And he wasn't too pleased about it either. 'To the manual arts room, boys.'

I'd say there would've been about sixty of us kids in all and he lined us up in two long rows. 'Out with your hands, boys,' and he grabbed his cane and he started off down one side with two cuts each, on each hand — Thwack! Thwack! Thwack! Thwack! — and when he'd reached the bottom of that line, those of us who were on the other side, we were thinking how he might've lost some of the strength in his right hand. But no. When he got down to the bottom of the line he called out, 'Don't worry, boys, I'm ambidextrous.' And he was too. He swapped hands and he came back up the other line — Thwack! Thwack! Thwack! Thwack! — and by jingoes it hurt.

Balls

Hi Swampy,

Back from our sea trip. Had a ball both on and off the ship though I must report that, contra to what I had expected, there was no visible signs of sexual activity on board. Perhaps it's because we're all too bloody old.

Have attached a sort of diary-type rundown of a couple of my school days' memories. I realise they're not from the bush but who gives a shit. Anyhow please feel free to add, subtract, or otherwise alter my writings to suit your requirements. I might add that it is all factual; that's to the best of my aging recollections. I could have gone on for another couple of years but I thought that might bore you to tears.

Good luck with the book and I look forward to hearing from you soon.

Best wishes,

Frank Partington

In February 1945 I enrolled at Hampton High School; Hampton being a suburb of Melbourne. Initially I managed very well and, even though the headmaster ran a very tight ship, he insisted there be no corporal punishment meted out and that only deprivation of liberties was to be used for misdemeanours. This was a great relief to me, especially after my previous school experiences. But one of the headmaster's pet aversions was that of students arriving late. To that end, he provided a 'late-book' and every morning, immediately after we'd marched in from assembly, all entrance doors to the school building were locked by the prefects and school captains. That is, apart from the one door near the headmaster's office, which was where the late-book was situated, right where he could see it from his office chair.

To get to Hampton High I'd catch the Carnegie Tram No. 4 at the corner of High Street and Alma Road, St Kilda. I'd get off the tram at the rail overpass in Balaclava Road and I'd walk across to Balaclava Railway Station. After a wait of two or three minutes, the Sandringham train would arrive and I'd catch that right through to Hampton, then walk the remaining half a mile or so to school. It all worked like clockwork until one particular chilly winter's morning. I'd alighted from the tram and was heading across to Balaclava Station when I heard my train cross the overhead bridge and pull into the station. By the time I'd scampered up to the platform the porter had locked the gate.

'The train's early,' I pleaded. 'Look, I got a ticket.'

But, no, he dug his heels in and he wouldn't let me onto the platform until after the train had left. So I had to catch the next train. But the thing was, I was now late for school and, as I ducked in the only open door of the school building, and was trying to sneak past the headmaster's office, a loud shout stopped me in my tracks. 'Partington, sign the late-book and write down your excuse.'

Naturally, I wrote down that I was late because my train had come early and I'd missed it. That was that. I had a decent excuse — or so I believed. Next thing I know, the headmaster walks into my classroom like he's some sort of supersleuth and he's going on to me about how the Melbourne trains are never early — never — and so it's obvious that I had already been running late before I missed the train.

'That's not correct, Sir,' I said in my own defence. 'The train left Balaclava Station early, fair dinkum.'

'Son, trains never run early,' he snapped and so the crime of being a 'liar' was also added to my already growing conviction list and I was sentenced to detention during the next sports afternoon.

Detention was held in what was called the 'detention room'. The detention room was a double classroom with sliding doors that, if need be, could be closed to make two single classrooms. It usually housed about fifty students from all classes — Form 3 to Form 6 — who'd been sentenced for a variety of misdemeanours. I among them. There was just the one supervisor in charge. Anyhow, when me and my fellow detainees arrived the next sports afternoon, up there on the blackboard was chalked twelve different sets of eight-figure numbers. Our task was to multiply those twelve different sets of numbers, by themselves, if you catch my meaning. And let me remind you, there were no calculators in those days. Now, I'd just like your readers to take a moment and give a little thought to the task of multiplying eight-figure numbers where, for instance, the last row of numbers in the expanded multiplication procedure needed seven zeros added to it before the multiplying started. Then, of course, there was also the addition. In short, it was no easy task.

Now I managed the first four sets then my brain clogged up and so I just estimated the others. Unbeknown to me there was a system in place to catch unsuspecting detainees like myself, who tried short cuts. Anyhow at 4 p.m. we were directed to write our names on our papers and pass them back to the student behind us to be marked. The minimum acceptable number was to have six correct answers. I got only two right so then I was ordered to spend another couple of weeks in the detention room attempting to solve the same mathematical problems, instead of playing sport. This certainly improved my skills at multiplication and addition. Though, my missing sport was a different matter.

I loved my sport, especially Aussie Rules. Even if I do say so myself, my ball skills were pretty reasonable and though I was a bit slow around the ground, footy was something that I aspired to at the highest level. Any perceived 'lack of talent' never entered my mind. As I said it was winter and so naturally, for my chosen winter sport I'd put my name down to play Aussie Rules. But now, due to these circumstances beyond my control, footy training had already started and so I wasn't even considered to be picked in any of our organised teams. Instead, after my stint of detention was finally over, my sports afternoons were spent playing the mindless game of 'kick-to-kick', which pissed me off no end.

Anyhow, two of my mates were into soccer and at that stage the school was struggling to get enough players to form a side. So then I went to the sports master, Mister Boil — known to us kids as 'Fester' — and I asked if I could be considered to play in the soccer team. That was okay. The change was granted and I spent the next couple of weeks in practice, trying my best to keep my hands off this strange, alien, rounded ball.

As to what happened in our school practice games: we'd have two captains and they'd take turns in picking players for their teams. By the third practice game I'd been relegated to being the last one of a team chosen, and it was a game to remember. It was played in the pouring rain. To use the term 'glue-pot' to describe the pitch would be an understatement. The mud was ankle-deep and the soccer ball resembled a round mud brick. By half-time I'd been penalised three times for picking up the ball and running with it, and twice for taking spectacular marks. I somehow got the feeling that my mates were losing confidence in me, rapidly. But with no substitutes in sight, I ploughed on regardless and late in the game the scores were locked together, nil all. Then with seconds to play I found myself wandering aimlessly around near the opposition's goal square, and when I heard the shout of 'Partington', I looked up into the sky and there was the ball, coming in my direction. My first instinct was to leap above my opponent and take yet another spectacular mark. But, no, as if they were reading my mind, my team-mates started shouting, 'Head it! Head it!' So I quickly gauged the angle that was needed for me to head the ball into the goal. I then shut my eyes and leapt into the air with my head stretched to its limit. My moment of glory had arrived.

Anyhow, I must've somehow miscalculated because, next thing, the mud-soaked ball whacked into me, just above the right ear, nearly knocking my noggin off. Such was the force of the whack of the sodden soccer ball that my legs went from underneath me. Down I went like a sack of spuds. Splat into the mud. So much for my ball skills; well, my soccer ball skills, anyway.

There was no sympathy from my team-mates either. In actual fact, they suggested that I report back to Fester and ask to be transferred back to Aussie Rules. 'No, far too late for that, son,' he said. 'It's the middle of winter now. The season's half over.' Then he had a bright idea. 'Look,' he said, 'how about I send you down to the Brighton Beach Baths to swim with the Brighton Icebergers.'

Which I did, and to my surprise, the teacher-in-charge turned out to be a nice young chap. On some real cold afternoons he'd let us go home early, though he always insisted we got properly wet first. To that end some of the lads would slowly edge their way into the water. But not me. I took my own life in my hands and chose to dive off the high tower where there was no chance of turning back once you were in mid-air. And that method of entry must've had some sort of positive effect because, later on, I ended up representing my school house in the high-diving event at our internal school sports.

But anyway, that's where I completed that particular winter. But shit it was cold. Absolutely freezing, and on those icy winter days, I swear, my testicles went into hibernation — they completely disappeared into 'brass monkey' territory — and that continued right up until I was able to excuse myself from the Brighton Icebergers and begin cricket practice.

Better than the Circus

Though slightly exaggerated, these couple of incidents happened when I was teaching at a little place on the central coast of New South Wales called Kinchela. Kinchela's a small dairying community between Kempsey and South West Rocks. There wasn't really a town there as such. Other than the school, there was just a butcher's shop and a general store and that was about it. There wasn't even a pub which is perhaps why the few mums and dads that lived in the area had so many children. I don't know, I can't be sure, but there were only about four or five families living close by and there were seventeen children in the school; that's Kindergarten right through to the end of primary school. Like I said, big families.

But it was a great little community and they were a great mob of kids. Truly great. And always willing to be of help. I remember the time we set up a small flower garden beside the pathway leading from the entrance gate to the steps up onto the single classroom. Anyhow, one time we had the school inspector coming and the flowers in this garden — well, to be honest, they weren't travelling too well. Most of them were dead and those that weren't dead were wilting. In fact the whole garden looked neglected; not quite the look that would help cause the inspector to give me a positive report. But some of the kids were bits of larrikins — particularly among the older lot — and they came up with an idea to impress this inspector feller. What they did was, they cleared up the dead and dying plants from the school garden, then they went home and they cut some gladiolas from their own gardens. Then on the morning of the school inspector's visit they brought these cut gladiolas along and they just stuck their stems into the ground to make a nice display. And it *was* a nice display, too. It looked good.

Later on that morning, the school inspector arrived and as he walked through the entrance gate, that was the first thing he saw: this small bed of gladiolas. And you could see how impressed he was. For a moment, he just stood there admiring the garden. I even thought I heard him mutter the words, 'How beautiful,' which was all fine and dandy — until it apparently got too much for him and he knelt down and plucked one of the gladiolas from out of the garden. To his surprise, instead of it being attached to any root formation, it just magically came out of the ground.

Well he wasn't too impressed with that, was he? Naturally he thought it had all been my idea. 'Not impressed, Mister Hayes,' he snapped with an uppity snarl, and strode off to the classroom. 'Not impressed at all.'

So that's just one little story. Then at the Kinchela School they had those pit toilets. You know the type — the long-drop toilets where they dig a hole and place a can with a toilet seat over the top of it. Anyhow, it had been a very dry season so the level of the waste in the toilet was down a long way; probably about five or six feet down. Well down. That was all okay and then one day, one of the little girls came up to me and said, 'Mister Hayes, Sir, there's a snake in the toilet.'

So I went down and lifted the lid and, by the filtered light that was coming through the toilet roof, I could just make out this big carpet snake, down there in the pit of the toilet. I could only see about a couple of feet of him but, from what I did see, he was as thick as your arm. Absolutely huge he was. Now I'm not too fond of snakes of any kind so I said to the kids, 'Oh, he's only a carpet snake and he's down there pretty deep so he won't hurt you.'

'No way, Sir,' came the chorus. 'There's no way we're gonna go to the toilet while there's that big snake down there.'

'All right,' I said, 'I'll just have to shoot him.'

Actually I was hoping that by suggesting I'd shoot the snake, it might put the kids off. But no, it didn't, and there came a chorus of, 'Yes, Sir.' 'Good on yer.' 'Shoot 'im, that's what me dad'd do.'

Oh, okay then. I was now in a bit of a spot. I didn't have a gun at school of course so I said to the kids, 'Well do you know who might have a shotgun?'

Again there was a chorus of suggestions, the closest being an old farmer chap who lived down the road a bit, and over the creek. My wife had taken the car for the day so the next problem was how to get there, to this chap's place. Now one of the families had about seven kids attending Kinchela and they used to ride to school, two or three on each horse. 'Can I borrow your horse?'

'Yes, Sir.'

'Good.'

But this horse was quite strange. I'd say that someone — a man — must've belted it around the head at one stage because it was as docile as anything with kids, and any of the women could catch it no problem. But with a man, it'd pull its head right back — shy away — and carry on like anything. Anyhow, with some help from the kids I managed to get the bridle on this horse, then I hopped on and I rode it about a mile or so down the road and I tied it up to a fence post near where this little boat was. Then I rowed the boat across the creek, and walked a couple of hundred yards up to the old farmer's place. Luckily he was home. I explained the situation about the snake in the school's toilet and he gave me his double-barrelled shotgun and a couple of cartridges.

'Thanks,' I said and I walked back down to the boat, rowed it back across the creek, then when I went to get back on the horse, he yanked his head right back. In doing so he snapped the reins and off he cantered. So now I had a bloody mile or more to walk back to the school. When I eventually get there, I'm not in a good mood and I stride straight over to the toilet, shotgun at the ready. Of course, all the kids have gathered about, wanting to witness the action. 'Sir, Mister Hayes, Sir, can we come in and see?'

'No,' I said.

'Oh, come on, Sir.'

I relented a bit. 'Okay then, but stand right back.'

I enter the toilet with the kids shuffling in tight behind me. 'Go on, Sir. Shoot 'im, Sir.' I lift the lid of the toilet and point the double-barrelled shotgun down into the semi-darkness. I know that the level of the waste in the toilet is quite low but, just in case there's a bit of a splash, I close the lid back down onto the barrels of the shotgun. The kids shuffle in closer behind me. One ... two ... three ... and I pull both triggers. 'Boom! Boom!' and when the gun went off, the percussion from the blast blew the bloody lid clean off the toilet. Just about hit the roof it did and, oh, what a mess.

Now while I'm on about it, here's just one more incident from the school at Kinchela that I really must tell you about. I had one student there and, when he was a couple of months shy of turning fifteen, he wanted to leave school. That was okay by me but, because he wasn't quite of school-leaving age yet, the department wouldn't let him leave. So I took him back into the school — the primary school — where he bided his last couple of months until he turned fifteen. That's only a bit of an aside to this particular story because the same young feller plays a part in what I'm about to tell you.

Anyhow, because of constant flooding in the area, the school was built about two and a half metres above the ground. There was also a part-railed fence running right around the actual school building. One day, the Hereford bull from the paddock down the road got into the school playground, came over and stood at the bottom of the stairs running up to the classroom and, no matter how hard we tried to shoo him away, he just wouldn't budge. He just stood there, which meant that the kids couldn't get outside to have their lunch.

So I got this young feller — the one I was talking about before — I got him to climb out the back window of the classroom, where he got on one of the other kids' pushbikes and he raced around to get his father to come over on a pony and drive this bull out of the playground and back into its paddock. But when his father arrived, the bull still wouldn't budge. Not an inch. It just stood there looking up at the kids in the classroom.

Plan B was to try and make the bull so angry that it would chase the pony. The idea there was that, when the bull chased the pony, the father would ride through the gate, down the road a bit and into the bull's paddock and he'd be home and hosed. So the father riled this bull up until he got him good and angry and, as the bull turned around to have a go at the pony, the father took off out of the playground, out the school gate, and up the road toward the bull's paddock, with the bull in hot pursuit.

Now a couple of hundred metres up the way there was a short lane that led into the bull's paddock. The gate was open — which was how the bull had got out in the first place — and so with the angry bull close on his heels, the father wheeled the pony down the lane and through the opened gate and into the bull's paddock. Problem was, when the father stopped and turned around, there was no bull. Instead of following the pony down the lane and back into its paddock, the bull had gone straight past and continued on, up the road.

So then the father had to turn the pony around, go back down the laneway, back out onto the road and head off in hot pursuit of the raging bull. So now, instead of the bull chasing the father on the pony, the father on the pony was chasing the bull. Of course, by then, we're all out of the classroom, watching things unfold. Anyhow, when the father finally caught up with the bull, the bull took one look at him and he must've remembered that he was supposed to be chasing the father on the pony and not vice versa. So the bull then turned around and it started to charge them. Next thing we see, back they came, but now the bull's again in hot pursuit of the father on the pony.

Oh, I tell you, just at the sight of it all, the kids, they just thought it was a huge joke. Some were cheering on the bull. Some were cheering on the father on the pony and there were those that were crippled over with laughter. 'This is better than the circus, Sir,' I heard one of the kids call out.

And it was.

Anyhow, back down the road they came with the bull in hot pursuit of the father on the pony. Through the gate and back into the bull's paddock the father went. But the bull, it didn't even bother to go through the gate; instead, it jumped clean over the barbed-wire fence and that was okay because at least he was now back in his paddock. So then the father wheeled around again and he rode back out of the paddock, shut the gate and the bull was left, running around the paddock in ever diminishing circles until it just about collapsed from exhaustion.

Oh, and these kids, they just reckoned it was the best day's fun they'd had in ages. 'Better than the circus.'

Big Bogong

My name's Ray Rushby and just before I tell you my story, I'd like to relate to you a quotation I once read about someone else's experience at school. It went along the lines of, 'Latin is a language, as dead as dead can be. It killed the ancient Romans, and now it's killin' me.' So there, that's a quote I once heard, and I reckon it's pretty true too.

Any rate, on to my story. Now I'm going to change the names of the two blokes in this story because they were piss-pots and I don't think it's fair to mention their real names because they were actually very good to us kids. Along with changing their names, I'll also have to change the name of the racehorse. Not that the racehorse was a piss-pot but because of its connection to the two blokes who were piss-pots.

Okay, well, I grew up in the Kiewa Valley area of Victoria, near Mount Beauty. Places like Tawonga and South Tawonga, Clover Flat and Bogong are all a part of the Kiewa Valley. Then there's Mount Bogong. I don't know if you've ever heard of the Bogong moths. Well these Bogong moths used to breed all up through the mountain areas around there and every now and again there'd be a huge plague of the buggers — just huge. And in them days there was no electricity for lighting or things like that; we only had candles and kerosene lanterns. So when the Bogong moths were on the fly you had to be very careful because they'd come down for the light and they'd just about swamp the place. Big buggers they were too, some of them. I'd say they'd probably get up to about four inches long and six inches wide with their wings spread out. And it's also legendary how, in the olden days, the Aborigines used to go up into the mountains and they'd have this big festival kind of thing where they'd have a good time and they'd have their initiations and their corroborees and they'd eat these Bogong moths. No, I haven't tasted one myself but I've heard that they're okay; like they won't kill you or anything like that.

Anyhow that's the area I grew up in and that's where I went to school in a little one-room building. I'd say it would've only been about thirty foot long by about fifteen foot wide — so it was small — and it was made from bush timber; like the off-cuts from the local sawmill and that. We had just the one teacher and he taught every grade from Kindergarten right through to Sixth Class. Then after Sixth Class we had to go to one of them bigger places like Tangambalanga or somewhere for our high schooling.

Yeah, so how many kids were there? Let me think. It was a fair while ago now but, from memory, there was one, two, three … I don't know, probably about twelve or fourteen kids in all I suppose and as I said they was ranging from about this high to twelve or fourteen years old or thereabouts. Back in them days you could leave school when you were fourteen, which is what a lot of us did.

Now I could go on forever but there's a bit of background to this story that I've got to tell you first, and this is where I've got to change the names. See, a bloke by the name of Bob Stephens owned a big property near where we lived in the Kiewa Valley. From my five-year-old point of view, Bob Stephens was classed as a millionaire. I don't know if he really was or not, but that's how us kids saw him. I'd estimate that Bob would've been about sixty years old or so. I mean it's pretty difficult to describe ages when you're only five years old yourself, because back then anyone who was over the age of ten was considered to be old.

So there was Bob Stephens and he was like the boss of the place; then there was Johnny Johnstone. Johnny was an ex-jockey who'd retired from the game and he'd become like Bob's best buddy, as well as being his valet, his cook, his chauffeur, his house cleaner, his butler, his drinking partner and whatever. Johnny would've been about forty, so there was a big difference of age between the two of them.

Any rate Johnny and Bob both enjoyed a drink. To be more exact, let me put it this way: they'd been known to have one or three on a hot day. Or even one or three on a cold day, for that matter. Or any day, really. And when they got on the plonk they used to argue like all hell, and then they'd start fighting. And Christ Almighty, did they fight! There'd be Bob prancing around like a world heavyweight champion, threatening to knock Johnny's block off, and Johnny would be dodging and ducking and diving and he'd be shouting at Bob, 'Yer can't even catch me, yer fat old bastard.' And Bob was a big man, you know. He was about six foot something and he weighed about fifteen or sixteen stone and there was Johnny and, of course, being an ex-jockey, he was about seven stone, wringing wet. But you know, that's just the way they lived their relationship.

So that was Bob Stephens and Johnny Johnstone. Now I don't know whether you want me to get onto the story about Big Bogong the racehorse or not, because Bob owned Big Bogong and Johnny was the jockey that'd rode Big Bogong in the Melbourne Cup.

Oh, the bull story first. Okay, so Bob owned this big property right, and he had pigs and cows and horses and dogs and chooks and ducks and just about everything else that runs around on a farm. One time, Bob bought this prize bull. Just huge it was. Now, if my memory serves me right, I think Bob paid something like two thousand pounds for the thing, which was an absolute bloody fortune in the late 1940s. But as it turned out, not only did this bull cost a bloody fortune but it was a real cantankerous bugger. Real cantankerous. So this particular time Bob and Johnny went into the pub at Mount Beauty to get on the turps, which wasn't that unusual. Bob had this big Packard car. Just beautiful it was. Do you remember those old Packards, with the radiator grille and those huge big headlights on the front?

Any rate, after they'd had a few, then a couple more, they drove back home from Mount Beauty. It was night time and they were pretty shot by then and, when they got to the front gate of Bob's property, Johnny got out of the Packard to open the gate so they could drive the car through. Now, it just so happened that the front gate of the property opened onto the paddock where Bob kept this prized bull of his and for some reason this bloody bull, it suddenly took offence at the two shining headlights on the Packard. I don't know; they might've woke it up or something, but the bull charges the car and smashes into the headlights and the radiator grille. Of course, Bob Stephens, he gets very upset about this — he loved his old Packard — and so he goes straight up to the house and he grabs his shotgun and he comes back down and 'BANG': he blows the bull's head clean off. So there's a couple of thousand quid down the drain and the Packard's in need of a hundred quid or so's repair.

So that's the story about the prized bull and the old Packard.

Okay, so Bob owned this horse I was telling you about called Big Bogong that he'd once entered into the Melbourne Cup. Now I can't exactly remember what year that was but it would've been, oh, maybe around the mid-1940s or something and from my recollection the bloody thing run last. Well if it didn't run last then it came pretty bloody close to running last. But that didn't matter because it was Bob's great claim to fame, how he'd had a horse that had run in the Melbourne Cup. Yes, even if it didn't bring home the bacon.

He was a funny old guy, Bob. I don't know whether this has got anything to do with it or not but he used to have this big walnut orchard out the back of his house and when the walnuts were ripe they'd fall to the ground and he'd pay us kids sixpence a bag to go and pick up the walnuts so he could send them off to be sold. And when you were just young kids like we were, well, sixpence to us was like, oh mate, we were bloody millionaires, just like Bob was.

But it wasn't easy money, not on your life, because the thing was that Bob also had this bloody mob of pigs roaming around the place. And mate, these weren't your normal everyday domesticated kind of pigs. No way. These were more like your real feral variety. Real savage bastards they were and, what's more, they loved walnuts. So when it was time for us kids to go and pick up the walnuts, there was this big race on between us and the feral pigs as to who got to the walnuts first. There was myself, my brother and my sister and the neighbour from down the road, young Wesley, and when we went walnut harvesting, a couple of us would be scrabbling around on the ground, picking up these bloody walnuts as quick as we could, while the others would be running around with sticks, belting the shit out of the pigs to try and keep them away from the walnuts.

Any rate, that's just a bit of an aside story about the walnuts and the feral pigs. So now do you want to hear the one about Big Bogong? Okay, well I think by that stage Bob had given up on this racehorse of his because, after it'd run near on last in the Melbourne Cup, he'd put it out to pasture and the only exercise it got was when us kids used to ride it to school. Now, I don't know how this is all going to pan out but Johnny Johnstone was a real character and I remember how, after Bob had said we could ride Big Bogong to school, Johnny turned up to give us riding lessons. It must've been a very hot day because Johnny had had a few. In actual fact, it must've been a stinking hot day because he'd had a few more than a few. In fact he was as pissed as a newt. He said, 'I've come ter give you kids ridin' lessons. First lesson's all about how to mount the 'orse.'

It was all barebacked back then of course, and so after all us kids had managed to help Johnny scramble up one side of

Big Bogong, the horse gave a couple of steps sideways — and arse over tit Johnny went and he disappeared clean off the other side of the horse. Crunch. Fair on his noggin. So we scampered around the other side of Big Bogong to check if Johnny was all right, which he must've been because he just sort of gave us a bit of a shy grin then, when we picked him up, he shook the dust off his clothes and he turned to us kids and he said, 'There yer go, kids, I jus' wanted ter demonstrate to yers about how NOT ter mount a 'orse.'

So we never got any further with our riding lessons that day because by then the heat must've been really getting to Johnny, and he decided it'd be better for his health if he abandoned classes for the day, so he staggered back off to the house, looking for Bob. Any rate, that didn't bother us kids. There was about five or six of us in all and we learnt to ride Big Bogong pretty quick all by ourselves. After that, each school morning we'd go over and we'd put a bridle on Big Bogong and then we'd all pile on — barebacked — and away we'd go, on the three miles or whatever it was to our school. Then after we got to the school house, we'd all pile off and Big Bogong would turn around and wander off back home.

But the funny thing was, right on the knocker of 3 o'clock in the afternoon, just as school finished, that horse would be back there waiting to take us kids home. And he done that all by himself. True, fair dinkum, he came back just to pick us kids up and take us back home again. You just wouldn't read about it, would you, and so that's the story of how us kids got to ride to school on a horse that had run in the Melbourne Cup.

Bird Calls

Burragate. Yes, Burragate was a village where time stood still. It was an easygoing community where the people were very countryfied. I was teaching there between 1953 and '58. Burragate's down near Eden, on the far south coast of New South Wales. To get a better feel of it, it's on the Towamba River between Eden and Bombala.

A bloke by the name of Ben Boyd opened up a lot of that area down there. Ben Boyd was a Scot who'd done well as a stockbroker in London; then he came over here to Australia around the mid-1840s. He was an entrepreneur really. He got involved in just about everything, from banking to whaling. He was also a ship owner, grazier and pastoralist. At one time he was said to be one of the largest squatters in the country, with cattle and sheep stations everywhere from the south coast of New South Wales, right through to Deniliquin, which is in the Riverina area of New South Wales, and down to the Port Phillip region of Victoria. He even ventured into politics. Anyway, as an early settler, Ben Boyd built Boydtown, just south of Eden, and he used to take his cattle up the Towamba River, up onto the Monaro.

But then things started to go bad. He had his fingers in too many pies I believe, and he got into economic strife. So he headed off overseas where he disappeared under mysterious circumstances in the Solomon Islands. Some say he was shot soon after he'd landed on Guadalcanal. Then afterwards there were rumours that he'd escaped to get away from all his money troubles. A big search was set up but they only found his belt. So you don't know, do you?

Yes, so anyway, to Burragate. Burragate was set in extremely hilly country. Very windy. Very isolated. The roads were poor. Not sealed. Some of the roads had been given names like the Snake Track and Big Jack and things like that, which might give you some idea. A heavily timbered country it was. Even when my wife and I were there, in the mid- to late-1950s, there were still two or three families involved in sleeper cutting who brought timber out of the hills with bullock teams. We had open fires at the school and bullock teams delivered our firewood. We paid something like thirty shillings for a load of wood and this fellow, it'd take him about a day to round up his bullock team and go out into the hills, then a day to cut and load the wood and then another day to come back and unload it all at the school. So it was quite a laborious job really.

I was the only teacher there at Burragate. I had around eighteen to twenty students on the roll. It was an interesting school really, in as much as it went from Kindergarten right through to the Intermediate level. It was a big spread to teach but I coped. The kiddies who were doing secondary, they did their schooling by correspondence and if something popped up during the day that they couldn't handle, my comment was, 'Look, just go on to another subject and come and see me after school and we can sort it out then.'

My wife and I, we lived right in the village, on the school grounds, in what they called a 'vested' residence. The school playground was quite large: about five acres. One memory that immediately comes to mind was when I started a vegetable garden out the back of the residence. See, most of the locals had a house cow and, of course, as I said, there were a couple of bullock teams in the town. So I offered one of the pupils a shilling for each billy cart load of manure he could deliver. Anyway my wife and I, we went away for the weekend and when we returned the whole front lawn was covered in a mountain of cow manure. I tell you, that kiddie must've got all his friends and relatives to give him a hand because he'd collected a hell of a heap of cow poo. So much, in fact, that it ended up costing me something like two pounds and, mind you, two pounds was a hell of a lot of money back in those days.

That's one thing that springs to mind. But then the big day of course was Bird Day. Bird Day was the inspiration of the Merimbula school's principal, Jack Lynch. Jack was a bit of a legend in that area. He spent something like twenty-five years at Merimbula School. Anyhow, it was a fantastic event. Always much anticipated. It was an annual bird-calling competition and all the small schools in the area would go down to Merimbula to compete. So there'd be Merimbula of course, and us: Burragate. Then there'd be Pambula. There was Wyndham, Rocky Hall, Towamba, Kiah. Then you'd also have Eden. Nethercote. You'd probably have Wolumba, I think it was. You had, oh strewth, I can see the teacher there as clear as day. The school was just out from Pambula. I'll think of it soon. There was also a place called Palestine but I can't recall if they entered in the bird-calling competition or not. But anyway, there were quite a few schools.

On the big day, other than the bird-calling competition, we also had bird-painting competitions and choirs and folk dancing. Then to finish the day off, you had your gymnastics. I got quite involved in the gymnastics side of things because I'd either somehow found, or borrowed, a vaulting horse. I'd then made a springboard, and we'd put on these gymnastic displays in the Burragate Hall. Oh, you'd see kids flying through the air in all directions. It looked quite impressive, actually.

But this Jack Lynch, he did a great job there at Merimbula and, oh, Bird Day was a big thing. Very big. All the pupils got involved and at Burragate, leading up to Bird Day, instead of hearing laughter and chattering at recess you'd hear a cacophony of bird calls echoing around the playground, with all the kiddies practising their various bird sounds. There'd be the sounds of magpies, kookaburras, wonga pigeons, owls, whip birds, doves, crows and gulls. You'd even hear the odd duck. 'Quack, quack.'

Then to enter the competition you'd have to have something like half a dozen different bird calls up your sleeve. It was individual choice. And each school would encourage their kiddies to enter and, on the day, to start with they'd all line up and have elimination heats and if you were successful in the elimination heats, you'd then progress on to the finals. Mind you, if you ended up being among the winners you were given quite an impressive trophy. Very impressive, actually. But no, it was a big day — fantastic — and those Burragate kiddies would get so excited and involved and wrapped up in it all because, as I said, Burragate was a very isolated place and so we didn't get out to visit too many other places that often.

Breaking Bread

I was born on the east coast of the North Island of New Zealand. My parents were farmers in Poverty Bay, near Gisborne. Dad got the property through a rehabilitation programme after he'd come back from the Second World War. I presume it was something similar to your Australian soldier settler's blocks.

I loved the upbringing on the farm. It was a dairy farm and, like a lot of the young boys do on farms over here in Australia, from the time I was about nine I was driving a tractor and helping Dad out on the property. Dad started out with twenty-five cows, and twenty-five years later he was milking one hundred and seventy-five cows. He then sold that property and bought out his father's property, and we went over to cattle, sheep and cropping, plus he put in a few acres of grapes. I was thirteen at that stage and with the new farm being only three kilometres from the beach, it was a great place to be as a teenager. All you had to do was to ride your horse over the hills and you'd be right at the seafront.

My early education was at Manutuke School. Manutuke's quite famous actually. It's where Captain Cook had his first encounter with the local tribal people. Throughout that whole area the majority of the population was Maori — the Indigenous New Zealanders — so much so that, back then, I was one of just three *pakeha* — white European people — in my class of around thirty-six. Then for high school, we caught the bus into Gisborne.

As far as religion goes I guess we were pretty typical of the time. My older brothers never recall Sunday School as being an enjoyable experience. Though that might've had something to do with Dad's military ways, where getting to church was a matter of having to shine your shoes, pull up your socks, put on a tie and 'Stop crying or else'. Then as soon as we hit the church, Mum and Dad would be all smiles. As kids you sort of thought, What's going on here? But later on in the 1960s things got more relaxed. The mortgage had been paid off and it was a time when there was a lot of demand for our primary products in both the European and British markets.

After my schooling I went into engineering. But I'd always been a part of the church and one day the minister said to me, 'Colin, why don't you consider the ordained ministry?'

By that stage I was married with children. But I didn't mind either way. I was enjoying my job. It had a pastoral aspect to it anyway. I was managing an engineering workshop with about twelve staff and when they came in grumpy or whatever I'd never crack the whip. I'd just sit them down and say, 'Well what's the problem?' and we'd talk it through. I also enjoyed mentoring the young apprentices. Though, upon thinking more about the minister's suggestion, what an ordained ministry would give me was the licence to work with a broader scope of people. So with that in mind, I decided to go with it and the church, in its wisdom, sent me off to university for three years to study theology.

The uni was in Dunedin, in the far south of the South Island. Dunedin is New Zealand's version of Scotland. When the Presbyterian Scots first arrived, they landed in the north of the North Island and said, 'No, it's too hot here,' so they jumped back into their boats and they sailed all the way down to the bottom of the South Island and it was like, 'Oh great, this's just like home. It rains, it hails, it snows, it's freezing and the wind blows all year round,' and so that's where they settled and, in true Scottish fashion, they called the place Dunedin.

After I did my theology degree I served in a couple of small town parishes before I started a stint as a chaplain in the navy. I chose the navy not only because they have a sense of humour, but because it also meant we'd be based in the one spot, which provided a little more stability to a failing marriage. I still went out on ships of course. In actual fact, I wish I'd been allowed to do more of that because I believe it makes for a more effective chaplain. It gives you a greater understanding of what the sailors are going through while they are at sea. And it also helps in dealing with the families when they get back together again, on the land. I'd advise the sailors of how family life was being organised in their absence: 'They've got their set routine, so don't burst in and start bossing everyone around. Ease yourself into it.' Yet, even so, with all that, there's still a number of marriages in the armed forces that don't survive.

Okay then, so how did I make the transition from there to Alice Springs, Australia, and get involved with Frontier Services, the Isolated Children and Parents Association and School of the Air? Well I'd been in the navy for eight years. By then my own marriage had fallen apart, so when my contract with the navy was coming up I started looking around and I saw Frontier Services had a vacancy as a patrol minister in the Kimberley region of Western Australia. It was purely pastoral work; an area I really enjoyed and one I felt I'd been effective in, plus I thought that it could well be the time to return to some of my roots. I could relate to farming people and with having an engineering background, that could be of an advantage as well. Also, with the Kimberley job, there was talk about being an intermediary between the Indigenous people and the pastoralists and that really captured my attention.

Then I get halfway through the interview in Sydney and they say, 'How would you like to learn to fly?'

I said, 'Why would I want to learn to fly?' and when they explained they also had three flying positions in Frontier Services, and one was vacant here in Alice Springs, I could hardly contain my smile. 'Oh, okay,' I said, 'I suppose if that's what you really want me to do then I'll have to do it.'

So I got the job in Alice Springs and I got my pilot's licence and ironically the area I now cover is roughly about the same size as New Zealand. And I love it. But it's not all plain sailing. Alice Springs is a long way from family and my adult children. I've got grandkids now, plus my partner, she still lives in New Zealand and, even though it's easy to get from New Zealand to Australia, it's not that cheap to then get out here to Alice Springs. Still we do manage time together every six weeks or so. But I am enjoying the people here. I enjoy the landscape. That feeling of open space. In fact, I now much prefer to drive than to fly. You don't have chance meetings when you're in the air. Anyway, I'm not usually in a rush to be anywhere.

Though one of the great advantages of flying has been the relationship I've struck up with School of the Air. Now I must make it clear that I am a private pilot and not a commercial pilot, so while I am allowed to take passengers on my flights, they're not allowed to be paying passengers. There's rules about all that stuff, and I stick to them. Anyhow I was out at a station one day and the kids were all excited about their teacher coming out so I said to the parents, 'How do these teachers usually get out here?'

Then when I was told that they had to drive all the way out from Alice Springs, I said, 'Well, why can't I fly them out?'

'Oh, look,' they said, 'flying would make far greater sense because after having to drive for three or four hours over rough dirt roads, the teachers are quite stressed and tired by the time they arrive.'

Okay, so when I got back to Alice Springs I went to see Bill Newman, the second-in-charge of School of the Air here. We got on famously and it all grew from there really. So now if either the teachers or myself have a reason to go out to a station, we try and co-ordinate the visit. By doing that, instead of a three- or five-day trip for the teachers, most times, we can do it as an over-nighter. And the kids really love their teachers staying overnight. It's something special to them. So depending on the distance, we might head out in the morning. They get in half a day's teaching. We stay overnight and the next day they can get in another half a day's teaching before we fly back. And usually after we arrive, I head off with the owner or the manager of the property and I could end up doing anything from helping with the fencing to climbing up on the top of a windmill with a couple of monkey wrenches in my hand.

In all, it's an excellent use of resources. The teachers can now get out there more easily, and with less stress. The kids have a great time with the teachers. They learn more, and I get to meet and chat with the station people. Though, of course, if they don't know me, one of their fears could be that I'd arrive and start waving a Bible about, which would put us all in an awkward spot. We have a diplomatic way of sorting that out though, where it gives them the chance to say, without any embarrassment or conflict, 'Look, we'd rather not' or 'Yes, that's fine by us.'

It's all about forming comfortable relationships. Also what's helped is that, prior to working with School of the Air, I'd started to get involved with the Isolated Children and Parents Association, or ICPA as it's known. In fact I'm now the treasurer. Within my area there's thirty-eight families involved in ICPA and so, by that stage, we'd already had that all-important face-to-face contact. I don't know if you know about ICPA or not but, with the money they raise, they give out educational bursaries and grants and make donations to children in need of educational material or help and they also do advocacy work at a political level. Their main fundraiser up here is the Harts Range races.

So all those various contacts are coming to fruition, along with the tradition of Frontier Services and the Patrol Padre serving the people of the outback. It's all alive and well, really.

So I've been in the Alice for eighteen months now. The teachers are quite relaxed with me. The station owners and workers are getting familiar with who I am, and now I'll tell you one funny story. Every time we go out to a station I always take a loaf of fresh bread. That's because a) the kids don't often get fresh bread out there and b) the breaking of bread is important. So this one time, I turned up with a loaf of multigrain and the mum said, 'Oh, thank you. That's lovely.'

Then Dad came in. He took one look at the loaf of multigrain and said, 'Where the bloody hell did you get this bird seed stuff from?'

Okay, I'd learnt my lesson. Next week I go out to a different station, though this time I take a fresh loaf of white bread. I've wised up. The mother takes one look. 'Oh we always eat wholegrain. The only time the kids are ever allowed to eat white bread is when we go to town and we have it for a treat at McDonald's.'

Sometimes you just can't win, can you? So now when I go out to any of these places I take one plain white loaf of bread and one multigrain loaf of bread.

Burying God

Back in the late 1950s–early '60s, Whitton was the hub of the Murrumbidgee Irrigation Area, or the MIA as it's called. In fact, if you ever came across a road sign that read 'W 100 miles' or whatever, the 'W' wasn't one of the more populated 'W' places like Wagga Wagga. It was Whitton, because back in those earlier days Whitton was at the end of the railway line and, as such, it was up and going and thriving well before any of those larger MIA towns like Leeton and Griffith came along. Then, unfortunately, when Griffith and Leeton were established, Whitton was virtually forgotten. Now just as another historical aside: the township of Whitton was once known as Hulong. Then, in 1883, the name was changed in honour of John Whitton, the chief engineer of the railways. I think you'll even find a bust of John Whitton, these days, at Central Station in Sydney.

When we arrived in the mid-'60s — with myself as principal — we found Whitton to be an interesting place. Not only did it have a solid history but it had an extremely supportive community. In fact, it was the community members themselves who got together and built their own town hall. They'd raised the funds from the sale of two rice crops they'd grown, out behind the dump, on the old racecourse. At the time the Whitton Town Hall was touted to be the largest public hall in the MIA. And it was that same strong community spirit that came to the fore when the old double-brick, three-classroom school building was set to be demolished.

At that stage the P&C (Parents and Citizens) group were looking to raise money for the beautification of the grounds, plus to buy equipment for the new school that had been opened since 1967. With the P&C President also being a qualified builder, when the demolition of the disused old school building came up for tender, the P&C decided to put in for the job. And they were successful. As I said, it was a three-classroom, double-brick building and they did the demolition over a long weekend. Yes, over just the one long weekend, and they used the same ingenuity that they did when they'd built the large town hall.

Now, how they went about it was: the P&C got together and they decided to sell whatever 'scrap' they got from the old building, back to the community, and the money they raised from doing that also went into the school grounds and school equipment. The galvanised iron and the floorboards were in big demand, and the old bricks were even more sought after. That's because a lot of the farm roads would bog up in winter rains and those bricks could be used to stabilise the roads. So all the farmers put in their interest to buy the 'scrap' and they also offered their help by bringing in their trucks or their front-end loaders or whatever other equipment was needed to knock the old building down.

So the old building soon disappeared, leaving just the foundations. Now, by saying the old building, I meant that the school was built in two parts. There was the original building — that had been constructed in the early-1880s. Then the additional classroom was built in about 1920. But it was very interesting in as much as the technique they used for the 1880s foundations, with a deeper trench that had been packed with charcoal, sand, rubble and loose bricks, made the foundations as solid as a rock, while the much newer 1920s reinforced-concrete foundations were where the building had started cracking. Amazing, isn't it? And like I said, that had reinforced concrete.

So okay, the building was demolished and now we had to deal with the foundations. The question was, 'How are we going to break it up?' Then the fellow who was the builder —

the P&C President — he said, 'Let's just stick some explosives under it and blow it up.'

Now I'm not exactly sure just how many of us were experienced with using explosives. I certainly wasn't, so I was a touch nervous to start with. Anyhow you could liken it to a scene straight out of *Dad's Army*. So okay, we dug right down to the bottom of the foundations and we placed in the explosive. That done, we lit the fuse and we scampered back and dived behind these big mounds of gravel, dirt and top soil that had been brought in to fill in the large hole that the explosive was going to make. Then we blocked our ears and waited for the big explosion. The fuse was supposed to burn for no longer than a minute. Forty, fifty, sixty seconds passed and nothing happened. We waited some more. Two minutes, five minutes. No, still nothing, so we waited a while longer. By then we'd waited for a quarter of an hour and still nothing. We looked at each other. 'What's going on?' But no one dared venture out from behind the mounds to go and investigate.

It was nerve-tingling stuff. Time passed. Will we or won't we, and if we do, who's going to do it? Everyone was looking at everyone else. Still, no one offered. It certainly wasn't going to be me. So we waited a while longer and the explosive still didn't go off. In the end we waited for about half an hour or so, just in case. Then the P&C President plucked up the courage. 'I'll go,' he said and he crawled out from behind his mound and he edged his way back over to where the explosive had been laid. As it turned out, there was something wrong with the fuse and so he sorted that out and this time, up she went ... 'Boom' ... and it did the job. What a relief. That was probably one of the most tense moments of my life, waiting and not knowing when or if the explosive would go off, then watching the P&C President crawl over to investigate. Anyhow, we got the job done and it was yet another successful community effort.

But as I said, we were always trying to find ways to raise funds for the school. Another time we were out cutting wood for a 'guessing competition'. Normally you'd just run a 'raffle' but the Education Department wouldn't allow us to use the word 'raffle'. That sounded too much like gambling, so that's why we ran what we called a 'guessing competition'. What you had to do was, you paid a certain amount of money to take a guess as to the weight of this heap of wood that had been cut and the person who had the closest guess, they won the load of wood. As simple as that. But it couldn't be called a 'raffle'.

Okay, so we were out on one of the local properties this time, cutting up wood for this 'guessing competition'. We got this log onto the big mobile saw and just as we were about to saw it in two, a huge carpet snake popped its head out of the hollow in the log. As you may know, carpet snakes are very much in demand by farmers — grain farmers in particular — because they'd let them go in their shed or a hay stack where the snakes would control the rats and mice. Anyway, there I was and this big snake popped its head out of the log. So one of the farmers there, a bloke by the name of Young, he grabbed a chaff bag and said to me, 'Here, Les, hang onto this bag a tick while I stuff the snake into it. I want to take it home.'

Now I'm not that fond of snakes. To be honest, I'm petrified of them. Doesn't matter what type they are. But of course, I didn't want to let on that I was scared, did I? So I grabbed the bag and I held it as far away from myself and as wide as my arms would allow. The only trouble was that, as fast as he stuffed this huge snake down into the chaff bag, the thing was just turning its way around again and coming back up, and out of the bag.

'Get back in there, you beggar,' the bloke was saying, and there I was, standing there like a petrified sculpture, holding onto this chaff bag, while the snake was slewing itself around, right in front of my face. Frightened the living daylights out of me, it did. I reckon I lost about twenty years of my life that day.

That was just another of the 'hairy' moments we had when we were fundraising for the Whitton school, and gosh I'll never forget that one either. The other story I'd like to bring in at this point is about Geet. Geet was a very popular member of the staff. He was a dedicated classroom teacher who had a Lithuanian background, and that's where a few problems arose. See, because his parents were from Lithuania, Geet had grown up with English being his second language and so therefore he had an accent that could sometimes confuse the students.

Oh, just as an aside: Geet loved his music and I well remember the time he introduced the school students to the melodica, which culminated in Whitton School's participation in the Leeton Eisteddfod and the school concert. But, oh, the kids really took to these melodicas. They even took them home to practise where, unfortunately, the constant sound of the melodica started to get on some of the parents' goats. So much so that it was a common sight to see kids sitting outside their homes practising their melodicas, having no doubt been banished there by their tormented mothers.

But that didn't deter Geet. He just loved his music and when he later returned to his Australian home town of Newcastle he became very involved with the Marching Koalas. I don't know if you're aware of the Marching Koalas but they were a marching band, very much in the Yankee style, where they get dressed up in all their finery and march up and down the street. Apparently it's a big thing in America, and when they took the Marching Koalas over to the USA I believe they were received with high acclaim. Though mind you, the Marching Koalas didn't dress up as koalas and I don't think Geet was actually ever one of the kingpins in the band. He just might've been in charge of one of the sections; like the trumpets or whatever it might've been. So yes, Geet certainly loved his music.

Oh, and that's right. Another story has just come to mind. I recall Geet once making a statement in class about how all ginger cats were female. Of course, you're talking to bush kids here and so they all protested that he was wrong.

'No, no,' he insisted, in that accent of his, 'all ginger cat is female.'

'But, Sir. But, Sir.'

'No, no, no. All ginger cat is female.'

Then during recess one of boys raced home and he returned with his large ginger cat in his arms. 'See, Sir,' he said, pointing with pride to the cat's testicles, 'he's a male,' and Geet had to concede defeat, much to the glee of all the extremely interested bystanders. But in that case Geet must've got mixed up between a 'ginger cat' and a 'tabby cat' because, in truth, all tabby cats are female. It was just that he was trying to give a nature lesson and he used the word 'ginger' instead of 'tabby'.

So there was some sort of mix-up there, as there were on quite a few occasions with Geet's accent. As I said, at times, his spoken word could make for some confusion, and that same year I remember only too well when he decided to eliminate the overused word 'got' from the classroom vocabulary. To that end he told the kids to write the word 'got' on a piece of paper. After they'd done that, Geet told them to place their piece of paper into a small cardboard box. Which they did. Then they all went outside, grabbed a shovel, and they buried the cardboard box, with the word 'got' in it, in the school garden. It was quite an ingenious idea really though, unfortunately, the next morning a very concerned parent rapped on my office door and demanded to know what kind of schoolteacher would get their students to go out in the school flower garden and bury 'God'.

Characters Young and Old

In the early 1980s I got a promotion to principal in a place in far north Queensland called Irvinebank. To get there, first you have to get to Cairns, then you head south-west to Herberton and then twenty-three creeks out of Herberton, going toward Chillagoe, you'll come across Irvinebank. Back then it was a small school with about thirty kids and I was teaching the lot: Grade 1 to Grade 7.

Something about Irvinebank that may be of interest is that, at one time, it was known to have the deepest tin mine in the southern hemisphere — the Vulcan Mine. I was told that, just before the First World War, Irvinebank had been a thriving town with about ten pubs. Then during this boom the miners went on strike for more money. The only trouble was that by the time they went back to work, the mine was flooded and because it was so deep they didn't have the equipment to pump all the water out. That's when the big mine closed down and, following that, the whole town went bust, went belly-up. And so when we arrived, Irvinebank only had a population of a bit over a hundred and there were only a few little one- or two-man mining operations still working.

Actually our introduction to Irvinebank was an interesting one too because teachers usually get transferred around Christmas time. So, with it being the wet season, we drove up from Brisbane to take up the appointment and there was the usual flooding. I think we even had to hang over in Mackay for a while due to the Pacific Highway being under water. I was married by that stage, so there was my wife and the two kids — about eight and ten — along with all our gear, stacked into our little Cortina station wagon. So we eventually got to

Cairns and we were heading from Herberton out to Irvinebank through these twenty-three swollen creeks and we're going down this dirt road — well, mud really — and there's this guy limping along, carrying a guitar. He thumbed a lift, so I pulled over. 'Where're you going, mate?' and he replied with this terrible stutter, 'I'm ... m ... m ... Irvinebank,' he said.

'Yeah, same here. Would you like a lift?'

'Yeah ... yeah ... yeah ... yes please.'

Anyhow he crams himself and his guitar into the back of our overloaded station wagon, and the kids, they're trying to push themselves as far away from him as they can. So we're driving along and I'm trying to have a conversation with this bloke. I'd somehow found out that his name was Neil, so I said, 'How far to Irvinebank, Neil?'

'N ... n ... n ... not far.'

'Oh, okay.'

He said, 'W ... w ... would yer l ... l ... like me ter sing a s ... s ... song?'

I thought, Well this'll be interesting. 'Yeah, okay then,' I said.

Anyhow he starts strumming away on his guitar and he sings beautifully. Absolutely beautifully. Perfect. Not one word out of place. Not even a hint of a stutter, and when he'd finished I said, 'Gee, Neil, that was really great.'

'Oh,' he said, 'th ... th ... th ...th ... thanks.'

I found out later that, as a kid, he'd had an extremely severe reaction to an immunisation and that was the cause of his stuttering and his limp. So I reckon he would've had a real hard time of it at school. Nice bloke though, and a beautiful singing voice. Absolutely beautiful. But that was Irvinebank. It was a place full of larger-than-life characters. Mind you, because a lot of them hadn't ever been outside Irvinebank, they were a pretty rough lot too. Some had been there for fifty-odd years and they didn't even know where Cairns was, and Cairns was only a couple of hours' drive away.

That reminds me of another story: as I said, by the time we got there, all the mining was done by the little guys; you know, just a couple of blokes going out and following the tin seam along what was not much more than a rabbit hole really. But there's a story that they still talk about in Irvinebank, about a couple of old bachelor miners. These two blokes shared a little shack on the side of the hill and they used to love playing chess. Just loved it. Anyhow one of the guys — I'll call him Ted — well this Ted was getting a bit frisky so he decided to write away to one of those 'lonely hearts' clubs and find himself a woman. So he did that: he wrote away to this mob and after a couple of months this female turns up in town, looking for Ted. They get on okay and so she moves into this little shack where Ted's living with his mate. Anyway things are a little bit cramped with the three of them living in this small shack so eventually Ted says to his mate, 'Three's a crowd so how's about you move out.'

'Okay,' says his mate and so he wanders off and finds himself his own little shack down the road a bit. He got the boot, but they're still mates and they still play chess together. Anyhow, after a while, the second guy also starts to get a bit frisky and apparently this woman of Ted's was a bit of a 'good-looker' so one day he says to Ted, he says, 'What's about I play you a game of chess for her?'

Ted says, 'Okay, fair enough.'

So they have this game of chess and Ted loses, so the woman moved out of Ted's shack and she goes to live in the shack down the road with Ted's mate. Checkmate. Yeah, so it was a wild place.

The publican was another character. He's dead now, but out the back of the pub he had the ubiquitous double drop toilets — like two bowls. Trouble was, there was no partitioning between them so, when you wanted to go to the toilet, you'd just go and sit down next to your mate or whoever and have a chat while you did your business. It was all in together, which made it pretty comfortable at times. But this publican, he was never that keen on people. Like he'd serve you drinks but he didn't like cleaning glasses and stuff like that. So if you went in and asked for a beer you'd be handed a stubby. No glass. No washing up. No nothing. Anyhow, after we'd been there a while, my father-in-law came up and he went down to the pub one time and he asked for a beer and the publican handed him a stubby. Being used to drinking out of a glass, the father-in-law said to the publican, 'Can I have a glass please, mate?'

So the publican grabs a dirty old glass off the dusty shelf, he spits in it, swirls the spit around, gets a grubby old tea towel, gives the glass a bit of a wipe-around, then he hands it over to the father-in-law. 'There yer go,' he says.

Oh, and that's right, I remember, just after the school's attendance rose to thirty-six students, we got in another teacher. This second teacher arrived in town; he's got nowhere else to stay and so he goes down and he boards at the pub. After he'd been there for a few days I said to him, I said, 'How's it going down at the pub?'

'Not real good,' he says.

'Why's that?'

He said, 'I don't think the publican's that keen on cooking and stuff.'

I said, 'What happened?'; and he told me that when he'd asked the publican about the possibilities of getting some breakfast, the publican looked down his nose at him and said, 'Oh, so you want breakfast, do yer?'

'Yeah I'd love a bit of breakfast, if that's okay,' the teacher replied.

The publican said, 'What would yer like?'

'Have you got a bit of steak or something?'

'Yeah.' So the publican lights the burner on the hotplate and he's standing there, waiting for it to warm up. Then just to see how hot the hotplate is he gollies on it, then he squishes the spit around with his spatula, then he throws the steak in on top, and the teacher said, 'Look, sorry. Thanks very much but I'm not real hungry now.'

So it was a town of characters. But of course to fully relate to some of these people and places you really have to spend time living there. I mean even the kids were characters; always up to some sort of mischief or other. I remember my first teaching day. The Department had built a new teacher's residence about a mile down the track from the school and so each day I had to cross a small creek and then walk up this steep hill to the school. So on my first day, these couple of little characters came up to see me. Twin boys, they were; about ten or so. The moment I saw them I thought, Hello, here's a go. Anyhow, they said, 'Sir, Sir, someone's taken the new toilet seats from off the boys' toilet.'

'Oh, yeah, really, fellers.'

'Yes, Sir, aren't yer gonna come 'n' have a look?'

I said, 'Yeah, okay, I'll come and have a look.' So we trot down and we go into the boys' toilet and sure enough the seats had been taken off. They're missing. 'Oh yeah, you're right,' I said, 'there's no toilet seats.'

'What're yer gonna do about it, Sir?'

'Nothing, fellers. Nothing at all.'

'What, aren't yer gonna get some new ones?'

'No, sorry, can't afford to get new ones. You'll just have to sit on the bowl.'

'Oh. Oh.' So they stood there for a while, thinking the situation over. Wondering what to do next. They took a look at one another. Come to some mutual sibling agreement. Then they said, 'Sir, we just might know where we could find a couple'a more new toilet seats just like the ones what's gone missin', Sir.'

'Oh really? Do you reckon you could go and find them?'

'Yeah. Might.'

'Well, how about you fellers go and see if you can find those toilet seats.'

Anyhow, off they trotted, back down the hill, in the direction of where they lived, and that's where they found these 'missing' toilet seats and so they came back and they put them back on the school toilets. Mystery solved. Problem solved.

So yes, there were some real characters out that way, both young and old.

Cuts

When I was a kid at De La Salle Cootamundra, I April-fooled the teacher. For argument's sake, let's call him Brother Thomas. Now this Brother Thomas was the worst teacher to get the cuts from. He had a strap that was made out of rubberised linoleum and though it might not have hurt that much when you first got hit with it, ten minutes later your hand would start stinging and it continued on stinging worse and worse for at least a couple of hours.

Anyway because I was so small — I was a weed of a kid, really — I always sat in the front row of our classroom, nearest the door. So if anyone knocked on the door, it was my job to go out and see who it was. The set-up there was, you'd come in from the quadrangle, in through a main door, and into a little alcove, about six-foot square. If you went straight ahead you went into the principal's office, but if you turned right, that's where the door to our classroom was, and I was the first desk inside the door. This was back in the days when two kids sat at the one old wooden desk with the ink well in the top middle.

Anyhow it was April 1st and at playtime that morning the older kids had dared me to April-fool this Brother Thomas. Now I've never been able to resist a dare. Matter of fact, I still have trouble with it. So I'm up for this April-fool's trick. Then, after we went back into class and we got settled down, I said out loud to Digger Fuller, the kid who was sitting in the row beside me, I said, 'Digger, was that a knock on the door?'

Digger said, 'Not sure. You'd better go 'n' see.'

I go out to see, and of course there's no one at the door. It's all pretend. It's April 1st. So I walk back in and I say to this

Brother Thomas, I said, 'Mrs Ruskin's at the door to see you, Brother.' Mrs Ruskin was one of the kid's mothers.

And so Brother Thomas goes out into the alcove and, when he comes back, he's not looking too impressed. He says, 'Simpfendorfer, what's going on? There's no one there.'

I call out, 'No, yer big April fool.'

And dead silence. The whole classroom went quiet. You could've heard a pin drop. And Brother Thomas, he's angry. He doesn't like being made a fool of, does he? He's that angry, he's going from red to redder. And everyone's waiting to see what's going to happen. Expecting me to get hauled out and given the cuts. And Brother Thomas, he's up for it. He's fumbling around in his robes looking for his strap. But he can't find it. He's so blinded with rage that he's forgotten he'd put it on the desk in front of him. He can't see it. I'm thinking, Well you're in for it now, Simpy. I start breaking out in a sweat.

Then from out of the dead silence this bloke, John O'Rourke — Chook O'Rourke we called him — well he started to laugh, and Chook's laugh was more of a cackle. That's why he was called Chook. And when he started laughing, it broke the tension and everybody else joined in. So Brother Thomas, his anger subsided and eventually after we'd all had a good laugh, everybody went back to work and I never got the strap. Well, not that time anyway, lucky me. Then about ten minutes later Brother Thomas came over. He'd obviously been thinking about it because he said, 'Who dared you to do it, Simpy?'

I said, 'No one, Brother. No one dared me.' And that was the end of it.

But that Brother Thomas, he could really give the cuts. Like I said, his strap was made out of rubberised linoleum. Then we had another Brother — we'll call this one Brother Felix — well Brother Felix had a thick strap and because it was so thick it didn't hurt very much. I remember the time Brother Felix was giving Fartin' Frankie Macauley the cuts and when the strap hit his hand, Fartin' grabbed hold of it and he ripped it out of Brother Felix's hand. That didn't go down too well either.

Then there was another couple of blokes; one was Tony Keyes and the other one was a feller named Michael Privett; Privett lived just out of Muttama. Anyhow, Tony Keyes and this Privett bloke, they had a competition to see who could get the most cuts in a month and Tony Keyes won it by about fifty cuts. He got over a hundred.

We had another Brother — we'll call this one Brother Robert — well this Brother Robert, he had a strap made out of leather and one time one of the other Brothers gave me a message to take to Brother Robert. Actually Brother Robert taught my elder brother, and it was in his class. Anyhow I arrived at Brother Robert's classroom just as he was about to give a bloke by the name of Graham Boyce six cuts. I don't know what Graham Boyce had done but Brother Robert, well, I reckon he might've even been trying to impress me. I don't know, but he said, 'Simpfendorfer, you just stand there for a minute, right, and watch this.'

So I stood there and watched Brother Robert give this Graham Boyce six cuts. Then after he gets his six cuts, Graham Boyce, he walks back and he sits down at his desk and he calls out, 'Thanks very much, Brother.'

And Brother Robert wasn't too impressed about that, was he? So it's out the front of the class again and Graham Boyce gets another six cuts. Back he goes to his desk. Sits down. 'Thanks very much, Brother.'

Out for another six. That's eighteen. Goes back. Same again. 'Thanks very much, Brother.'

Out for another six. But Graham Boyce didn't say anything after that last set of six cuts. Not a thing; just went back and sat down at his desk. Not a whisper. Twenty-four. They'd never get away with that these days, would they?

But that Graham Boyce, gee he was good at sports; athletics in particular. Then one day he was practising in the long-jump pit and on one jump he broke both the main bones in one of his legs. You could hear it; you know, it was like a shotgun going off: 'BANG' — 'BANG'. Just like a shotgun.

But the Brothers at De La Salle Cootamundra, not all of them were bad. See, sport was always a big part of the school and most of them were pretty good sportsmen themselves and so they liked nothing more than to go down to the park after school and kick the footy around with us kids. So in spite of the cuts and all that, I remember them as being good old days with lots of fond memories.

Dead on the Dunny

I grew up on a station property called Dalgety Downs, which is about three hundred miles inland from Carnarvon, in Western Australia. Dalgety Downs was around 760,000 acres, roughly, and all my primary school education was via Carnarvon School of the Air. The most positive thing about School of the Air was the flexibility. If there was a gymkhana to go to or mustering to be done and that sort of thing, you could go and do that, then catch up on your lessons later on. And given the shortage of staff that we had, it was pretty much a whole family affair anyway. Everyone pitched in, doing various jobs — the wives, the mothers, the kids, the lot.

The actual school lessons came out on the mail truck and we did those under the supervision of either Mum or a governess, then we also had our on-air time over the radio with the teachers from Carnarvon. We covered the usual subjects like maths and English. Obviously science wasn't a big part of it because we didn't have all the apparatus that you'd have in a large school. But we did basic engineering, which I enjoyed because it related to what we were doing on the property, and of course we had a proper workshop on the station. There was also mechanical work, which suited me.

To start with, Mum tried her best to supervise us kids, but she soon got sick of that and she had to find a governess. The main criterion there was to be able to find someone who was, first, capable, second, had the patience to put up with us and, third, someone who didn't mind the isolation. Most of the time the governesses weren't much more than kids themselves, really. They weren't even trained as teachers or anything. The vast majority were just city girls, pretty much straight out of school, looking for a job. I mean, the sets of lessons we got were pretty much self-explanatory anyway so they just had to have the ability to get us kids to enjoy doing our lessons and follow them through.

Usually, the governess stayed in a bungalow, separate to the main homestead so her living arrangements were independent of ours, but she'd come over for meals and for our lessons and that sort of thing. I guess we must've been a handful at times because we did get up to a bit of mischief; like when they replaced the old pipes that went through the asbestos wall into the bathroom area of the bungalow and the holes that the piping went through were never completely patched up, so us boys, we'd try and spy on the governess. I guess we thought of it as being an extracurricular biology lesson, plus it was great entertainment. That's until we got caught.

But we were very studious at that age, especially when it came to things like biology. I remember when there were some water pools out along the river system and we'd drive the governess down there to go swimming with us. Yes, us kids used to drive. We were about eight or nine and we could only just reach the pedals of the old Land Rover. But that was okay. By then we were already driving out on windmill runs around the property and that sort of thing. Anyhow, we'd take whatever governess who was with us at the time down for a swim and we'd try and talk her into going in the water without her top on. But unfortunately we had limited success there.

We'd also play a few pranks on them. One occasion we tied a kangaroo into the bed of a governess with our father's brand-new plaited leather belt, then waited to see what reaction there was when she went to bed that night. And there was a good one. There were screams, the works. She hit the roof. The kangaroo hit the roof. She took off in one direction and the kangaroo took off in another, still wearing Dad's precious belt. That didn't go down too well either. We got into a bit of strife over that one, especially from Dad.

Then there were the goannas. We had a bit of fun with them; you know, stick one under the governess' sheets and wait for the reaction. Of course snakes would also somehow appear in various places, in an attempt to scare the living daylights out of the governess. That always worked. Then, because there were graves scattered around the place from the former settlers, we'd always stir them up about how their bungalow had ghosts in it. That would put the wind up them too.

I'm not too sure how many governesses we actually ended up having because they didn't seem to last that long. As I said, they were pretty much city girls and isolation was a problem. But we did have a farm girl at one time. She was a bit more adaptable and resilient and gave as good as she got. Though she did get caught up in a prank of Dad's one time.

See, we had a young jackeroo guy working for us by the name of John, and he and another fellow were racing their motorbikes out on the way to a muster. We'd had some heavy rains and the roads had been washed out in a few places. Of course, in those days occupational health and safety was the last thing anyone thought about so they weren't wearing helmets. Anyhow this John, he was going flat out and he hit a washout and was thrown off his bike. Over he went and, when he came down, he whacked his head on a rock and knocked himself out.

He wasn't too good, but by the time they got him back to the homestead he'd regained consciousness. The flying doctor had been called but it was going to be an hour or so until the plane arrived so they gave him some drugs and a couple of whiskeys to help dull the pain. But what'd happened was, when he'd hit his head on the rock, the top part of his skull had mostly come off. It was flapping around and when you lifted it up, you could see his brain.

Anyhow by then a few people had gathered around the kitchen, either trying to help or just to have a look.

Our governess at that stage — the one with the farming background — Dad had her running around outside getting bandages and that. So John was sitting in the kitchen with the top of his head off and Dad said, 'Look, John, when the governess comes back in, I'll tap you on the shoulder and you kick your leg out.'

'Okay,' says John, so then, when the governess came back around the corner, into the kitchen, there's Dad, he's got a fork and it looks like he's lifted the top off John's head and he's poking around inside his brain. At just that one look she went as white as a sheet. Then when Dad gave John a tap on the shoulder and he kicked his leg out, that was it. She fainted. Down she went, CRUNCH, and then we had two people with cuts on their head, though one more severe than the other, of course. Anyhow, all ended well. The flying doctor came and took John away and eventually he came as good as gold. He didn't lose any of his sight or anything. So I guess you could describe that as being one of our extracurricular anatomy lessons.

But Dad was always coming up with one prank or other. Another time I remember — this was back when Mum was teaching us — for some reason we were doing lessons at night. Dad was up in the yard and he'd just killed a sheep for meat and he thought he'd pull a joke on Mum. He was wearing one of those old army greatcoats that they wore in winter. At that stage Mum had two Rhodesian Ridgebacks. Beautiful dogs they were, and big. Very big. They were pretty good guard dogs, too. Extremely protective of Mum, particularly the male dog. Anyhow after Dad had killed this sheep, he took out one of its eyes. As I said we were finishing late with our schoolwork, it was dark, and there came this moaning at the door. It was Dad, and he's calling out to Mum, 'Margot, Margot, for Christ's sake come and help me. I've popped my bloody eye out.'

Obviously schoolwork's completely forgotten and we're thinking, What's he done?

With it being so dark and him wearing one of these greatcoats, Dad knew the dogs wouldn't immediately realise who he was and that they'd most probably come out and have a go at him. So when he opened the door, he stepped aside and, sure enough, the male dog went sailing past. It then turned around and had a sniff. Oh, that's all right, it's someone he knows. But Dad didn't think that the bitch would be so protective. But in this case she was because, as Dad stepped back into the doorway, with the sheep's eye in his hand, the bitch went for him. It latched onto the arm of his greatcoat and started shaking it like hell. By now, Mum's right behind the dog. She's just about to call it to heel when this eye shoots out of Dad's hand. Up into the air it goes. Mum's aghast as she sees the eye shoot up to the roof. Then she watches it come back down, hit the ground and start rolling around the floor. By now Mum's gone into hysterics. 'How are we gonna put your eye back in? It's all covered in dirt.'

Amid all this kerfuffle, the dog realises that it had just attacked Dad. But it's too late, Dad's now down on the floor, he's got these big fang marks embedded into his arm, and he's crying out in pain. That's when Mum notices that his eye's not really missing at all. 'You rotten bastard,' she calls out. 'Serves you right,' and that was the end of lessons for that particular day.

Oh, and that's right, there was another time our lessons came to an abrupt halt. We had an old retired pensioner who pottered around the place doing odd-jobs like gardening and that. He would've been in his seventies. I'm not sure what his history was but he'd been around a long time. That's all I know about him, but he was a typical old-timer of the area. He'd given himself a tough time. As soon as he got money he'd go into town and set himself up in the pub and he'd stay there until all the money had gone. Then he'd come back out to sober up and earn some more money and he'd go back in and do it all again. That was how he lived, so his body would've been fairly well pickled to start with.

Anyhow, one time this old feller went missing. We were having our lessons with the governess, when Mum found him in the outside toilet. He was dead. Pants down around his ankles. A pained expression on his face. What had happened was, he'd apparently been constipated and he'd gone to the toilet, sat down, and he'd exerted himself a bit too hard, and he'd had a heart attack, and that's where he stayed — dead on the dunny. Apparently it's quite common with older people. So beware when you get constipated that you don't overdo the effort when you go to the toilet. Anyway, Mum came in and got the governess to help her get this old feller out of the dunny.

As I said, he'd been missing for quite a while so by this time rigor mortis had set in, and the poor old bugger was pretty much set in his ways, sitting on the toilet. In fact, he was as stiff as a board. Anyhow, Mum and the governess had to then, somehow, extricate him out of the toilet and bring him down to the homestead, ready for the police to come and pick him up. Trouble was, he was stuck in this upright sitting position, and he wasn't a lightweight either. Still, they somehow managed to get him off the loo but, because of his weight, and his rigid, awkward position, they had difficulty manoeuvring him out of the close confines of the toilet.

That's when Mum came up with a great idea: to save any further damage to his body, and for greater ease getting him through the door, she decided to roll him up in a blanket. So Mum and the governess gets this poor old dead feller wrapped up into a blanket. And it worked. They managed to drag him out of the toilet but then, as they were taking him down the steps, they dropped him, and out rolled this stiffened corpse. Of course, Mum being Mum, she immediately bursts out into hysterical laughter. Meanwhile the poor governess, she didn't know how to react; you know, whether to laugh or to cry or whatever. She was one of the city girls so I doubt if she'd even seen anything that was dead until that stage, least of all a human body.

Anyhow she must've been pretty upset over it all because, as I remember it, lessons were cancelled and so there was no more schoolwork that day.

And that's about it really. But those sorts of things are more about what went on outside our actual School of the Air lessons. As far as actual classroom stories go, I just can't recall any specific ones at the moment. Though, when Mum was teaching us, there was a lot of rulers involved. And wooden spoons. Yet, for the life of me, I don't ever remember being that difficult of a student.

Dobbed In

My daughter rang the other night and said, 'Dad, I've just been reading this great book about outback towns and pubs and, in the back of it, it said that if anyone had a story to tell about the old times and their school days to get in touch with the feller and sort out an interview.'

I said, 'So yeah?'

'Well,' she said, 'I've emailed the feller and told him you'd be up for a chat.'

'What do you mean?'

She said, 'I've dobbed you in.'

I said, 'Well, thank you very much.' Because to be honest I haven't actually read any of your books and so I wouldn't have a clue what's going on.

Anyhow, so what would you like to know?

Okay, well I grew up in western Victoria, on a property called Tochra. Originally it had been part of the Tarrone Homestead, which is a pretty well-known place down in those parts. Then after the Second World War it was divided up into soldier settlement blocks. Our block was one of the biggest. It was a grazing property of about five hundred acres and we were running around fifty head of Angus cattle, two and a half thousand Corriedale sheep, and about a million rabbits.

Yes, rabbits. Well, when Dad first arrived on the property the rabbits were in such plague proportions that they used to go out on 'Sunday rabbit drives'. What they'd do was, they'd string up some wire netting in one corner of the paddock, then they'd hunt up the rabbits by walking across the paddock, beating the ground with sticks and hitting spoons on the back of saucepans. Actually, in an old *Weekly Times* from the 1950s there was a photo showing rabbits stacked up at least a metre high, against a fence. There would've been thousands of them.

Like lots of people did, Dad used to trap and sell rabbits. He reckoned they were in such large numbers that he just about had to pull rabbits out from the mouth of the burrow so he could make room to set his traps. That's true. That's what he used to say. So anyhow, he'd trap these rabbits. Gut them. He'd leave the skins on, hook their back legs together and then hang them over a stick down by the front gate. Then a couple of times a week the rabbitoh would come by and he'd leave something like a shilling a pair in the bread box by the gate. So there was a bit of money in it.

Dad reckoned that he once made enough out of selling rabbits that he could afford to buy some more sheep. He'd trap them most of the time or he'd just dig out a burrow and wring their necks as they were trying to get away. Occasionally he'd pop them off with a pea-rifle. But in the summer you could only hang them out on the night before the rabbitoh came or otherwise they'd get flyblown, and that's when Dad came up with a great idea. What he did was, he put a cage on the back of the old Model T truck then, as he was digging out the burrows, instead of wringing their necks, he'd throw the live rabbits straight in the cage. Then the night before the rabbitoh came he'd kill and clean them and take them down and hang them out by the front gate, so they'd be nice and fresh. Anyhow the old rabbitoh pulled in one day and he said to the old man, he said, 'Can yer keep yer eye open, Wallace? Someone 'round here's keepin' live rabbits.'

And the old man said, 'Oh, yeah? How can yer tell?'

'Well,' the rabbitoh said, 'when somebody keeps wild rabbits alive they fret 'n' so when you kill 'em, their meat doesn't set. It goes off.' He said, 'So if yer hear anythin', Wallace, can yer let me know?'

'Yeah, okay.' And so the old man went and he dismantled the cage off the back of the truck and he never kept live rabbits again. But Dad reckoned the rabbitoh knew it was him. It's just that he got his message over to Dad in a very diplomatic way, that's all.

Now another story my daughter might've mentioned was how, when I was a little kid, I wouldn't eat rabbit. Hated it. This was back when Mum was still alive and we had lots of rabbit stews and so forth. Now no way known was I going to eat rabbit, so Mum separately prepared me a very special dish that was called 'undergrown mutton'. Unbeknown to me, it was the same thing of course. All she'd done was she'd taken the bones out. But it tasted pretty good to me — much better than rabbit, I can tell you.

But I was one of four children. When our mum passed away, I was six. I had an older sister, then there was a four-year-old and a baby who was just four days old. After Mum died the baby went to live with an aunt in Melbourne, and from then on we basically had a revolving door of housekeepers. I guess they were a bit like governesses. You know, they cooked and they cleaned and they looked after us all. For that they got a small wage and their keep. But oh, we had some beauties come through: girls on the run from their husbands, girls on the run from this and that, girls looking for husbands, the lot.

Actually, Dad had been wounded in the Second World War and he was pretty much stone-deaf. He'd spent nearly two years in 'repat', in Heidelberg, Melbourne. That's where he met Mum. She was a nurse. But he could stand beside a telephone and he couldn't hear it ring. Now I don't know if you know or not, but years ago a feller called Titch Holmes had a book of poetry out and one of the poems in that book featured the old man. This poem was about the following event.

As I've said, we had Angus cattle, which are rather dark in colour, and whenever the Warrnambool sales were on, Dad used to drink in the Victoria Hotel. But because Dad was so deaf, when he spoke, he spoke very loud — almost shouted — so that he could hear himself. So Dad was in the Vic Hotel this time and a feller happened to mention to him how the Angus breed of cattle were a bit wild and Dad replied, 'The black bastards'd kick yer head off if they got half a chance.'

Of course, with Dad almost shouting, what he said echoed throughout the bar. The only trouble was, just as those words were being spoken, two young dark fellas happened to walk in and they thought Dad was on about the behaviour of the Aborigines. So one of them confronts the old man and starts having a go at him. Of course, the old man couldn't hear a word the young bloke's saying, so there's Dad, he's sticking his beak right in this fella's face, shouting, 'What? What are yer sayin', mate? Speak up a bit. I can't hear yer.'

Anyhow it all ended up in one hell of a blue, so I'm told, with the old man not having a clue as to what all the kerfuffle was about. The poem was quite good really. Humorous. If you can get hold of the book, have a look. It's by Titch Holmes.

Yes, so that was the old man. Then about three miles down the road from our property was the town of Kirkstall. We were at the start of the soldiers settlement blocks, then the closer you got into town the more intense was the farming, with dairying and potato growing. At that time Kirkstall only had a pub, two stores and a hall. There was also a state government–run primary school: Kirkstall Primary School, Number 344 I think it was. It's long gone now, but when I first started in 1958 we had about fifty kids. Kirkstall also had quite a strong Irish community so there was a Catholic school just around the corner. That had about thirty kids. Our school was a big old building, a bit like an old church really. There were two teachers: one for the juniors, the other for the seniors. A lot of the time we rode bikes to school, and in all sorts of weather — rain, hail, shine. When I got older, I'd occasionally ride a horse.

Then when I was in about Grade 3 they built a small demountable-type classroom. By that stage there would've only been about thirty kids. So it didn't take long to dwindle.

What with kids growing up and leaving the area and people becoming more mobile and the roads improving, by the time I left Kirkstall we were down to only thirteen kids, with just four of us in Grade 6.

A couple of memories stick out. One was that we had about three young single male teachers in a row who drove those little pommy sports cars. What the heck are they called now? You know, those little sports cars with the canvas take-down roof.

Another memory is that at the bottom of the hill from the school there was a creek, and to try and stop us kids from going down there snake-hunting and the like, they put up a wobbly old four-wire fence. Of course that was like a red rag to a bull to us school kids. We were through that fence and into the creek like a shot. They may as well have left it open for all the good it did.

Then another memory is of when the Catholic school closed down and some of the Catholic kids came across to our primary school. Things got a bit tense with that, and for a while there was a standoff between the Protestants and the Catholics. So that was the situation; then one day, one of the older Catholic girls was coming to school and this Protestant kid said something to her, and she out with her soft drink bottle and smashed it over his head. Mind you, this was back when all the bottles were made of glass. No, I don't know what he said to her. He might've even put the hard word on her for all I know. But whatever he said, he certainly didn't say it any more.

Then from Kirkstall primary I went to Warrnambool for secondary school. That was a hell of a shock. My older sister went to the Warrnambool High School and I went to the Technical School. The high school was more for the academic types while the Tech was more for us who wanted to go into the trades. But because they'd have to go around all the different little country roads to pick up us kids, it was an hour's bus ride from our place into Warrnambool. And I tell you, some of those old school buses were real shockers. Old Austins and the likes. They used to leak like a sieve and the wind would come howling in through the floorboards. Oh they were something shocking.

I remember one time when we were going along in the old school bus on the way to Warrnambool High School. I would've only been about thirteen. It was a woeful day — rain, hail, the lot. Then all of a sudden there was this huge explosion outside the bus, which was closely followed by a 'crack', as one of the bus windows shattered. A couple of girls were sitting right next to the shattered window and immediately one of them started shouting and squealing and crying and carrying on. What had happened was, a bolt of lightning had hit the bus and it'd gone right through the window and hit this girl on the shoulder. We never saw a flash or anything, just heard this huge bang, followed by the crack. Anyhow they carted her off to hospital and she recovered okay. I think my sister's still got the write-up of it in the local paper. But how lucky was that, ay? Pity they didn't have Lotto tickets back in those days because I reckon if she had've bought one, she might've won.

Dog Tired

Well I sometimes get accused of living too much in the past, and I probably do a bit. But it's my considered opinion that we should always keep reminding ourselves of our history because it's that history that's made us into what we are today. I'll give you an example: we've got a couple of grandkids and they're forever asking me, 'What was it like in the old days, Pop?'

Okay, let's just say I then start to tell them all about the old house I used to live in when I was a young kid and I mention the word 'mantelpiece'.

So it's, 'What's a mantelpiece, Pop?'

See they don't have a clue what a mantelpiece is. Naturally enough that's because we don't have mantelpieces any more. We've got gas and electric and oil heaters and so forth in our houses these days. 'What's a mantelpiece, Pop?' And so I've got to describe to them how, in the old house, we had an open fireplace, where you burnt logs of wood. Then jutting out from the wall just above the fireplace there was a wooden shelf-like thing and that was called a mantelpiece.

'Oh,' they say, 'and what was it used for?'

Then I tell them it's where you put things like your sporting trophies and wedding photos and photos of the kids and then to keep on your wife's good side you put the mother-in-law's picture up there as well. Of course, that's until she began to look at you so accusingly that, every time you lit the fire, you started feeling guilty about something or other you did or did not do. So you then took her off the mantelpiece and you put her over on the sideboard, where she was a bit further out of sight.

'What's a sideboard, Pop?'

See, things like that. I remember some years ago when the wife and I were playing Scrabble with the kids and the only word I could come up with was the word 'nib'.

'That's not a bloody word,' the youngest says.

I said, 'Oh yes it is, because back before you were born we used to write with a black watery stuff called ink and we had pens that had nibs in the end of them and, if you were the teacher's pet, the teacher would give you the privilege of being the Ink Monitor and each morning before classes started you'd make up the ink from powder and water and you'd pour it into little ceramic ink wells that were at the top-middle of the desk.'

'Really?'

'Yes, and if you broke the middle bit out of the old pen nibs you'd end up with two sharp points on each side and you could then use the pen as a dart.'

Oh, they were great darts. Do you remember doing that? Though mind you, I was never asked to be an Ink Monitor because I worked out it was far more fun to soak up the ink with blotting paper and make little round balls out of it, which you then stuck on the end of your ruler and fired off at the other kids. And gee, didn't that make a splotchy mess. Yes, so I guess I was a bit of a little bugger at school, ay?

Anyhow it's all that sort of history I think needs keeping. And to continue those stories on through storytelling is a great way of doing it. Mind you, they weren't always entertaining or humorous stories either. I had a little mate. This was when I was still in primary school at a place called Sheffield, which is in the north of Tasmania. Now, we're looking at around the time toward the end of the polio epidemic, right. Remember that? Late '50s, into the early '60s. Remember how you used to have to stand in line and wait to get your polio injections and there'd be kids fainting left, right and centre? And it always amazed me how it was the kids you least expected that had the most fear of the needle. Real little toughies they'd be at school but when they were shown a needle, they'd go to water, and 'plop' — they'd faint. Then of course, later on in the '60s the vaccine arrived over here in Tassie in the form of oral drops. Or they might've even put some of the vaccine into little squares of sugar or whatever, so it tasted better for the kids.

But anyway, this was back when they were doing the injections and I had a little mate. We were the best of friends. Did everything together. Then he died of polio. Oh, it broke my heart it did. Broke my heart. I'd say we would've only been about six, going on seven. That was at Sheffield Primary School. But oh it broke my heart when they told me he'd died. We'd had the needles at school and everything but my poor little mate missed out. It was too late for him. Just terrible it was.

So that's just one of my memories from my school days at Sheffield Primary. Then something else from my old school days that's perhaps on a lighter note. By then my mother had got a job at the local pub as a cleaner. We used to live there in the pub and so each morning I'd walk down to the Sheffield school, put in a hard day of getting up to as much mischief as I possibly could, then I'd wander back home to the pub again in the afternoon.

Okay, this time they must've had a pretty wild time in the pub and I'd been kept awake most of the night. So I was dog tired even by the time I got to school. Actually I remember the teacher going crook on me more than once for dozing off in class. Then when it got to the end of the school day, I was coming home and I decided to have a bit of a rest, so I sat on the back bumper bar of a car. Now, back in those days — if you recall some of the old Chevys and the like — the back bumper bars weren't integrated like the bumper bars are today. Back then they used to stick right out on a couple of solid metal arms.

Anyhow it was a pretty warm day, which didn't help matters that much and so I decided to have a bit of a rest on the back bumper bar of this car. Which I did. But I must've somehow dropped off and I fell asleep with me arse jammed between the back bumper bar and the boot of the car. Of course the driver didn't have a clue I was there and so when he and his wife came out from doing whatever they were doing they just jumped in the car and took off. I mean, it was kind of fortunate that the old cars didn't go so fast back then, really.

So off they went and they got a fair way down the road until someone caught up with them and started waving and going on and pointing to the back of the car. Anyhow the driver stopped to see what all the fuss was about and that's when they found me, still fast asleep, with me arse jammed between the bumper bar and the car boot.

Five-Star Welcome

I was frightened, the day I arrived at Yanco Agricultural High School. It was one of those times when you know your whole life is about to change and nothing can be done about it. Behind me lay my home town of Beckom (Pop. 64). A simple bush existence filled with friends of a lifetime, their laughter and grumbles, the warm security their presence held; smells so familiar that you only missed them when they weren't wrapped around you like a comforting cotton ball of aroma. A place where my parents had been just a shout away. Yet now, at the grand old age of eleven years, I suddenly feared they had jettisoned me, prematurely, into the vast unknown of my future.

There were six of us new arrivals gathered on Yanco Railway Station that stinking hot day. All of us had come from the sticks; from farming regions throughout the south-western and western regions of New South Wales, just raw bush kids really, flung together as if we were spare parts from an under-twelves jumble sale. We milled around the station checking each other over until a small Bedford truck came to pick us up. The tray of the truck was surrounded by a reinforced wire cage and stunk like it had just come from the saleyards. We picked up our cases and ran toward the driver's cab to get the most comfortable ride.

'In the bloody back, youse blokes,' a gruff voice barked out at us from inside the cab. 'Who do yer think yer are, a mob'a bloody Lord-High-'n'-Mightys or somethin'?'

We turned in our tracks and sauntered around to the back of the truck. One kid clambered up onto the cage and opened the wire gate. 'Welcome aboard. The name's John Ashton,' the kid said as he helped each of us up onto the back of the mucky truck. After we'd jammed ourselves and our luggage into the cage, John slammed the gate, yelled out, 'Take 'er away, mate,' and we set off on the last leg of our journey, the five miles out to the boarding school.

As we were driven out of the township Yanco, I, along with the others, pushed my way to the back of the truck. There we gripped onto the wire cage for support, watching the houses disappear. When I finally turned around again, John had made himself comfortable out of the wind, behind the cab. Drawn by his confident manner I went and squeezed myself in beside him. 'G'day, I'm Bill,' I said.

John shook my hand. He told me that he had a brother who'd attended Yanco Ag during the Second World War. He reckoned that everyone at the school went by nicknames, and he asked to be named 'Jug Ears' or 'Jug', as that's what his brother, Joe, had been called and they were keen for the family tradition to continue. He asked if I had a nickname. I told him it was 'Swampy', because my last name was Marsh.

Jug seemed armed with a wealth of information, passed on to him by Joe, about what lay ahead. 'Fer starters,' Jug announced with a loud voice of authority so that we could all hear him, 'the economy'a Yanco Ag runs on cigarettes, "herbs" as they're called. Money's not worth a brass razoo 'cept fer buyin' yer herb stash.'

Then he told us about 'Dad-ak', the headmaster. 'Me brotha, Joe, reckons that Dad-ak locks kids who muck up in the dungeon under McCaughey House and forces 'em ter live on bread, water 'n' rats for weeks on end. Joe says he rules the school with an iron fist and a huge bunch'a keys. 'N' steer clear'a "Ape", the Ag teacher. He once gave Joe such a canin' that 'is fingers came out lookin' like they'd been through a sausage mincer.' Someone in our group must've looked doubtful because Jug quickly added, 'No joke, mate. 'E's still got the scars. 'E's showed me.'

Now that he'd grabbed our attention, Jug continued. 'And youse ought to know about how privileges work. That's where anyone can order us First Years about. We'll 'ave ter make way in line fer anyone senior. They can make us clean their shoes. They can bot our lollies, "chews" as they're called. 'N' if they tell yer to do somethin', do it, else you'll be in big strife.'

Jug explained that the higher the year you were in, the more kids you held privileges over. Then in your final year, if you became a school captain or a prefect, you could roll the cuffs of your shorts up three times, give the strap to students who were 'insolent' or tried to buck the system and rule their lives with as much authority as Dad-ak or the 'Nits', as teachers were named.

As First Years, Jug said, we weren't allowed any privileges. 'Us First Years are called "Grots", 'cause a grot is dirty, ugly 'n' useless.'

Then there were the initiation ceremonies performed by the Second Years. Jug told us to expect to be given the 'Royal Flush', which was where we'd have our heads shoved down a toilet and the chain pulled. He warned that if we kicked up a stink during our Royal Flushing we'd be forced to do unspeakable things. Things that he said Joe had told him were too frightening to mention.

I was beginning to wonder about this brother of Jug's; if perhaps he'd invented these stories just to put the wind up Jug. I couldn't be sure. They were certainly putting the wind up me. It sounded more like we were going off to live with some barbaric African tribe than to a bush boarding school. But by the look in Jug's eyes when he spoke and his graphic hand actions, I had the dreadful feeling that he, for one, believed every word of it to be true.

'Me brotha Joe says that when 'e was in First Year one kid got so homesick 'e hung 'imself in the showers of McCaughey House. They found 'im next mornin' danglin' by 'is school tie.

All blue he was, with 'is eyes bulgin' out like light bulbs 'n' 'is tongue hangin' a foot out'a 'is mouth.'

We reached toward our crisp blue-and-gold striped school ties and loosened them. But there was to be no relief from this onslaught because Jug followed on with the macabre story about the bloke who jumped off the second-floor verandah of McCaughey House, fracturing his skull and breaking his arms and legs.

'Then there's the ghost who lives in McCaughey House, 'n' on a full moon 'e's been know'd ta murder First Years while they're sleepin' in their dorms. Why, Joe woke up one mornin' 'n' the bloke in the bed next'a 'im 'ad a meat cleaver stuck right through 'is noggin 'n' a couple'a yards'a hose wrapped around his throat fer good measure.'

We gasped in terror and morbid fascination.

'Dead as a maggot 'e was,' Jug added, shaking his head almost in disbelief at his own brother's story. 'Dead as a bloody maggot, Joe reckons.'

As we passed through the wrought iron gates at the school's entrance, displaying its sign — YANCO A RICU TURAL HIGH SC OOL — an emptiness came over me as if my body had been sucked of its blood.

'It's like a prison,' someone muttered.

To me, it was like entering a completely different world. The comforting summer browns, oranges and yellows I'd grown up with had disappeared. There were no towering concrete silos, which were the landmark of Beckom. I was now being swallowed up by a dense river gum bushland. There wasn't a hint of dust in the air, only the sickly scent of damp earth and muddy bark.

Up the gravel drive we were transported, trapped together on the back of the truck, a small flock of blue-and-gold school uniforms ... lambs to the slaughter. I had visions of being locked away forever; of never being allowed to see my parents again; of never seeing the outside world again.

'You all right?' Jug asked.

'I'm a bit scared,' I answered.

'We'll be okay,' he replied. 'We jus' gotta look after each other, that's all.'

After what Jug had told us, I fully expected to see mobs of kids living in an encampment of grass huts and dressed like natives, with big boiling cauldrons waiting to stew us up. But when we drove out of the thick bush I could hardly believe my eyes. With a clang of the truck's caged gates we were unloaded outside the main entrance of McCaughey House. It seemed exactly as the school's brochure had said: manicured lawns and picturesque gardens lay before us. The collection of rare and ornate roses formed a pathway down to the man-made lake. Willow trees dangled their finger-like foliage into the lake's muddy waters. Three massive pine trees guarded an arched wooden bridge which stretched over to the main islet in the centre of the lake.

I turned to take in McCaughey House. It was the largest building I'd ever seen, almost like a brick-and-sandstone castle. The ground floor was curtained by huge arches. Behind them were large windows encased in thick wooden frames. I squinted up at the second storey verandah and felt dizzy at imagining a naked body, scorched with strap marks, falling in a flail of arms, legs and cries of desperation and homesickness.

'Youse the new Grots?' came a snaky voice.

Lowering my eyes I found that we were being surrounded by a mob of blokes dressed in the school's day clothing of khaki shirts, shorts, socks and sandals. As one, we First Years grabbed our suitcases and shuffled into a loose huddle.

'Look like a piss-weak bunch'a poofs ter me,' said another voice.

This brought a touch of ironic laughter from the growing khaki forces. We said nothing, only closed ranks.

'Hey, you. You got shit all over yer precious school uniform,' said a bloke who had the cuffs of his shorts rolled up.

We searched among ourselves for the accused.

It was me.

'Hey, Thommo, wha'da we do with a Grot who shits his school uniform?'

Thommo stepped forward and announced himself as Arthur Thompson, the school captain. He wasn't as rugged looking as the rest. He was tall and slight with snowy hair and rosy cheeks. I tried to explain that the mess had come from the sheep who'd been in the truck before us. Thommo completely ignored my excuse and barked a decree to the khaki troops that anyone who soils their sacred school uniform deserves to be taken to the lake and given a thorough dumping and washing.

Amid the cannibalistic cheers that these words brought, Thommo called, 'Go sick 'im, Rags,' and a kid not much older than me shot out from the pack like a starving dog. He grabbed me by the tie and dragged me away from my group.

'The name's Rags Kelly,' he hissed.

I tried to recall if I'd ever stood in front of such a large group. I remembered the previous year's inter-school sports carnival at Temora when I won the hop, step and jump, after most of the opposition had been disqualified for getting their hops mixed up with their steps and jumps. But that Temora crowd had looked bored and lethargic. This mob was different. They looked wild and mean and restless. Their eyes burned for action. I stood before them, clutching my brand new Globite suitcase, terrified.

'You touch 'im 'n' you'll 'ave ter deal with the rest of us,' came a voice from our group.

It was Jug Ashton. His brave words were supported by a couple of unenthusiastic, half-grunted whispers.

Rags Kelly dropped his stranglehold on my tie and lunged toward Jug. As he did, I instinctively spun around and clocked him one over the back of his head with my suitcase.

***

The brawl erupted on the gravel outside McCaughey House. It rampaged onto the manicured lawns. Suitcases were flung and torn, and exploded into loose balls of clothing. The tempest ploughed into the picturesque gardens. It rioted over the rare and ornate collection of rose beds. It cascaded toward the man-made lake.

All became a frenzied blur. The background echoed with the blood-curdling chant of 'Fight! Fight! Fight!' At anything resembling khaki I took a wild swing. At anything resembling a school uniform I shouted encouragement. Then I was in the water. Someone was jumping on me. Someone was pushing my head under. My aching arms kept swinging like windmill blades gone crazy. Then suddenly a deathly silence enshrouded me. I lay there floating head down in the lake, with no one pushing me, no one jumping on me.

Even without looking, I knew Dad-ak was standing on the bank above. He had an eerie presence the like of which I'd never felt before. I tried to keep my head under the water, hoping he'd go away.

But I ran out of breath.

Jug had described him to a tee. Dad-ak stood short and squat like an Italian dictator I'd seen in one of Dad's war books. His brown beady eyes glared down at me. His stumpy fingers held the largest set of keys I'd ever seen. Keys that were made to fit every kind of lock imaginable, including dungeon locks. Beside Dad-ak stood Arthur Thompson. A self-satisfied smirk plastered over his dial. My friends, saturated to the bone in their ragged and ripped school uniforms, were slumped on the lake's grassy bank. The khaki army hovered in the distance like a circling pack of dingoes.

Arthur Thompson pointed down at me. 'That's 'im, Sir. That's the bloke who started it all. Whacked poor Rags Kelly clean over the back'a the scone with 'is suitcase 'e did, Sir.'

'To my office, boys,' Dad-ak spat down at us and spun around, striding back toward McCaughey House. His piston-shaped legs pounded over the debris of loose clothing, shredded suitcases and uprooted roses. We stumbled along behind, attempting to pick up our belongings.

Into McCaughey House we poured, chasing the high-pitched ring of jangling keys. At the top of a double staircase a brilliant, leadlight collage of a shepherdess tending her sheep caught my eye. We slushed our way into the office and shuffled into a line in front of Dad-ak's desk. He examined us one by one.

Then he got to me.

'In all my years at this school,' he spoke, 'I've never witnessed anything as disgraceful as what happened outside there today.'

'We were jus' stickin' up fer ourselves … Sir,' I stammered.

Dad-ak picked up a pencil and began to tap it on his desk. He stared at me as if I no longer deserved to exist as a human being.

My head lowered with a shame unknown. As I stood there, shaking all over, listening to the tap-tap-tap of Dad-ak's pencil and the nervous squelching in my wet shoes, I shut my eyes and tried to fight back the tears by thinking of my beloved home town of Beckom. But in my mind, all I could hear was the aching sound of wind through the silos, whistling my childhood goodbye.

For Your Own Good

My name is Roman Kulkewycz. My parents were from the Ukraine and they were held as prisoners of war in Germany. After the Americans liberated them, that's when I was born. Then when I was a very young child we migrated to Australia and I began my schooling in 1952. That was at St Joseph's Convent, at Maffra, which is in the central Gippsland area of Victoria. I completed my schooling there in 1958 and I would like to share some of my experiences of that time.

Back then all of the teachers at St Joseph's were Josephite nuns. I don't know about the Australian kids but, in those days, there was none of this mum or dad taking us by the hand and leading us to school with a box of tissues at the ready. Us migrant children, we went on our own. No mum. No dad. The day before school started it was prearranged that we would tag along with some of the other migrant children who were already attending St Joseph's and it was their job to help orientate us to the school environment and the daily routine. My younger brother, Andrew, had it easy compared to me as, being the eldest, I was to be the groundbreaker.

Though little did I realise how much of a shock my first day of school was to become. I remember it vividly. With Ukrainian being the only language we spoke at home, I didn't even know that any another language existed. So when I arrived at school I was confronted by all of these kids speaking in a tongue that I didn't understand, and neither could they understand a single word I was saying.

The atmosphere between us migrant kids and the Aussie kids was, at first, rather hostile and frightening, though it is interesting to note that even though we could not understand the Aussie kids, nor they us migrants, we were still able to communicate effectively. A punch on the nose soon gave me the message that I was not welcome to hang around with one particular group of boys. I then kept close to the kids that I could identify with and who could understand me a little and it was they who provided me with some safe sanctuary.

Any communication with the nuns was also just as difficult. To get my point across I would first have to say something to another migrant pupil, who would then translate it into broken English to the nun teacher. I remember asking for a cup of hot cocoa on my first morning at school and receiving a kind and sympathetic smile from Sister Ilma as she sat there wondering what I was asking her for.

On that first day I felt abandoned and very disillusioned — abandoned by my parents who 'dumped' me in this place where I could not understand a word of what was being said, and disillusioned and worried about what was going to happen to me in the future. At lunchtime I sat at the base of a huge eucalypt tree and bawled my eyes out. Years later I was sorry to see that gum tree felled as, whenever I passed it, memories of later better times would spring to my mind. The old school was also eventually pulled down. A St. Vincent de Paul store now stands on the site and it is named the 'Jack Kelly Store' in honour of a parishioner. Only the convent remained but, with the nuns leaving the district, unfortunately, even the convent has now been sold off.

Yet, although the discipline was very strict, I'm sure those saintly Josephite nuns turned a blind eye to the many pranks us boys got up to and, to those of us who *were* caught red-handed while doing these pranks, it was explained to us by the nuns how our punishment was ... 'for your own good'. The nuns were simply wonderful, holy people who truly lived out their vocation under extreme difficulties. I do not mean to offend but I do not think that today any teacher could equal the zeal, the compassion and the stamina that those nuns had.

Today we have Integration Aides and funding for schools in an attempt to make a teacher's life easier but those dedicated nuns, as well as helping us learn the English language and religion, they also taught us the core subjects to equip us for careers in later life. To me, most importantly, they imparted the Catholic faith. I attribute their teaching and the way they led by example and through prayer to the fact that, today, I still go to the Traditional Latin Mass.

Of course, our facilities at St Joseph's Convent were very basic. Our entire school consisted of three very large rooms with a cloakroom, which always seemed to be chock-a-block full of bags and coats. At home time it was like a lucky dip when it came to finding your belongings. There was no lighting, and heating consisted of an open fireplace which was lit by the senior boys who were placed on a daily roster during those cold winter months. But with the rooms being so large and with such high ceilings, by the time our frozen bodies felt any of the heat from the fireplace, the day had usually started to warm up anyway. I must add at this point that, later on in my schooling, wood heaters were installed and they were the type that were able to be turned down overnight and brought back to life in the morning by allowing air to enter the fireplace.

A strict school uniform was also adhered to. We were never allowed to wear long trousers, not even on cold frosty mornings and I still can remember how my legs felt like ice. But boys being boys, one of our winter pastimes was to try and break the surface of every frozen ice puddle of water we came across. Needless to say that, by the time we got to school to start our lessons, many were the times that our shoes and socks were soaked through and our toes felt like painful wooden pegs. But we didn't seem to care, somehow.

A continual source of embarrassment to me at that time was my lunchtime sandwiches. While the Australian children had tomato, cheese, Vegemite and jam as fillings, I had things like salami, which could be detected at quite a distance from my bag in the cloakroom. Back then, the Australians considered the eating of such foods as being detestable and 'daggy'. The basic Australian diet consisted of meat, potatoes and vegetables. Today, much to my amusement, Australians now see the food that I was eating as being 'fashionable' and they are treated with reverence and great respect. Back then, wine and olive oil were something that only the Italians had. But look how much they are in vogue today.

I also recall how the school and the convent were separated by a thick cypress hedge. This was the perfect setting for a young boy's recess and lunchtime adventures. We would start at one end of the hedge and slowly climb our way through the twisted branches. With the hedge being so long, it took many weeks to get from the start to finish and so, when we reached that finish, it was considered by our peers to be a very great achievement. It was like, once you'd completed the journey, you were seen to be the wearer of an invisible badge of honour. In fact, it became such a challenge to all of us schoolchildren that, if someone stood back and looked at the hedge from a distance, they would see this constant moving and twitching right along its entire length. It was like the hedge was alive — a sight that would baffle even the most respected scientist. Then when we went back to the classroom we'd smell like pine trees, which was something else to be very proud of.

The seasonal activities also kept us busy. One that I have fond memories of was what we called the 'loakie hunts'. This was the process of flooding out cicadas while they were still in the ground. It became a real obsession, not just for us Catholic boys, but for the boys of the whole town, as there was a certain air of achievement if you flooded out a 'black beauty'. We also hunted the hatched cicadas in the trees which, depending on whether they sang or not, were called either 'singers' or 'pissers'. It was a marvellous form of adventure that rolled over into our every waking hour. So much so that we'd always carry bottles of water just in case we came across any cicada holes. This activity was also a great preparation for 'ferreting', which we graduated onto when we got a little older.

In those days I absolutely hated football. I could see no fun at all in competing for a muddy, slippery, odd-shaped ball in all sorts of weather. Father Frank Rowe was then our school football coach. Away from the football field Father Frank was a very good and holy priest. He was a huge man who would coach so enthusiastically from the boundary, he'd put the fear of God into us with his equally huge booming Irish voice. His most used instruction was the roar of 'Get rid of it, man' which seemed to happen every time someone got possession of the ball. Yet, even though his attention always seemed to be on the game, he still found the time to check if us migrant kids were competing or not. If he saw us congregated in a corner of the oval, talking about anything other than football, he'd become so angry and frustrated that his human nature would overcome his priestly nature. His jugular vein would stand out and pulsate and it would be like the start of World War Three, and he'd give us a real 'spray'.

I also recall the school milk programme which was funded by the government. Each day crates of half-pint milk bottles were delivered and plonked right in the middle of the quadrangle, where they would wait until recess time. Now that was all right in the winter, but during summer it didn't take long for the milk to go off. Nevertheless, no matter what condition it was in, we were forced to drink it. There were no health regulations in those days so it didn't matter if someone had an allergy or whatever to milk, we still had to drink it. Then some of the more innovative children started to bring along containers of drinking chocolate or other flavourings to add to their milk in an attempt to change its taste. But no matter what, off milk is off milk and, to me, it still tasted awful. Seeing that milk in cartons was unheard of in those days, the empty milk bottles were rinsed out and returned to the dairy where they would no doubt go through a thorough washing and sterilisation process before being refilled again.

Then once a week we all received an iodine tablet. This iodine tablet was a little white pill, with a funny taste, and we were supposed to swallow it. I'm unsure where all the tablets that were not swallowed ended up, but one can only imagine. Though again, whether we wanted to or not, just like the punishment we received and with the milk we were forced to drink, we were told that we had to take the pill ... 'for your own good'.

Freddy the Frog

J — I'm Joyce. I've just had my eighty-ninth birthday so I'm now heading for ninety and this is my younger sister, Doris. How old are you, Doris? I've forgotten.

D — Eighty-six, heading for eighty-seven. We're going downhill fast.

J — Yes, well, anyhow we grew up on a cattle property called Woleebee, which is about three hundred miles north-west of Brisbane, between Jackson and Wandoan, and about forty miles out of Miles. It was pretty isolated back then. The mail only came out once a week, on the Saturday, and the mailman would drop the mail off at our front gate then he'd continue on to the end of his run and he'd come back through on the Sunday, heading back to town.

D — The mail was delivered by horse and buggy, wasn't it, Joyce?

J — Yes, and our house was four miles away from the front gate and we had to ride a horse down there to collect the mail. Then if anything needed an urgent reply, Mother had to sit down and write it that night and Dad would ride back down to the mailbox early the next day, before the mailman came back through. It was a sixteen-mile ride, you could say. But Mother had four children within four years — boy, girl, boy, girl — and because there wasn't a school within cooee, when my brother and I were old enough we went to live with our grandparents, on our mother's side, at Wallumbilla and they had a school there. That's a story too, because Mother's parents were the first settlers up that way. They were from Germany and the family had to go from Germany, over to England, to catch a boat to Australia and Grandfather was so well-educated that he taught the children on the boat coming out. Yes he did, though, sadly, he and his wife started out on that journey with a young child and I believe she died at sea, didn't she, Doris?

D — I think that was the story, Joyce.

J — Anyhow, after they arrived in Australia they went up to Cairns, where Grandfather worked in the sugar industry. They then had a second child — a baby girl — but, soon after that, his wife died and Grandfather couldn't look after that second child and so she went back to Germany to live with her grandparents back there. After that he got married again and that's when he became the first selector up at Wallumbilla. That's where our mother grew up. She was the second daughter of the second marriage.

So, for our education, my brother and I, we went to live at Wallumbilla. That was in 1926, when I was about four. Our grandparents' property was about a mile and a half from the school and I remember how we always got a ride to school in the horse and sulky but then we had to walk home. The school was just an ordinary state school with two teachers. The head teacher was a man and he was all right; then there was a woman teacher and she was quite good too. I forget the exact number of students that were there.

We didn't stay that long at the school because, when the next two children in our family were also old enough to go to school, our grandparents said, 'Well, we can't take the whole four of you.' It was just asking too much so Mum and Dad bought this house, here in Miles, and Mum and us children came into town to live. So we left Dad out there on Woleebee, looking after the property, and he'd come in to see us about once a month in his old Whippet car. Yes, to this exact same house. So that's how long Doris and I have lived here. And that just goes to show how keen our parents were on giving us an education, Mum in particular, because she'd known a family who didn't believe in education and when their son got married he couldn't even sign his name on the marriage certificate, and Mum said she wasn't having any of that.

D — There was no correspondence schooling back then either, so that's why we had to come into town.

J — Yes, so then we arrived in Miles and the lady from across the road said to Mum, 'Whatever you do, don't send the children to the state school.' Apparently it had a bad reputation, you know with uncontrollable children and all that. The lady said, 'Send them to the Convent.'

Now, we weren't Catholics but Mum sent us there anyway and we all did very well. They didn't seem to mind Protestants going to the Catholic school, did they, Doris? I mean, at first, we weren't very popular and the other children called us 'ignorant Protestant bastards' and things like that. Oh yes they did, didn't they, Doris? But we weathered all that, and anyhow, as it turned out, we were an asset to that school because I remember when the school inspector came by and I heard him say to the head nun, 'Are these two any relation to the two out there in the infants room?' and she said, 'Yes, they're the same family,' and he said, 'I thought as much.' And that was because we were all getting top marks at our schooling because we didn't muck around like the other kids did and we concentrated on our schoolwork during the day and also Mother taught us at night.

D — That was with the old kerosene lantern on the table, wasn't it, Joyce?

J — That's right, there was no electricity in those days, and Mother, she had beautiful handwriting. Both she and her sister and our uncle had copperplate handwriting, and Grandfather always despaired at our handwriting, didn't he, Doris?

D — Oh, he had a beautiful hand, too. Mind you, with us, it was all slate and pencil to begin with.

J — The pencil was made of something similar to the slate I believe. Actually there might be a scrap of one of those old pencils in that tin over there next to you, Doris.

D — Oh, damn it, I've spilt them all now. Something had to give.

J — Then after the slate and pencil you graduated up to pen and ink.

D — We used lead pencils before we got to pen and ink, Joyce.

J — Yes, that's right, and we sat at wooden desks, about six foot long, and you had five children in a row — girl, boy, girl, boy, boy — and the desks had little holes in them where the ink wells sat. And I always sat right at one end of the desk and the ones down the way from me — mainly the boys — they struggled with their arithmetic so I'd write the answers down, real tiny, on a wooden ruler, and the ruler would gradually move along the desk until it got to the other end and the boys would write down the answers. Anyhow the teacher soon woke up as to why the ruler was forever travelling up and down the desk and then the boys were moved down the front, well away from me. Do you remember that, Doris?

D — No, I was in a different class.

J — Then they changed the head nun at the Convent and the new one, well, it wasn't her fault really but the boys were absolute little outlaws and she just could not control them. She'd give them the cane and everything but, oh, they were little terrors. I remember after one of the boys was caned he said to the nun, 'Can I have some more, please?' And these boys, they just eventually wore that poor nun out and so Mum said, 'Well we came in here to get you all educated and now you're just wasting your time so I'll send you over to the state school.'

By then they'd changed teachers over at the state school and the new head teacher, oh, he was strict, strict, strict. So we went from the Convent to the state school and I continued on and I went up to Grade 7 and I did what they called Scholarship, then I left. I was fourteen. That was the earliest age you could leave school. But I liked school. I was good at it.

D — I know that slate pencil's here somewhere, Joyce, but I just can't find it.

J — But the head teacher at the state school, the strict one, he even put the clock down the back of the classroom so we couldn't see what time it was. And if you spoke in class you got into big trouble. So we were that quiet you could've heard a pin drop. But even though he might've been strict, if he ever saw a storm coming or the black clouds rolling in, all of those children who had to walk or ride any distance home, he'd let them out of school early, even if it was in the middle of the day. He was very good in that respect.

D — No I can't find it, Joyce.

J — Of course, I didn't play up like this little tyke Doris did, did I, Doris?

D — Oh, I didn't play up too much. I only used to tell the teacher when he was wrong.

J — That was a different teacher to the one I had.

D — Yes, he was a different teacher. The one I had, his name was Fred Something-or-other so I called him Freddy the Frog. He was hopeless at maths. Absolutely hopeless. It was like the blind leading the blind, really. By then Joyce had moved back up to our grandparents' place at Wallumbilla and when the teacher couldn't work something out, I'd send the questions up to Joyce and she'd write down the answers and send them back to me and I'd go and show Freddy the Frog how to get the right answer.

J — Of course, when I left school there was no work in town for women or girls, not unless you worked in the pub or a shop, and they already had enough staff.

D — And it also depended on what religion you were too, didn't it, Joyce? And so a Church of England person wouldn't employ a Catholic person and vice versa.

J — Oh, religion was very big in those times and so, when I couldn't get a job in town here, I went back to my grandparents' property and helped them out on the farm. But anyhow, Doris, I'm sorry, you can go on with your story now.

D — Well, like I said, Freddy the Frog was hopeless at maths and so I'd send the problems up to Joyce at Wallumbilla and she'd write down the answers and she'd post them back and I'd take them to Freddy the Frog and I'd say, 'Please, Sir, this is the way you're supposed to do it.'

J — That's how you win friends and influence people, Doris.

D — And oh, he did not like that. We weren't friends, I can tell you, because I'd show him up in front of the other kids. He thought I was a real smarty-pants and so he tried his best to ignore me; like I'd sit there with my hand up with the answer and he'd ask everyone else but me. Anyhow I'd whisper the answer to Mavis, the girl next to me, and she'd put her hand up and when she answered the question he'd go, 'That's very good, Mavis. How did you know that?' and she'd say, 'Please, Sir, Doris told me,' and he'd say, 'Well, Doris tells you lots of answers, doesn't she?' And I did too.

Then in my last year I had to nominate to do Scholarship or not. The exam was made up in Brisbane then sent out to all the schools in the state. Anyhow Freddy the Frog wanted me to nominate to do Scholarship but I refused. No way I was going to do it. Didn't see the sense in it. I dug my heels in and so he put all his efforts into Mavis. He gave her extra tuition after school and all of that, then at the last minute I said, 'Please, Sir, can I go for Scholarship?'

He said, 'Well, you've missed a lot of lessons.'

But I still did it and, well, who passed? This one. Me. And Mavis, the one he'd trained, well, she didn't pass, did she? Anyhow this Freddy the Frog had a real set on me, and another thing I did was to break the middle bit out of an ink pen nib, and when you did that you'd end up with something like a two-pronged fork. It was sharp too. Matter of fact, we had a dart board at home and we used to play darts with the broken pen nib.

Anyway, at school I'd often write the answers down on a tiny piece of paper and I'd pin them to the broken pen nib and I'd throw it into the side wall and the kids would get up to sharpen their pencils and, as they walked past the wall, they'd pull out the nib and open the piece of paper and see the answer. Then one day Freddy the Frog caught me and he sent me out of the classroom and I said to the lady who was doing the cleaning, 'Old Freddy the Frog's sent me out of class,' and she said, 'What did you do?'

I said, 'I had these pen-nib darts, see,' and I showed her one I'd hidden from Freddy the Frog and she said, 'How do they work?' and I said, 'Just like this,' and I threw it and it got stuck up in the ceiling. Anyhow the ceiling was too high and I couldn't get it down so, this cleaning lady, she had a broom and she helped me get up onto the table and she put a chair onto the table and I got up on the chair, on the table, and I'd just knocked it down with the broom when she called out, 'Doris, he's coming,' and so I jumped down just as Freddy the Frog walked in. Oh, I thought he'd copped me. But he hadn't. I'd just got down in time.

J — But you were a real little 'b' to that teacher, Doris, weren't you?

D — Well put it this way, Joyce: he resented me because he thought I was a smarty-pants. But I wasn't really. Yes, I was cheeky but ...

J — It was more of a personality clash, wasn't it, Doris?

D — Yes, we just didn't hit it off because I'd always show him up with his arithmetic. Anyway that's all behind me now, and he did come over to congratulate me when I passed Scholarship, which was quite nice of him.

J — And because none of us kids could milk properly, he also used to come over and milk our cow when Mum was away.

So I guess he wasn't too bad. And he taught us first aid and all those kinds of things, too. But his great ambition was to have one of his pupils come in the Queensland state top ten of Scholarship, and that never happened. Anyway they were fun days when you look back, weren't they, Doris?

D — Well, at least he could milk a cow.

George

I was raised on a dairy farm at a place in South Australia called Monteith. You'll find it on the Murray River, roughly halfway between Murray Bridge and Tailem Bend. Back in those days it was a very busy place, especially along the river flats and around the wharf area. These days, of course, it's not like it used to be.

Monteith Primary School was my first school. It was pretty boring, really. This was back in the era when teachers could wield the willow and I guess I got into the usual sorts of trouble young boys did, so I copped my fair share. It was basically a one-teacher school but the year I began we had sixty-three children and so the teacher chap roped his wife in to help out. She taught Grades 1, 2 and 3 and he taught the rest.

I guess, for me, the only real highlight — if you'd call it that — was that I was left-handed. Of course, in those days, if you were left-handed they tried to teach you to become right-handed. So if I got caught using my left hand I'd get a whack over the knuckles with a ruler or worse. I tell you, I used to come home black and blue at times. Now I've never actually delved deep enough into it to be exactly sure but, through different things I've heard and read, if you're left-handed then apparently you use different parts of your brain. Perhaps that's why a lot of left-handers are bank managers and so forth. I'm not a bank manager but that's just one of the theories anyway.

As for memories about my primary school days, I've got a few. I guess the main one was when the 1956 floods came through and the school ended up being surrounded by water, so they shut it down and we were taken by bus to Murray

Bridge Primary School for a whole year. It was a pretty big flood. Most of the dairy farms around Monteith were flooded and the farmers had to agist their cattle out to various locations. We were very fortunate in as much as our actual milking shed was just above the flood waterline so we were still able to use that. Though because of all the water, we had to bring in heaps of fodder.

But it's not so much my primary school years that I want to talk about, it's more about going to high school at Murray Bridge. It made for quite a long day really. Each morning us kids had to ride our pushbikes three or four miles out to the railway siding just to catch the 8 o'clock train to Murray Bridge. To put it into context, in those days there were a large amount of navvies and labourers working for the railways; you know, fettlers and people like that. Anyhow the railways used to run an early morning train, out from Murray Bridge, to take their workers to Tailem Bend. Then on its return trip, that same train, it'd pick up all us kids and it'd get into Murray Bridge in time enough for us to walk the fifteen or twenty minutes to the school. The same thing happened after school. The train would leave Murray Bridge and drop us kids off, on its way out to pick up the workers at Tailem Bend. It was a steam engine back then and it only had about four carriages; a couple for us boys and a couple of carriages for the girls. That's because we weren't supposed to co-mingle. Anyhow there was always a certain amount of banter going on, on this train to and from Murray Bridge and when I read in your last book about how you were writing school days stories I thought, Well, you might just be interested in this one.

See this was back when we still had Guy Fawkes Night and you could purchase firecrackers. So before we caught the train to go home after school, most of us kids had time enough to go to the shops and buy a drink or something to eat, or to purchase something that was needed at home. In those days most of us carried what was commonly called a kit bag, whereas today the kids have backpacks. Anyhow, in your kit bag you kept all your school books and you might have a tin as a lunchbox.

But there were some real characters. This particular guy I'm going to tell you about, his nickname was George. His actual name was Trevor but everyone called him George for some unknown reason. But he was one of those kids who could be hyped up into performing just about anything you wanted him to do. You know, he was as slow as a wet week but, if it was sports day and he was running the 880 yards, with everyone egging him on he'd get so hyped up that he'd perform above himself. It was like he'd go into overdrive.

Anyhow, it was around Guy Fawkes time and George had purchased some firecrackers. Back then you could buy some amazing stuff: Chinese lanterns, cartwheels and all sorts of firecrackers. But George was particularly proud of the fact that he'd just purchased these sixpenny bungers. I'm not sure how many he'd bought but he told us that he'd saved up all year for them. So there might've been a few. Now, I don't know if you remember the sixpenny bunger but they were quite a large fire cracker. What's more, they packed a fair amount of punch. So we get on the train and, of course, George says, 'Look at what I've got,' and he opens up a brown paper bag and he takes out one of these sixpenny bungers to show us. Huge it was.

"N' how big of a bang do yer reckon that'd make, George?' someone asked.

'Lots,' says George.

'Bet it doesn't,' says someone, egging him on.

'Bet it does,' says George.

'Go on. Show us.'

'Yeah, okay,' says George.

Now I just can't remember where the matches came from — probably from one of the kids that smoked, I guess — but anyway, in a flash, someone had handed this box of matches over to George.

'Go on,' someone says. It could've been me.

'Okay,' says George and he takes out a match and he lights the wick of this sixpenny bunger.

Now also on the train in those days were the older students. They usually stayed away from us younger kids, in the other carriage. But some of them were prefects and, as such, it was their job to take it in turns to patrol the carriages in an attempt to keep things in some sort of respectable order. So George had just lit this sixpenny bunger when one of the prefects appears out of the other carriage. In an instant George sticks the lit bunger back into the brown paper bag, along with all his unlit sixpenny bungers. He sticks the bag in his knapsack and he slips it under his seat, out of view. Of course, the prefect catches a whiff of burning wick, doesn't he? And seeing that George looks the most guilty out of the lot of us, he goes over to George.

'What's goin' on, George?'

'Nuffin',' says George.

Meanwhile there's this hissing sound coming out from under George's seat. The wick's burning away, and it's caught onto the remainder of George's precious sixpenny bungers.

'Are you sure?' says the prefect.

'Yep,' mumbles George.

No sooner had George uttered those words than there came an enormous explosion from under his seat. 'BOOM', 'BOOM', 'BOOM', off went all of George's sixpenny bungers. Now I don't know if you've ever seen anyone shit themselves but I reckon that prefect might've shit himself that day because, as he took off like a startled gazelle, back to his carriage, I could've sworn I saw a brown stain spreading out on the back of his strides.

Goats

I was born in western Queensland at a place called Dajarra but, because of the work situation, my mother and my father couldn't stay there too long and so they went back to the Northern Territory, out onto Gallipoli cattle station. Dad worked on Gallipoli as an engineer. He looked after all the station vehicles and the windmills and that sort of stuff. Mum and my sisters, we stayed there till it was time for me to go to school. So from Gallipoli, we moved back to Camooweal and we stayed in Camooweal till 1942 which was when we moved over to Mount Isa. All this time Dad was still working on properties around the place and so he only came into town to visit us when he could. He ended up going to Alexandria Station and he stayed there for quite a number of years before he went over to Creswell, and that's where he got sick. He got a poisoned ear and so they took him into Tennant Creek, to the hospital there, and when he was just about to get out of the hospital he died of a heart attack. That was later on, in 1956.

I was a young girl of about six when we went back to Camooweal. That was back in the early- to mid-1930s, and the little house we lived in was made from corrugated iron and bush timber, and it had a dirt floor. There was a little verandah out the front and we had a big rainwater tank and if we ever ran out of water we had to cart some in. This was before the water was laid on in town. There was no washing machines. All we had was wash tubs and washing boards and coppers to boil up the water for the washing. For a bath we had a big tub that we all had to share. So it was all in together — well, almost — and then we didn't get a shower till years later. There was no fridges. We had one of them Coolgardie safes. It was a square galvanised box thing with charcoal and mesh wire around it and then there was bags over all of that, that we had to keep wet so things were kept cool.

There was a lot of families living in Camooweal in those days. They even had a Shire Hall. That's still there and it's the same one that was there when I was a kid going to school. I remember how it was a real big thing for us kids to go down and watch the monthly dances in that hall. The CWA ladies used to do the catering and they'd organise the sandwiches and the cakes and they'd boil up the water in kerosene tins for the tea. But, oh, they dressed up for the occasion. They really did. There was some of the most beautiful long evening dresses — just beautiful — and there was an old feller who played the piano and someone else was on the drums, and they polished the floor up with sawdust so that everyone could glide around on it. Yeah, just glide around.

We didn't have a veggie garden at our place in Camooweal but there was this Chinese gardener; his name was Ah Wing. We all called him Ah Bah — that's the Chinese name for 'father' — and he was married to a lady from Burketown, Dora, and they had four or five kids. My sister married one of the older boys, Charlie Ah Wing and she now lives in Mount Isa. But Ah Bah had everything in his garden. He had a well and he drew up the water with the old horse going round and round and this old horse was all rigged up so the buckets of water would come up and they'd get tipped into a trough that was up high, then the water would run from the trough, out into his garden, out along the drains. All handmade. No hoses or anything. He had it really well laid out and he provided veggies for the people in the town and also to a lot of the station people who would come in to get their veggies: pumpkins, potatoes, everything you could name. He even had fruit trees. You wouldn't think so nowadays, if you saw Camooweal, but he grew just about everything you could name.

The Ah Wing family have gone from Camooweal now and a lot of the Aboriginal families from out Lake Nash way, they've come to live in Camooweal. Remember that big thing about the Aboriginal people out on Lake Nash Station years ago, when they all went on strike for equal wages? Well, when the white station owners were forced to pay award wages on the cattle stations, they couldn't afford to pay everyone, so a lot of the Aboriginal stockmen and their families, they sort of drifted into Camooweal. But now, since they've given some of that land back to the Aboriginal people, they've gone and set up their own community out that way.

So I started at Camooweal State School in 1935. There's a picture of the old school there, in that book called *The Border and Beyond: Camooweal*. It was written specially by Lilian Ada Miller. She was originally known as Ada Freckleton. The Freckletons used to have the main grocery store in town. Freckleton's Store is all closed up now and Ada's brother Joe, he was the only one that remained living in Camooweal, and he did that up till his death.

Anyhow, a few years back they had the Camooweal School Centenary reunion and I went back for that and I got a centenary cup and a cookery book and also my sister gave me that book by Ada, *The Border and Beyond: Camooweal*. I forget exactly when that reunion was now, but it says here that the school was established in 1893. So that would make it 1993, wouldn't it? But a lot of people came back to that reunion, yeah. I remember how we all signed the roll book and had our photos taken and each of us planted a tree and things like that. But I don't know if the trees would still be alive now. It gets too dry in Camooweal and when the school holidays are on there's no kids about the place so I doubt if the trees got any water at all. But I haven't been back since the centenary. I usually go through that way by bus and the bus just goes straight through town and out the other side, and I just stay on it.

The school's still there, though. It's been renovated since. But in that picture, in Ada Freckleton's book, that's how it looked when I was there. It's one of them off-the-ground types of buildings that are typical of that area. I think they built them that way because it got a good air flow underneath — you know, like a breezeway — because it gets real hot out there. We also used to play a lot of games and stuff underneath the school. We even ate our lunch there. I guess it's like what the schools these days call a 'wet area' — a place where the kids can go when it's raining. Though it didn't seem to rain that much out at Camooweal and, of course, the King of England and the Commonwealth was still alive back then and so when the bell rang we all stood in line, and when the boys raised the flag we sang 'God Save the King'. Then after we'd done that, we marched up the steps and into the school to a marching tune. I can't remember what the tune was just now but if I heard it I would.

When I first went to Camooweal it only went up to Grade 7. We had two teachers: a lady who taught all the lower grades, then there was a man, who must've been the headmaster, and he taught the higher grades. The teachers were all right. The man, he married a local girl, one of the Riley girls. The woman teacher, she was pretty good too. But the cane was in, in those days, and I used to get the cane quite a bit because, see, I was writing with my left hand when you were supposed to write with your right hand. So I'd try and write with my right hand and I'd still end up getting the cane because my work wasn't that good. It was too messy. But then if I pulled my hand away before I was hit with the cane, I'd get a few more. But I wasn't a naughty child. Not really. It was just that I was left-handed and I think that might've sort of affected me.

So I was forced to write with my right hand. But when I was out of the classroom I did everything with my left hand. To this day; yes, I still write with my right hand but do everything else with my left hand. I iron and I cut things up and everything with my left hand. Poor old thing's got arthritis these days. It's funny because, back then, all the tools and things were made for right-handers so I guess they figured out that the right hand was the right way for everyone to go. There was nothing made for left-handed people like me and so I sort of taught myself to knit upside down. And because it was war time we were all knitting squares that were to be made into blankets then sent off to our soldiers. Everyone was knitting back then; socks and gloves, everything, and with all those complicated patterns it was quite a skill because with the socks, you've got to knit the heel and then you knit the top. It was the same with the gloves. But we got quite good at it. Then I learnt how to crochet. That's why it's hard for me to teach anyone how to sew or to crochet, because I'm left-handed. I can only teach a left-hander. A lot of my family, like my grandchildren and my great grandchildren, they're left-handed too, just like me.

So this was way back, say between 1935 and 1942, and in your first years at school, you'd write on a slate with chalk. I'd say the slate was about a foot by a foot; something like the A4-size piece of paper that they use these days. Then when you'd learnt how to write properly on the slate, the next year you were given a lead pencil and you learnt to write with that on paper, and if you made a mistake you rubbed it out with a rubber. Though you dare not call them 'rubbers' these days, do you? They're called erasers or something like that. So you'd do that for a year or two then maybe from Grade 5 upwards you started writing with pens that had ink nibs, and each morning the boys would mix up the ink powder with some water and that would be your daily supply of ink. The desks we used to sit at were two-people wooden desks with iron frames — I think they had iron frames, anyway — and the ink well was up top, in the middle, and we had blotting paper, to blot up any ink splotches we made.

Then we played lots of different games; games like all-rounders. I think that's like softball. We called another game 'basketball' though these days it's more like netball. So, yeah, we played all them. Then there was always our big sports day at the end of the year. Oh, that was a big thing. With the end-of-year break-up, when we had our sports day, we had running races and three-legged races and egg-and-spoon races. But the really big thing out at Camooweal was when the boys had their billy goat races. That's true, yeah; billy goat races. Well, they put reins on their billy goats and then they sat on their backs and away they went. No saddles. It was all bareback, and a lot of the boys had their own goats that they'd trained special for the race. They didn't ride them to school. They only just had them special for the races. There's a picture in Ada's book with about five or eight boys all dressed up with braces, shirts, shorts, socks, boots and hats — some of them are wearing straw hats — and they're all sitting up there on their goats with their halters, bareback, ready to take off and they'd race for about a hundred yards. From the look of it, I'd say that that picture could've been taken at one of our school sports days.

But we all had goats. Everyone had goats. They cost nothing to feed because they just ate the weeds and all the rubbish. In return they gave us our milk, and when times were bad, they were our meat. You could also make butter and cheese from their milk. We didn't, but you could. Then you could also use their skins as rugs for the floor. You could ride them. Some people even used them for carting wood and water. Oh, you can't beat a goat. In Ada's book it says here that, and I quote, 'There are those of us who believe that there should be a monument to the goat in Camooweal, so great was the people's dependence on the animal in the early struggling pioneering days.'

I agree with that because that's how important goats were to us. Before my school day even started, I used to go and help Mum milk the goats of a morning and then she'd let them out of the yard and off they'd go, off to the town common.

Then, when they were ready to come back for their afternoon milking, me and a couple of my girlfriends from school, we'd go out and meet the goats as they were wandering back in and we just went in behind them and put them in the yard and we'd milk them and then they'd spend the night in the yard. Oh yes, the goats knew where to come back home to. They were well trained. All we had to do was to check if they'd had babies during the day — you know, kids, as they call them. So if you had a few goats and some veggies and you had a few chooks, then you were just about right in a place like Camooweal.

Gotcha!

TREVOR — You're listening to 'Summer all Over' with Trevor Chappell. Matthew from Roxby just wants to say 'happy birthday' to his daughter who's camping with her grandparents on the Tassie west coast. Happy birthday, Catlin, from Matthew. Good morning, Lance. Lance has a school days story.

LANCE — Good morning to you and all the best for the new year. Now mine's an unusual one. I'm eighty years old but back when I was at school, during the war, we used to go out to Mascot aerodrome because we were fascinated by aeroplanes. Anyhow there was this big American feller out there, this time, and he gave us a book. It was a rude book. He said, 'Here you are, boys, have a look at this and you might learn something.'

Well, me and my mates, we took it home for a look and then I took it to school the next day and I gave it to one of my other mates to have a gawk at and I said, 'Don't look at it in school, whatever you do. Just take it home and have look at it, then bring it back to us when you've finished.'

Anyway, silly boy, he decided to have a look at it in school, and he got caught, didn't he? The teacher nabbed him and he confiscated the book. 'I'll take that, thank you very much.'

But see, I had a pretty fair idea as to what would happen. So at lunchtime, a few of us, we crept around the side of the staff lunchroom and when we spied in through the window, sure enough, here's all the teachers, gathered around, looking at this book. And so it was … one … two … and then on the count of three we yelled out, 'Gotcha!'

Well you should have seen it. These teachers, they didn't know what to do. They dropped the book and us boys, we took off for our lives. They didn't find out who it was but I tell you what, those teachers got one hell of a shock.

TREVOR — It's even better when you catch the teachers out.

LANCE — Yes, that's what I was saying ...

TREVOR — Good on you, Lance. Swampy, you're bound to get heaps and heaps of stories here.

SWAMPY — Yes, I've already got a couple of very short ones that I've picked up on my travels. The first one's about a little boy in country Victoria. The apple of his mother's eye he was. She was just so proud of him and, of course, she wanted him to look well presented at school. To that end she used to shine his school shoes until they almost sparkled. But the thing was, she only allowed him to wear those shoes while he was at school — not before he got to school, and not even after the school day had finished. So every morning she dressed him up to the nines then she made him put his shiny shoes and his socks in his school bag. So then he had to walk, barefooted, along a dirt track, the mile or so to the school gate. And it was only at the school gate that he was allowed to take his socks and the shiny shoes out of his school bag and put them on. So he'd wear them all day, while he was at school, then, in the afternoon, he had to take them off again at the school gate and he had to walk back home, barefooted, through all the bindi-eyes and dirt and stuff.

So that's one little anecdote. Then there's one I heard about when I was up in the Northern Territory, at Tennant Creek. As you might know it gets as hot as hell out there, especially during summer. Anyway there was this little kid; for the sake of the story we'll call him Tommy. Now, like many of the kids are in those outback places, this Tommy was a real rugged little individual. Anyhow, this summer's day, the temperature's over a hundred in the water bag and he's mucking around in class, something chronic.

The teacher's had enough so he says, 'Outside, Tommy. I'll deal with you later.'

So little Tommy shuffles outside and the teacher continues on with his lessons. A couple of minutes later little Tommy reappears. He walks straight back in the door, past the teacher, and he goes over and he sits back down at his desk.

The teacher says, 'I thought I told you to go outside?'

'Yes, Sir, you did.'

'Then why are you back here?'

'It's too bloody hot out there, Sir.'

Then the last one — and I'll be quick about it — was a story I heard when I was travelling through outback Queensland. A new teacher had arrived out at this small town way out in the middle of nowhere, and he was trying to familiarise himself with the dozen or so kids in the school. Anyhow after the first week he had all their Christian and surnames down pat. He even had a pretty fair idea as to their nicknames and how they'd come about. But there was one young feller by the name of Wally Smith and he just couldn't work out why all the other kids were calling this lad 'Shorten'. I mean the kid wasn't small, by any stretch of the imagination. Anyhow, for the life of him, this teacher just couldn't work it out. So he went to one of the more senior kids and he asked, 'Hey, why does everyone call young Wally Smith Shorten?'

And the kid said, 'Well, Sir, that's because his brother was nicknamed Curly.'

Hair Today, Gone Tomorrow

This was back in the '70s. I was about twenty at the time, and it was my first year as an art teacher. Back in those days, while they were teaching you to teach, you only got paid fifteen bucks a week so I dressed in op-shop gear. You could say that I had that real 'art student' look. Though I guess what really made me stand out from the rest was that I also had very long hair for a bloke, down past my shoulder blades. It was great. A work of art in itself.

Anyway I'd just found out that my first teaching job was to be at a small town over on the west coast of South Australia. I won't mention the name of the place but my first comment was, 'Where the hell's that?' and I had to grab a map to see just where I was being sent. Next problem was how to get there. Seeing that I didn't have a car, bus was my only option and the only bus going out that way arrived in the town at four in the morning. Mind you, this is also in the middle of winter so it was going to be cold.

Still, I didn't have any alternative so I packed my worldly possessions into an old cardboard box, got on the bus in Adelaide and headed off, and at 4 a.m. the bus emptied me out in the town. I looked around. Nothing. No one. Not a soul. It was like Dry Gulch. I waited for the tumbleweed to blow past but when that didn't even arrive I thought, Well, I'll just grab a bit of sleep on a nearby bench and when the place starts moving I'll go and see if someone can point me in the direction of the school and the principal.

So that's what I did. And seeing as it was freezing, I grabbed a few extra warm clothes out of my cardboard box and I wrapped them around me, then I went to sleep on the bench.

When I woke up there were all these people standing around me. Gawking. 'Good God,' I heard someone say. 'Disgraceful,' was another comment.

Of course, with seeing me lying there, dressed as I was, with a partially unpacked cardboard box of op-shop clothes beside me and with my long flowing hair and all, they assumed I was some sort of hobo who'd lobbed into town. Little did they know I'd arrived to teach all their little darlings. Anyhow, I explained my situation and they got word to the principal and when he arrived, he wasn't in the best of moods. He took me over to his place and we had breakfast and he basically told me how disgusted he was with the manner of my arrival.

Then he gave me the rundown. He said he was 'ex-army' and that's how he ran his school. Discipline was his catch phrase. Discipline and authority, and he expected his staff to follow his every order, his every command, to the nth degree. As straight as a die he was, as was the rest of the community. As I was soon to find out, they were not only ultra-conservative, but they also had an extremely strong religious base. Anyhow, the principal went on to say that if I, as a member of his staff, was to be respected by students and parents alike, I had to dress in a presentable manner with proper pants — trousers, as he called them — and a belt and I'd have to wear a shirt and a tie every day. And I had to have a haircut.

That's how it all started. And to start with I did try to look respectable; well, the best I could. I wore a tie, and for the first week or so it stayed around my neck. A week or so later it had slipped down to around my waist, where it came in handy holding my op-shop pants up. So yes, in a funny sort of way, I did end up wearing a belt. But I steadfastly refused to get my hair cut. As I said, I liked my hair the way it was. It was my signature look, if you like.

So me and this principal were at loggerheads from day one, and that's how it continued. Though in an attempt to keep myself sane and rebuff some of his ultra-militarism I started drawing humorous cartoons about him and the deputy principal. And they became very popular. Like, every Monday morning, I'd paste a new cartoon onto the noticeboard and there'd be a line-up of staff and students waiting there, ready to have a good laugh at my latest gag.

Then one day I was asked into the principal's office. 'It's good what you're doing with those drawing things of yours,' he said, 'but I'd like you to put more of an emphasis on the actual humour.'

'Well,' I said, 'that's what I thought I was doing. Everyone seems to enjoy them.'

'That may be so,' he said, 'but what I'd like to see is more real humour and less about me and the deputy principal.'

'Oh,' I said.

'And if you don't do as I say you'll be moved on from this school.'

So I was kicked out of the office, under threat of being moved on and ordered not to draw any more cartoons featuring him and the deputy principal.

Anyhow, next Monday's cartoon was a ripper; one of the best I'd done, even if I do say so myself. Everyone got a huge kick out of it, bar, of course, the principal and the deputy principal. So true to his word, I was moved on. I'd only lasted there three months and they found me a school further over on the coast, and that's where the story about the haircut came in. This new place was another ultra-conservative community and, me being me, with my op-shop clothing and my long flowing locks, I can understand how I may have appeared as being a little different than their general run-of-the-mill, religiously-orientated-farming-short-back-'n'-sides type of bloke. Well, for starters I wasn't into sport or stuff like that.

Now at this new place they held ram sales and whenever any of these sales happened all the farmers would end up in the pub having a great piss-up. This particular time a ram was sold for something like $43,000. Yes, for just the one ram. It blew everyone out. So all these farmers ended up back at the pub and they were getting absolutely pissed as. And I overheard one group of these tanked farmers going on about how just because someone else had been paid $43,000 for a ram, that it didn't mean they were now all well-off. Times were still tough, they reckoned, and they were still scratching to make a living.

Anyhow I was there having a few beers with a mate — he was a not-so-conservative local — and when I overheard their whingeing and wailing I said to them, 'Haven't you guys got some sort of co-operative going where you can share your wealth around? Like if someone gets paid heaps for a ram, then they can share their money with blokes like yourselves who are struggling.' It all seemed quite logical to me but they looked at me as if I was stupid. So I said, 'You don't always have to own everything for yourself, you know.'

Well they didn't like that. Not one little bit. 'What are yer,' they said, 'a fuckin' Commie or somethin'?'

'I'm definitely not a Commie,' I said, 'but have you got any idea of just what "collectivism" is?'

Anyhow they said, 'Oh come over 'n' join in a beer with us.'

Me being a greenhorn I said, 'Yeah all right,' and so there I was, now having a few beers with these guys, trying to explain about collectivism. But they just couldn't get it. They still thought I was a Commie and so things were getting quite heated. Anyhow, while we were drinking and going on I started to get the feeling that things weren't quite right; that they were up to something and whatever that something was, it was no good. Then after we'd had a few more beers they said, 'We're gonna have something to eat out the back, why don't yer come 'n' have a feed with us 'n' yer can explain a bit more about what yer on about.'

Stupid me, I said, 'Yeah, okay,' and so I stumbled out the back of the pub with these guys.

But unbeknown to me it was just a big set-up because one of these guys had previously snuck outside and he'd grabbed some hand shears out of his ute and before I knew it, they'd jumped me and they'd started hacking at my hair.

Anyhow the mate I'd been previously drinking with, he knew these guys and, what's more, he knew what they were like when they were tanked. So thankfully he'd kept an eye on me and when he'd seen what was going on he shot out the front, got into his car and drove around the back. So there I was, down on the ground, getting my hair hacked about when, next thing, there's this shotgun going off: 'BOOM' — 'BOOM'. And when I looked up, there was my mate, standing beside his car, car doors open, with his shotgun in hand.

'Quick,' he shouted, and while the tanked farmers took off for cover, I made a break for it and I jumped into my mate's car and we pissed off out of there pretty quick-smart.

So I managed to escape from that one but then, of course, the next morning when I rocked up at school I had to face the principal and explain my unusual haircut. That didn't go down too well either.

Hiz

I met my husband when I went to New Guinea in the late 1960s. At first we were farming in the Markham Valley. We had a number of different things on the go; we started with peanuts, then we went into sorghum and, with sorghum being a grain crop, we developed a sideline of laying birds, for their eggs. At one stage we were also growing rice, though that meant a lot of investment in as much as you needed to farm wetland rice to keep the army worm at bay. Then in the late '70s we moved to the highlands of the Morobe Province, where we were growing coffee and, when we could eventually afford it, running some cattle.

During that time we had three children, a girl and two boys, and in those earlier days, in the Markham Valley, with the national language being pidgin English and there being no school nearby, their education was pretty much left up to me. Our first born was a girl. She was a wonderful student who took on board everything I said. The next one, the first boy, was more questioning and I remember to this day the time I was teaching him to read and write and he said, 'Why does the word "his" end in an "s" instead of a "z", like it sounds?'

Might I say at this point, pidgin English is written phonetically and as such it's a very straightforward and logical language. For instance, we were once on leave in South Australia and my father said to my son, 'Now, you won't be a naughty boy, will you?' and my son looked him dead in the eye and said, 'Yes.'

At that reply, smoke started coming out of my father's ears. But I said, 'Hang on, Dad. Listen, he is giving you the right answer.' I said, 'It's like French. You've given him a double negative question — "You won't be a naughty boy, will you?" — and he's agreeing with you by saying "Yes" that he won't be a naughty boy, and that's exactly how they would answer in pidgin. You'd say, "Yes" because it is, logically, the correct answer.'

Another problem of learning to speak and think in pidgin then transferring it to the English was: in New Guinea, if your pencil's broken you'd go to the teacher and say that the pencil is 'buggered up', and just imagine if you said that in an Australian school, you'd be in trouble for swearing, wouldn't you? But in pidgin, 'buggered up' is actually the expression for anything that goes wrong.

Okay, all that aside: so there I was teaching my first son and he quite logically asked why the word 'his' ended in an 's' rather than the more phonetic 'z', and my answer was, 'I don't know, but English is a funny language. That's the way it is and you just have to learn it.'

Well he looked at me and he said, 'Mum, you're telling me to learn stuff that you don't even understand.'

That comment shocked me. He was absolutely right, so I swore to myself I'd find out the answer because a) I'm a mum, b) because I'm logical and c) my degree was in Science, and with science you never say, 'I don't know' without ending the statement with, 'but I will find out'. Scientists don't go in for mystery or supposition. We believe there's a reason for everything, and so that's what I set out to find.

Of course there were many obstacles in my way. By living in New Guinea I was isolated, geographically. I also had other things to do, with three children to teach. I was also a farmer's wife, and we all know what that entails. Plus we had a large number of workers on the farm and I did the sick line, which was when the workers would line up for basic medical treatment. I also had to do all the buying and selling of supplies via the trade store. I was a very busy person. But I did not let that deter me. When I visited Australia I asked many quite knowledgeable people as to why 'his' hasn't got a 'z' but they all said, 'Don't know. English is a funny language. Just learn it.'

To my mind that type of attitude just breeds a proportion of children who are going to think they must be dumb and everyone else is getting it. Or else they're going to say, 'The schoolteacher's dumb or the system's dumb and I'd rather play a game that has rules like football.' Nobody minds rules in football. It's what the game is founded on. In fact, that's why the game is called 'Aussie Rules'. Yet whenever I speak to people about spelling they say, 'Oh there are a few rules but there's that many exceptions, it's not worth learning them.'

'Well,' I then ask, 'what are the rules?', and they actually don't know.

Anyway I've just spent the last twenty years of my life researching and writing a print-on-demand book called *Reading with Rules: thirty thousand words with their spelling rules, reasons and rebels*. At present it's self-published in paper form and basically it's a book that parents or teachers can refer to when a child asks why a particular word is spelt the way it is. It also gives the reason for each rule, plus the explanation for each rebel.

For example, I'll give you a couple of the rules. First of all, the reason why 'his' ends with 's' rather than 'z' is that, even from the very early Roman days, they had a fear of writing the letter 'z'. That's because the letter 'z' came from the Phoenician word *zayen*, which is the sign of the dagger. They didn't like it so they didn't write it. This then carried through to other languages, including English, where, to negate the use of the letter 'z', we put one 's' for 'z' and a double 'ss' when it comes after a stressed vowel in a word like 'hiss', as in the 'hiss' of a snake. When you get to the end of a word which is unstressed it's not so important. The word 'omnibus' for example, doesn't end in 'ss' and when you shorten it to 'bus', it keeps its single 's'. The word 'yes' doesn't end in a double 'ss' because it comes from the relatively modern 'yea so' and, as such, has been combined into the one word of 'yes'.

Another very simple rule is that all important words in a sentence have to have at least three letters. By important words I mean the nouns and their adjectives and the verbs and their adverbs. That's why, when we write the word 'axe' we place an 'e' at the end of it. Because, if you can't double a letter, you add a silent 'e'. Then if a child asks, 'Why has the word "egg" got two g's?', that's because it's an important word. It's not just a little joining word within a sentence and it's not just a pronoun, and when we say noun we mean noun and not pronoun, because 'he' and 'me' have two letters.

In essence, what I'm saying is that there are rules, and there are sensible reasons for any of the exceptions. Then the words that disobey the rules are known as 'rebels' and they are usually rebels with a reason and if they don't have a reason I call them 'rascals', and there are only twelve rascals in the English language. So when a child sees that there is a system here, they then realise that English is not such a silly language, as most of their teachers tell them it is. I mean, how awful it is that we're told our language is strange and weird and not like other languages.

My further research has also revealed that after Johannes Gutenberg of Germany 'invented' the metal typograph in 1430, and letterpress printing of books began to spread throughout Europe, people said, 'If we're going to have all these books we must make sure as many people as possible can read them, so we'll simplify our spelling.'

Take Italy for example: to this day you can virtually read Italian even if you don't know the language. That's how simple it is to read, and there's very little dyslexia in Italian schools. I've heard they don't even have spelling tests. There's no need. The French also simplified their spelling. But then with English, the simplification of the spelling proved to be more difficult. Firstly, William Caxton had done his studies in

Holland, so when he came back to England in 1475 and set up his printing press, a lot of Dutch spelling was thrown into the mix. Added to that, England had been conquered so often that the language was, by then, a mix of many languages. Some words remind us of the Germanic and Viking days, as in 'knot' where the 'k' is silent. It's still said 'k-not' in Germany. The French couldn't stand the letters 'k' and 'w' so they got rid of them. The word 'Queen' originally started with 'Cw' until the French changed it to 'Qu'.

So English spelling was in a mess and it wasn't until the 1800s that they thought they should come up with a standardised dictionary of words. To that end they decided to get a committee of men together, all of whom had to be both 'learned and leisured'. By 'learned', they meant that they not only had to know French and German but also Greek and Latin. But unlike other countries, this committee feared that if the general populace started reading, they would get a lot of new and different and strange ideas and there'd be a revolution like there was during the late 1700s in France, where the peasants cut the King's head off, and following that they had that terrible thousand days of cutting off thousands of heads. The Napoleonic Wars was also a spin-off from that uprising, with more death and destruction. Taking all that into account, this English Committee decided on a fixed plan not to simplify spelling so that it is easy to read and they justified that decision by saying, 'We can't simplify our spelling too much or we'll lose our culture.'

In stating all this, I'd like to make the point that I'm not English, myself. My mother's father was English but all my father's people were from Scotland and my mother's mother's people were from Holland, and before that from France, and before that from the Pyrenees. Only a fraction of me comes from England. And I'm just stressing that point because I believe that the English establishment would never want to publish a book — and in this case something as hugely important as a dictionary — which explains that their spelling is like it is because they'd been conquered so often.

Then also around the mid-1800s there were two streams of thinking. Charles Lyell had published his book on geology where he believed that you could see the history of the world in its rocks; and you did that by reading the different minerals in the rocks and the different ways a rock was formed — igneous or sedimentary — and by reading the fossils. On the other hand, Charles Darwin's book on evolution — *On the Origin of Species* — though it had not quite yet been published, his view was that all living things evolve to suit the environment they're in, which is how I look at spelling, as an evolving thing. Now this committee, being learned men, had read Lyell and so, after deciding that each word in this dictionary should have just the one way of spelling, they then decided that that choice of the spelling should be reflective of its past. To that end, this dictionary was to be called *The New English Dictionary on Historical Principles*.

It proved to be a long, drawn-out process. Then after that first committee had gone broke, the Oxford University stepped in and said, 'We'll save it. We will do it,' and it eventually came out in 1888 as *The Oxford English Dictionary*, without the additional tag of 'on historical principles'. The reason there was that, with it being such a huge job, Oxford University decided to only give a short overview of each word rather than having to go through the more exhaustive process of explaining the 'historical principles' for each of the words.

Anyhow, I think I've talked enough on all of this. But you can probably notice the passion that's there, and I certainly haven't done all this research and writing to get myself a higher degree. That's useless to me. I live in the bush, for God's sake. To me, all this has not been worth doing unless it helps as many people as possible with their reading and writing and their understanding of it. That's why I've set out *Reading with Rules* in a simple manner, explaining things in ordinary everyday terms, as well as supplying a CD. Unfortunately I've exhausted all avenues and I am still yet to get a sponsor to make it available for free online, on the world wide web. I've even approached teachers' colleges and universities but no one seems prepared to take it on, so now I'm looking to, somehow, get it online.

I must add too: remember the rule I was talking about 'that important words have to have three letters'? There are only four exceptions to that rule: one of the words is a noun; the other three exceptions are verbs. The noun is one of the most ancient words we have in the language and the verbs have been used so often that they've been worn down. I'll leave that to the reader to ponder on, to try to work out. The only other thing is that abbreviations and slang words do not have to follow the rules.

So yes, that's been a focus of my working life for the past twenty years, and it all began with my son's question as to why the word 'his' ends in an 's' instead of the more phonetic 'z'.

How it Was

I just want to make it very clear that this story is not meant to be a criticism in any way, shape or form. It's simply a tale of how it was back in my early school days.

I grew up on a dairy farm at Gleniffer, which is on the north coast of New South Wales, near Bellingen. I was the eldest of two other brothers and a sister. We were producing cream and pigs at that time. Dad said that electricity had come through our valley around the Depression era back when they were trying to give work to as many people as possible. And so, even though we'd long gone beyond hand-milking, it was still in the days of the old milk can.

The whole area was basically just cream and pig production. Everyone had what was called a 'separator', which is a machine that spins at high revs and separates the cream from the milk. So the cream came out of one spout and the milk went out another spout, and we sold the cream and the milk went to feed the pigs. So the milk was basically a by-product. Then a lorry would come along about three times a week to pick up the cream. Now, apparently cream keeps quite well just as long as you have good ventilation.

Later on, of course, in the early '50s, when they converted from cream production to milk production, that's when the milk lorry came twice a day.

We lived about five mile from the Gleniffer school and I started going there in the late '40s. From memory there were about thirty-eight kids. It was a one-teacher and one-room school. The toilets were the old drop type and they were set away, away to the back of the playground. Then there was the weather shed, about a hundred metres from the school building. Everything was made from sawn hardwood timber, the school included.

One of the local farming families had started up a regular school service that did the rounds, picking up all the kids. Now, I can't be a hundred per cent sure, but I think that when I first started at Gleniffer they used an Oldsmobile Utility. It was definitely a ute of some sort, anyway. I was probably champing at the bit to go to school because, before I'd reached school age, I just remember seeing the old ute going past. So I just assumed that the natural thing to do in the progression of life was to go and climb up over the tailgate of the ute and head off with the rest of the kids. So that's what I did and there were about eight or ten of us kids squashed into this old ute by the time we finally arrived at school.

So that old ute was what I was first taken to school in. Then about a year later we were part way down the road, on our way to school, and steam started pouring up out of the radiator, and that was the end of the Oldsmobile ute. That's when the Bedford truck — or lorry as they were called back then — that's when it came along. It was owned and run by the same family. It had dual wheels at the rear. Headlights on each front mudguard. Sort of a vertical grille, typical of a Bedford. It had a Bedford cab, naturally, and then they'd made a plywood canopy to go over the back of it. In fact, if you can imagine, it sort of looked a bit like a horse float or something that hippies would drive around in these days, as a caravan. There was no seating. We all had to stand up. Actually, I think if we'd had seats it would've been a bit of a shambles because the roads we travelled on were pretty rough. They were surfaced with river gravel and as one old feller once remarked, 'That type of gravel never stops rolling till it gets back to the river.'

Then sometimes, after we were dropped off at school, the owner of the Bedford lorry would go back to his place where he'd take the canopy off and he'd go and pick up offal from the butter-and-bacon factory at Bellingen. As I said earlier, all the farmers were cream and pig producers and so these people would bring the offal back out to feed to their pigs. Nothing was ever wasted. Everything did the whole circuit. Then before the afternoon school run, the owner would just back the lorry into the Never Never Creek, give it a bit of a clean down, whack the canopy back on, and come to the school, pick us kids up and take us back home.

Actually, something of interest was that we always called it the 'Never Never River' and these days they call it a creek. But there was a string of these creeks that were all tributaries of the Bellinger River and, where the creek ran through our farm, believe it or not, it never never dried up. And gee it was a beautiful stream of water. Though I don't think they called it the 'Never Never' because it never dried up, because, see, there were also some other interesting place names in the area. One was called Promised Land. There was Tallowwood Point. Buffer Creek was nearer to us. There's a bit of a controversy over the spelling there: some call it Buffer — ending in an 'er' — and some call it Buffa — ending with just the 'a'.

So anyway this feller would drive the lorry down to the creek, he'd throw a few buckets of water over the tray, give it a bit of a scrub down, then he'd whack the canopy back on and come and do the afternoon school run. And I tell you, it's hard to get rid of the smell of offal because, after he'd done one of his offal trips, there was still quite an aroma hanging around in the back of that lorry, I can assure you.

As I said, the roads were pretty crook around that area and so it got to the stage where the canopy had been shaken about so much that it was just about falling to pieces so then they just left it off. The lorry still had its crate-like sides on. It had like old hardwood fencing along the sides. But after a while, with the picking up of the offal, the blood stains got imbedded into the timber, and even to this day I still squirm at what the young twins from a neighbouring property would do. You know how, when little kids are getting their bottom teeth, they like to gnaw on things. Well these kids just loved to chomp into the blood-stained timber.

So that was the Bedford lorry. Then came the Ford Mainline Utility. It had a canopy as well. The canopy was just like what you see on the back of four-wheel drive utes these days. It was a moulded type, made from some sort of timber product. The Ford was smaller than the Bedford, which was a bit of a problem because, by that time, we had a few extra kids at the school and so everyone had to really squash up.

Then when they closed Gleniffer school down, things changed and all the kids had to then start going to school in Bellingen. Though, in our case, the Ford Mainline still kept on doing a feeder service into Gleniffer where it'd meet the school bus that went into Bellingen. But by that stage, due to the road conditions, the exhaust fumes were almost overpowering. So I don't know how much longer it lasted. Like that old feller said, 'That type of gravel never stops rolling till it gets back to the river.'

If You Could

I was born in the UK. Grew up there. Was educated there, and then after I'd completed an undergraduate course in Economics, I went to work in that particular area. But I was always chopping and changing, unsettled, and so after a few years I was wanting to do something more fulfilling. At that time my job had taken me to Kazakhstan, where I was selling advertising space in a financial journal. Anyhow I decided I'd had enough of that and so I packed the job in and caught a train into north-west China.

It was incredibly remote. I was on my own. I had no guide book, no map. I couldn't speak Chinese. No one spoke English. There weren't even any road signs in English. Over in China they have hotel rooms that are set up like a travellers' dormitory. So I was staying in one of those and this day a Chinese chap came in and he said, 'We urgently need someone to come and teach English for a month at a university summer school. Could anyone here do it?'

Immediately my hand shot up: 'I'd love to.'

It all went from there really, which was brilliant because I could've spent a whole year in that part of China and not understood a thing, simply because I couldn't communicate. But by teaching these kids English I got to know an awful lot about the Chinese and their culture. So that happened purely by chance. Then when I got back to the UK it was a case of, 'Well, what am I going to do now?' and one of my mates said, 'Well, James, if you enjoyed it in China so much, why don't you become a teacher?'

I said, 'Don't be silly. I can't be a teacher. Not me.'

But then I thought about it, and I'd really had a great time in China and so, yeah, I decided to go down that route. I went to

Brighton University, qualified as a teacher. That was about five years ago and I've not looked back since. And then, basically, my partner, Lexy, and I, because we think it's important to teach different types of children, in different ways, we started thinking about having a teaching adventure. We were actually looking at going to either Canada or Australia but when my dad renewed his Australian citizenship, it meant that I was then eligible for 'citizenship by descent'. So it was like, Right, we're off to Australia and let's try and work in the outback. It'll be an experience. It'll be an adventure, and perhaps we can also be of help to some of the Aboriginal kids.

Then after we arrived in Australia I got work, pretty much straight away, in a school in Melbourne and Lexy got a job in a coffee shop. Anyhow one of Lexy's dad's cousins was living in Melbourne — his name was Trevor Pratt — and Trevor invited us to a barbecue over at his place. During the afternoon we got chatting to Trevor and he was very interested as to why we wanted to work in an outback school, and in particular, with Aboriginal children. When we explained to him just why we wanted to he then told us that he was chairman of an organisation known as the Mitchell Plateau Association who, among other things, were trying to get the government to set up a school at an Aboriginal community in the far north of Western Australia. The government was apparently taking its time over the matter and so one of the Indigenous grandmothers had been helping the kids with their education through Derby School of the Air. But now that she was in her seventies, it was all getting a bit too much for her, and so they were trying to raise some money for private tutors to go up there. Of course we let it be known that we'd be very interested.

'Okay,' he said, 'if anything happens, I'll get in touch.'

We let it go at that and, after a while, when we hadn't heard from Trevor we thought, Oh well, we may as well buy a camper van and go on a trip up the east coast of Australia — which we did. Then two weeks into our trip we got the call: 'It's all go. We need you up there straight away.'

So we sold the camper van in Sydney, hopped on a plane, and off we went and, as Lexy said, here we are, we're now living in a modified shipping container at Kandiwal Aboriginal Community. It might sound a bit rough but it's actually a really nice place, our little donga. We've set it up well now and, what's more, because it used to be refrigerated, it's insulated, which is just as well. Because coming from the UK we've never known heat like this. Not only that but, after we came back from Christmas holidays, we caught the tail-end of a cyclone. It was incredible. We had about four hundred millimetres of rain in four days. It just did not stop, and it came in with such driving winds that the rain was horizontal. Water was everywhere. Whereas normally, to get to the school, it's just a ten-minute stroll along a bush track, but all the creeks were running so high and fast that we were completely cut off. It even got to the stage where the parents were so eager for us to come back and teach their kids that one of the elders got in touch by satellite phone and said, 'Come on, guys. I'm sure you can cross the creek now.'

Actually we were pretty keen to get back to school too. By that stage we'd bought a four-wheel drive Toyota Hi-lux in Darwin but something had gone wrong and it was only running on two-wheel drive. Anyhow we had a good look at the creek and it was like, 'There's just no way known we can get across there.'

Next day, same again. The rains had stopped but the creek was still full of rushing water. Then Brownie, one of the local tour guides, he got across in his four-wheel drive and he said, 'Yeah you'll be right. It's okay now.'

We'd already told him that our vehicle now only had two-wheel drive, but he must've forgotten. He also must've forgotten that our Toyota Hi-lux was a lot lighter than his Land Cruiser. Anyway we took another look and it was, 'Well if Brownie says it's okay, then it must be okay,' so 'VROOM' into the creek we went.

As soon as we hit the water the front wheels shot up. The back wheels started spinning. The bonnet rose and we began to float downstream. So it was a quick reverse, and I only managed to pull the car just a little bit out of the main flow of the creek before it conked out. We then had to leave it stuck there, climb out onto the roof and jump off onto the bank, then walk back up to the camp to get Brownie to tow us out. So we approach swollen creeks with a lot more caution these days. But talk about wanting to go on a teaching adventure. That really put the wind up us.

Okay, now a bit about Kandiwal Community. It was established in 1987. Prior to that, Rio Tinto had been looking to mine in the area. For whatever reason nothing came of that but they left a couple of houses and they also left an airstrip. Two tourist operators have since built it up. So you've got the community there. Then about five hundred metres away, in a north-easterly direction, is one of the tourist camps. Then about eight hundred metres from the community, in a slightly more easterly direction, you've got the second of the tourist camps. They're all no more than ten minutes' walk apart, but there's trees and creeks in the way so you can't see each other. The camps are quite well established. For accommodation there's luxury tents, plus they have laundry facilities. We usually eat at one of the camps, along with the guests, then after dinner we give a talk about what we're doing and then the guests send up books and things for the kids. In all, it works well.

Even though it's not a dry community, there's no problems with alcohol. If someone goes into town they might come back with a couple of slabs of beer. But that's about it. You never see anyone drinking during the day, and unemployment isn't a problem. A few of the teenage girls work in the tour operators' kitchens. Some of the men are employed by the tour operators as manual labourers. Some work with the park rangers. Others work for the Department of Environment and Conservation, where they go out trapping and recording animals for research. So they've got plenty to do up there.

And I know Lexy's already said it but they're the most fantastic children. We teach a total of sixteen kids; most of them are primary school age. They basically come from three main families and they've usually had a good upbringing. But if any of the kids starts to do it tough they immediately get taken into the bosom of the community where they're looked after by a grandma or an aunty.

And these kids, they're so genuinely friendly. They even take us out camping. One time they took us to a little spot beside a fast-flowing creek, and they were in the water all day. They'd start upstream and float down with the current, then they'd duck-dive underwater and make their way through the trees that had fallen into the water. Then they'd get out at the bottom and walk all the way back up the top and do it all again. I mean, Occupational Health and Safety would've had a nightmare, but these kids just had the greatest of fun. It was fantastic, and they were fishing; pulling out fish and slinging them straight on the fire for a few minutes, then we'd eat them with our fingers. Oh, and we were all in those dome tents and, that night, just as they were getting off to sleep we heard this frantic rustling sound then this little kid started shouting, 'Mister James. Mister James. Help. Help. Help.'

So we rushed out, 'What's happening? What's going on?' and it was a little boy of about twelve. He'd forgotten to peg down his tent and he'd had a nightmare and there he was, rolling about, all caught up in this tent, trying to find his way out, bless him. And he's calling out to me for help. I was really quite touched by that: you know, him calling out my name to come and help him.

So that's about it. That's our story. It's been just the greatest of adventures and along the way, Lexy and I, we've been able to help the kids with their education. And just on that, I don't know if you can squeeze this into your book or not but the Mitchell Plateau Association was basically set up by the guy, Brownie, who I mentioned had crossed the creek in his Land Cruiser. Well, he got on board a group of retired business people to help him form the Mitchell Plateau Association, of which Trevor Pratt is currently the chairman, and they work with Kandiwal Community in a variety of areas. One of the main ones is to try and get the lease back for the community.

Then, as I mentioned, they're also trying to get a state-run school up here. That's been dragging on for about ten years now and, to be honest, the government's just been giving them the right runaround. You know, like, you need to have X amount of kids before we'll set up a school. You have to get the appropriate teacher housing before we'll set up a school. Another time the government said, 'Okay, we'll give you a school if you get the power and water supplied.'

Naturally there's very strict regulations about all that and so you're looking at a million-dollar investment. So the government's rubbing its hands and thinking, Great, a small place like Kandiwal will never be able to raise that sort of cash. But the community's very forward-thinking and, for it to move forward, they know they need to educate their kids. Otherwise it'll go backwards, and nobody wants that. So everyone involved got together and they said, 'Okay, we'll put in the money for the power and the water.'

Of course, once that happened, the government backed out of it again, didn't they? Which is one of the main reasons why we're now up here as private tutors. But bear in mind Kandiwal is a permanent community. We've got excellent attendance. Much better than in most of the Aboriginal communities we've heard about; so it's obvious that the kids want to learn. And the parents are supportive. From the time Lexy and I got here everyone's been one hundred per cent behind us. If we wanted to change things or teach the kids this or teach them that, they've always said, 'Yes, go ahead with it.' No questions asked.

What's more, they're also willing to get the proper teacher housing up here. So in the scheme of things the state government wouldn't really have to spend that much money to help educate these kids. All you're looking at now is getting teachers in, and what's a teacher's salary out here in Australia? It'd be nothing compared to the millions of dollars they plough into Aboriginal policies and initiatives. Anyhow, it'd be greatly appreciated if you could somehow get it into your book and let your readers know that a state-funded school at Kandiwal is not just viable, it's also something the community really wants and needs.

Ingenuity

I'll send you the piece out of the newspaper if you like. It concerns an incident that happened to the younger brother of the Taskis family, Ronnie Taskis, and it's about the coolness and ingenuity within a crisis shown by his two elder brothers, Douglas and Laurie Taskis. It's true too because it says here in the clipping that a 'Mister A.O. Jarrett of Mullengandra Station confirms these particulars'.

Now I believe the story appeared in the Melbourne *Argus* in about 1931 which was when the Taskis boys were attending Mullengandra Public School. Mullengandra, or Mully as it's more commonly known, is about twenty-five miles north of Albury, on the Hume Highway. It's sort of halfway between Albury and Holbrook, and I've actually spoken to Laurie Taskis' son and he's very happy for me to tell you the story. Neither Douglas or Ronnie Taskis married and, unfortunately, now all of the three brothers who were involved in the incident are dead.

As it goes, there was a group of seven children walking to school on this particular day. Mully was only a small one-teacher school, situated on the banks of the Sweetwater Creek. At that time a Mister Wailes was the schoolteacher. Anyhow, somewhere along the way young Ronnie was bitten by a snake. I'm not sure of just how he came to be bitten but I'm presuming it was on his hand. Of course there was no immediate medical help available. In fact the school didn't even have a decent first aid kit. So the two older brothers, Douglas and Laurie, what they did was, they took the laces out of their school shoes and fastened two ligatures above the wrist and the elbow of young Ronnie.

None of the group had a knife to bleed the snake-bite wound and so the two older brothers raced down to the nearby Sweetwater Creek and they grabbed some sword grass. Now you mightn't know just what sword grass is but, to give you some idea, it wasn't named sword grass without reason. It's very sharp. So then Douglas and Laurie got this sword grass and they made incisions in the snake-bite wound with it. Then just to make sure that they'd extracted as much of the snake poison as possible they went and caught some leeches out of the creek and they put them on the wound. Leeches being renowned blood-suckers.

From there I'm not sure how they got help, but it goes on to say here in the news clipping that young Ronnie was hurried by his father to Albury Hospital for medical treatment. As I said Albury was about twenty-five miles away and it was noted how the doctors at the hospital were extremely impressed with the quick actions of the two older Taskis boys. In fact they said, and I refer once more to the paper clipping: 'the doctors declared that it was only the prompt attention of Ronnie's brothers that saved the little fellow's life'.

So there's a story about how these two young schoolboys, Douglas and Laurie Taskis, saved the life of their younger brother, Ronnie. And as Mister Jarrett was quoted as saying to the newspaper people, 'Not one man in twenty would've done more in a crisis.' And I very much agree with those words. Then just to end it off, after the news-making story hit the city papers the school was presented with an up-to-date first aid kit.

Now, while we're talking about ingenuity, I have another little story that you may be interested in. It's also from the Mullengandra Public School but this time this incident happened in the mid-'40s. Apparently Mister Wailes was still the teacher. So Mister Wailes must've been very settled in at the school and the parents must've been very happy with his teaching abilities. Anyhow there was this lad who was about twelve or thirteen. As you'll come to appreciate I don't think

I should mention his name. But due to his father having to work away from home quite a lot and his mother not being in very good health, the boy was given a special driving permit just in case his mother took a bad turn and had to be rushed to hospital; you know, while his father was away or otherwise indisposed.

It was mid-winter in Mully. Cold, wet and miserable. So when the children came out of school at the end of the day they were met by driving rain, and that's when this particular boy came up with the idea. He looked around and he noticed his father's utility parked just a couple of hundred yards away, outside of the Royal Oak Hotel. In those days everyone always left the keys in their cars and that. Not like nowadays. So the boy nipped down to the hotel and he jumped in his dad's ute and he drove it back to the school. The children then loaded their pushbikes in the back of the ute, before they clambered in the cabin and off this boy went, down the highway, and he delivered them all to their various homes en route to his own house.

Now I know that that's also a true story because my younger sisters were at Mully school at that time. The only trouble was, they lived in the opposite direction to where this young lad lived and so they weren't offered a lift. They had to get on their bikes and pedal home in the rain, and they got a good drenching, they did, too.

So there's just a couple of quick stories for you. And, no, I'm not sure what happened to the father who was in the Royal Oak Hotel. I guess he just stayed on there, drinking; either that or the young lad drove back and picked him up at a later stage.

Just Like a Sentence

I grew up in the Gulf country of Queensland where we lived on a cattle station four mile out of Normanton. When I say 'cattle station' it was really mainly more of a depot for my father and my uncle to run their horses because, at that time, they were big drovers all through that country. So it was only a small place, only about twenty-six square mile. Yeah so, even though we did run a few head of cattle, the property was more set up as a droving operation than as a cattle station. Besides having the brood mares for breeding they also had hundreds of other horses. See back in them days they didn't have motor vehicles, they only used horses when they went droving, and they used to have about two different droving plants a year. A 'plant' is what you call the whole works; like all the horses, all the cooking gear, the saddles, swags and all that sort of stuff — the whole box and dice — and only one plant would do just the one trip, then you'd get together a fresh plant for the next trip. That's why they had so many horses.

But that's all besides the point because Normanton was also where I did my primary schooling, and someone was saying the other day that if I was going to tell a story about my school days, then I had to tell you about the time I was about ten and Mum was taking us into school in our old bloody Ford and I fell clean out of the back of the car and got hooked up on the back bumper, and all the other kids were yelling out for Mum to put the brakes on pretty quick but she didn't and it was only when she saw me trailing along behind in the dust that she decided to stop the car. So that's the story, and from memory I was none the worse for wear from it. Mum just threw me back into the car and off I went to school and I don't even remember having any days off school because of it. But it wouldn't have been the best of starts to a school day, ay? Anyhow, that's the story.

At the Normanton school, back in the late 1940s and into the early '50s, there would've only been about thirty of us kids. There were no Aborigines but we had one family of Chinese and one family of, I think they was Kanakas or something. You know, Kanakas was those Islanders that they brung over here to work on cane farms and that. Anyhow I think that's what they were but they were definitely a different race other than the Aboriginal.

Even so, for a small place like Normanton, there was a fair swag of us kids and when I was in my last year at primary school there was four of us in Grade 8. The school only went to Grade 8. In Queensland, back then Grade 8 was called 'Scholarship'. I don't know why it was called that because I wasn't on any sort of scholarship or anything. These days, Grade 8's the first year of secondary school, though back then it was the last year of your primary school. But with the old Normanton school, everything's gone now. It's a completely different school now. It used to be a three-room wooden building, about three foot off the ground on stumps, with a verandah right around it, and we always had a cut lunch because back then there was no cafes or shops or a school canteen or whatever, so you had to bring your own grub or you'd starve.

I remember one particular kid; he used to wag school a fair bit and one time the principal or whoever it was got a message to the police that the kid was skipping school and so the constable heads off on his pushbike to go and find this kid. So he went around to the family home and he rounded this kid up and then the copper made him plod all the way back to school with the front wheel of the pushbike right up his arse. I forget the kid's name just now, and even though I wasn't that real bright, I still struggled through my Scholarship all right. I enjoyed social studies, which was like history and geography combined sort of thing. Two subjects all mixed in together. But English and maths were the two subjects that mattered most. I mean, it meant bugger all if you got bloody one hundred per cent in social studies; it was what you got for maths and English that counted.

Still, I got through in the end. Then after Scholarship I went to boarding school at Abergowrie. Abergowrie's about sixty mile inland of Ingham. Ingham's right over on the coast, between Tully and Townsville. Actually, my older brothers went to Mount Carmel in Charters Towers, so I was the first of the Gallaghers to go to Abergowrie and that was probably because it was a little bit closer to home. Less far away.

Any rate we had a cousin who was also going there, to Abergowrie, a feller from Julia Creek called Peter Dawes, and apparently Dad had talked to Peter and his parents and they all reckoned it was a pretty good school. So that's where I went. It was an all-boys agricultural boarding college back then and, of course, I was a little bit more interested in agriculture than what I was in English and maths, even though in one of my exams I did get an A for chemistry. I don't know how that happened but, yeah, maybe I should've been a chemist or a doctor or a scientist or whatever instead of being a drover and a butcher like I am now. I might've even found the magic of DNA or something like that, ay? So who knows?

But I have to tell you: when Dad first took me down to Abergowrie it took us about a week just to get there. So she was a pretty long trip, ay? We flew out from Normanton to Cairns on the old DC 3 aeroplane and that would've took probably four or five hours by the time you'd landed at Croydon and Abingdon and all them little places along the way to Cairns. It was what's called a 'milk run', meaning that the plane stopped everywhere. Then we stayed overnight with an uncle in Cairns and the next day we caught the train from Cairns and that was going to take us right down to Ingham, but we only got as far as Innisfail and we couldn't get any further because she was a pretty primitive sort of railway track in those days and all that Tully country was flooded, which wasn't that unusual I might add. But this was in about 1957. The big cyclone went through Cairns in '56 and then we had the big floods in '57 and that's when we went through, in '57.

So then we got stuck in bloody Innisfail for about four or five days, just waiting till it was safe to go on by the train, and luckily we had a friend who was living in Innisfail and so we used to go around to their place every day for a feed and that. Anyhow, when we eventually got through to Ingham, Dad just had to drop me off at the train station and skedaddle because he had to head straight back to Cairns so he could get there in time to catch the next plane back out to Normanton. See, there was only one plane a week on the Cairns to Normanton run and if he hadn't got back to Cairns in time to catch the old DC 3, he would've been stuck in Cairns for another week, and that's the last thing he wanted to do.

Anyhow, when he dropped me off at the Ingham railway station, there was a mob of other Abergowrie kids waiting there and luckily I knew this Peter Dawes, the cousin from Julia Creek I was telling you about. So I stuck close to Peter and he showed me the ropes till the bus came to pick us up and take us out to Abergowrie, and that would've took another couple of hours or so. So in all, she was a pretty long trip, ay?

But boarding school was okay. It was nothing special and anyway I knew right from the start that I was only going to be stuck there for two years so I just had to do me time and get accustomed to it. But I always wanted to be home. I didn't want to be down there. I might've got an A in chemistry one time, like I told you, but really all I wanted to do was stock work and to go droving and ride horses. That's all I wanted to do, so I just looked at it like it was almost a two-year sentence for a crime I never done, then I'd get me ticket out of the place.

Little Scoundrel
In memory of Yvonne Stokes

This story is about my brother, Bill; the little scoundrel. It was soon after the First World War when we were living in Lynden Street, Camberwell, Melbourne. I would've been about six and Bill was about five, and we were both going to Canterbury State School. But he was the type of boy who was always up to some sort of mischief. In fact, you could liken the story to how — not — to win friends and influence people.

Back in those days each school day began with us standing in the quadrangle singing 'God Save the King' as the Union Jack crawled up the flag pole. That done, we'd march — if you could call it marching — to the deadpan beat of a drum, from the quadrangle into our classrooms. Those days we sat at wooden desks; two by two. Bill was in the class below me and he was a real boy, he was; you know, the type who'd always be out to improve his standing among his so-called mates. Then at lunchtime I remember seeing a group of boys gathered at the far end of the school ground, near the incinerator. Usually they were a rowdy bunch but this time there was a suspicious quietness about them as they stood around someone. At a closer look I noticed that Bill was the centre of their attention. Uh oh, what's he up to now? I thought. But I let it be.

Then as we were leaving school that afternoon all the boys acted more friendly than usual toward him. 'See yer tomorra', Bill. See yer, mate.' Now Bill was very good at keeping secrets — very good — and so there was no use in me asking as to why, all of a sudden, he was so popular. So I didn't.

The next day I just happened see a couple of Bill's 'new' best friends in deep conversation with their teacher, Mister Martin. Then after school that day, Mister Martin handed Bill a letter to take home. Very few kids took letters home from their teachers so it was obviously something special; most probably about the upcoming school concert in Canterbury Memorial Hall. Anyhow, that afternoon, eager to find out what the letter contained, we didn't even stop to play in Highfield Park or hang around Miss Simpson's lolly shop, we went straight home. Mum always had sandwiches and drinks ready for us after school and it was while we were tucking into our snacks that Mum opened the letter. Well she just took one look and she went as white as a sheet. 'Oh my goodness,' she gasped and ran from the kitchen into her and Dad's bedroom.

This's a bit odd, I thought as I heard her opening drawers, then slamming them shut. I gave Bill a questioning glance. He was looking a bit sheepish, but he kept munching on his sandwich. Then Mum stormed back into the kitchen. 'Go to your room at once,' she shouted at Bill, 'and stay there till your father gets home.' Mum hardly ever told us off, so I knew Bill must've been in big trouble.

It was always best for me to disappear if ever Mum got upset so I wandered down to Pearl's house under the pretence of seeing how the baby was going, though, in reality, I was also hoping to be offered a biscuit. Pearl was Mum's best friend. They were about the same age — in their late-twenties. The baby seemed well and happy and I was offered a biscuit. That was good and so after I'd finished the biscuit I decided to make my way home again, to see how things were. Not too well as it turned out. Bill was still locked in his room and Mum was still upset. So then I decided to go and visit our next-door neighbour, Mrs Foster. Mrs Foster always offered me a biscuit when I went to see her. It was no different this time. I said 'yes' to one of her gingerbread biscuits, and while I was eating it she inquired about Bill.

'He's been sent to his bedroom,' I said.

'Oh, really,' she replied, with a raise of her eyebrows. She then offered me another gingerbread biscuit which I accepted, partly because I was beginning to wonder, with the way things were, if I'd be getting any dinner at all. So I stayed there with Mrs Foster for quite a while and had another biscuit and when Mister Foster arrived home from work I thought it was about time to go back home and check on things there.

It still wasn't good. I could even feel the tension as I went up the back stairs. I could see Dad was home, which usually meant that Mum would be setting the table for dinner. But she wasn't. She was in Bill's bedroom with Dad, who was talking to my brother in very earnest tones. The door was closed so I hung about outside straining to listen in, but then Mum appeared. 'Go and wash your hands, Yvonne,' she snapped.

Well at least it seemed like dinner was still on. So I washed my hands and I went and sat at the kitchen table. Mum came in. She was very quiet, so I thought better of asking her what was wrong. Bill and Dad finally arrived. It was very rare for Dad to get angry but I could see that he was very upset. Bill on the other hand was red-eyed and solemn. Mum served our meal. We ate in silence, then she said, 'I'll take the children to school in the morning and I'll go and see Mister Martin.'

'He seems like a sensible young man,' Dad said, 'so we should get them all back.'

'All what back?' I asked.

'Little pigs have big ears,' Mum replied and that was the end of the subject. No more was said and, of course, there was no chance of getting anything out of Bill.

Next morning when Mum took us to school there were several other mothers there, also waiting to see Mister Martin. Oops, I thought, this looks very bad; very bad indeed. Anyhow they all went off to have some sort of meeting while us kids did our usual thing out on the quadrangle with the flag and we sang to the King, before shuffling off to class.

During the day the story emerged about how my brother had snuck into my parents' room, where he'd taken Dad's war medals, slipped them into his school bag and smuggled them to school where, in an attempt to impress some of the most influential of his classmates, he handed them out as gifts. Of course, most of our fathers had been soldiers during the First World War and we knew just how personal and precious those war medals were. And now Dad had lost the lot, thanks to Bill. Of course there was a big ado about it and eventually all of Dad's medals were returned. So I guess it turned out to be quite a happy ending for everyone, apart from Bill that is. Bill's popularity was back to zero.

Manners

One time I was teaching in a 'Special School' at a town down in the south-east of South Australia. With it being a 'Special School' a lot of the students either had some sort of disability or had come from a disadvantaged background. There could've been troubles at home or the parents might've been struggling on welfare for whatever reason. Stuff like that. So some of the kids I was working with were real little roughies. And I remember one day this little boy got really annoyed with me for some reason or other. I forget just why that was, at this moment, but this little kid, he spun around at me and he snapped, 'Piss off, Miss.'

Of course, I immediately replied with, 'Excuse me. In this school we always use our best manners when we talk to teachers and adults. So what should we say, then?'

And this little kid, well, he looked up at me all sheepish and he said, 'Well then, Miss, piss off, PLEASE.'

Miss Sunshine

Living in a small bush town and working as a teacher in a one-teacher school has its positives. Mind you, it also has its drawbacks, particularly when it comes to everyone knowing everything there is to know about everyone else in the place, and that's including yourself. I was once appointed to a small town such as that. It was a few hours' drive out from Geraldton, which is a shipping port city, on the mid-west coast of Western Australia.

In this school I was sent to teach at, there were only twenty-four students and, on my first day, the kids were testing me out, particularly one young boy, their ringleader, little Teddy Thompson. When I told him to settle down he ignored me and continued mucking around; showing off and so forth.

'Right, Teddy, that's your final warning,' I said.

'Final warning for what, Sir?' he replied and started to laugh.

'That's it,' I said and so, as you could do back in those days, I hauled him out in front of the class and I decided to really give him something to think about. I gave him a smack. Not hard, but just hard enough to bring him to his senses. It was amazing just how quickly things settled down after that and I could get on with my job of teaching. Good, I thought. Well done. I didn't like doing it but it got things back under control.

At that time I'd just started boarding with a local family, the O'Briens — Elizabeth and Arthur O'Brien. I'd only been there a week and so I didn't know them that well but, as I was soon to discover, Elizabeth O'Brien's maiden name happened to be Thompson; that's Thompson of the same family little Teddy Thompson belonged to. The Thompsons lived just across the road from the school and apparently, the instant little Teddy had arrived home, he'd regaled his tale of woe on to his mum; most probably something along the lines of, 'Sir whacked me real hard 'n' I done nothin' wrong.'

Of course, Teddy's mum was then straight on the phone to Elizabeth O'Brien to tell her about what her heartless new lodger had done. What's more, this Elizabeth O'Brien, nee Thompson, also happened to run the local telephone exchange. Next thing, Elizabeth's on the phone to whoever and with it being an old telephone exchange, the whole district's listening in on the party line, aren't they? So everyone within cooee now knows what's happened. They're all in on the act, and my God didn't they have a field day. Before I'd even arrived home from the school that afternoon, all the gruesome details about how I'd spanked poor little Teddy Thompson were out in the open. What's more they'd all formed the opinion that I was the 'baddy' in all of this. So the moment I step into the house, Elizabeth O'Brien greets me with, 'What a terrible, terrible man you are. You are just so cruel,' and off she went, 'blaa, blaa, blaa'.

'Look,' I said, 'I am not putting up with that sort of rubbish.' I said, 'I've got twenty-four kids to teach and there's just no way I can teach twenty-three of them while the twenty-fourth is being rude and disruptive.'

Anyway, the long and the short of it is, from then on, yes, from time to time Elizabeth and I still did have our little disagreements, but she proved to be one of the most lovely and genuine of people. She was superb, and her husband, Arthur, was one of nature's true gentlemen. Every morning we'd get up for breakfast and we'd have lamb chops. Every morning.

As it happened, this community was very strongly Catholic and, being so, everyone had large families. That's why such a small place could muster up twenty-four primary school students. The O'Briens themselves had five children. Then there were the Thompsons, they had four children. Down the road were the O'Rileys. They also had quite a few children. And I must say that, after those initial few weeks of school, those kids proved to be a fantastic bunch. Absolutely beautiful. What's more the families were great as well. They were as honest and straight as the day is long, with extremely solid values, both moral and spiritual. So you can't get away with anything as the only teacher in a small town like that.

Anyhow I was very comfortable there. Loved it, actually, even if it did leave a little to be desired when it came to the more 'social' aspects of life where a) any eligible and/or suitable women were as rare as hen's teeth, b) the moral and religious guidelines were set in stone and c) your every move was scrutinised to the nth degree.

Then near the end of one particular school week, when I was cleaning the car, I started wondering what I could do on the weekend. As usual there was nothing much happening in town, so a mate and I, we decide to go to Geraldton, where we'd heard there was a dance happening on the Saturday night. Geraldton was about a three- or four-hour drive away.

Saturday comes, and off we go. When we get to Geraldton we go to the dance. And I remember this girl, she was wearing this, kind of like, a white ballerina dress, and boy didn't she look a million dollars. Absolutely stunning. I asked her for a dance, and she accepted. Perfect. I asked her for another one. She said that was okay, but she told me how it had to be our last dance together because, with her being the current Geraldton Miss Sunshine, she was also obliged to dance with some of the other fellers as well. It was her duty. We then floated into that second dance, and we were getting on like a house on fire, me and Miss Sunshine. Mind you, she was an exceptional dancer too. She said she even had the medals to prove it — a point I did not dispute. I told her that the only medals I had were from the Royal Life Saving Society. She found that funny. We laughed. She had a great laugh. Obviously she had a good sense of humour as well.

Anyhow, as that second dance drew to its close, as you do when you meet someone as attractive as she was, well, I wanted to find out a bit more about her, didn't I? So before she went off to fulfil her evening's commitments I said, 'May I drive you home after the dance tonight?'

Of course this was in the days when the only reason you drove a woman back to her home after a dance was to try and get up to a bit of mischief in your car. Back then you were never even allowed into a woman's house until you'd been properly introduced to her parents and well and truly vetted.

'Thank you for the offer,' she said, 'but unfortunately I've come to the dance in my father's car.'

So that was it, I'd drawn a blank.

'Perhaps some other time?' I asked.

'Perhaps,' she replied as she floated off into the clutches of one of her many other male admirers.

After driving all this way to Geraldton I didn't want the night to come to nothing, so I then homed in on someone else. She wasn't anywhere near as beautiful as Miss Sunshine, nor was she as good a dancer. But you know what it's like when you're a young, single, hot-blooded male. It's tough sometimes. Very tough. Anyhow I had another dance or two with this other girl and by then it was getting near the end of the evening, so I asked her if she'd like me to drive her home.

'Yes,' she said.

Things were looking up. After the final dance — a slow waltz — I drove her home. I pulled up outside her place and I'm just about to try my luck when I hear the front door of the house open. The verandah light comes on. I look up. It's the father. He's standing there. Arms folded, and he doesn't look too pleased to see me in the car with his daughter. I've run into another blank.

'Good night,' I say.

'Thanks for driving me home,' she replies.

As I pull away from her house, I mumble, 'Thanks for nothing.'

It was a long and lonely drive back to the small town where I was teaching. I forget what happened to my mate. I actually didn't care really, because I wasn't in the mood for company — well, not male company anyway. To say the least, the night hadn't turned out anywhere near as well as I would've liked. In fact it had been a complete disaster. But as I was driving along, the memory of Miss Sunshine came back to me. Miss Sunshine: the sweet smell of her perfume. Her stunning beauty. The way she glided me across the dance floor. Her easy manner. The way she spoke. Her infectious laugh. It all seemed so darn comfortable. And when I'd asked if she'd like to go out with me some other time, she had said 'Perhaps', hadn't she? Which was far better than a flat, outright 'No'.

Problem was, I'd been enjoying her company so much that I'd forgotten to ask her what her name was. Yes, I knew she was the current Geraldton Miss Sunshine. Yes, I knew she'd won medals for her dancing. But that's all. Without her name I couldn't even ring her up or anything.

It wasn't until after I'd long gone to bed in the early hours of the Sunday morning, and to sleep, that I was awoken by a sudden blinding flash of brilliance.

The next morning — the Monday — I walked to school with a spring in my step. I might've even been whistling. I fronted the class, the whole twenty-four of them. 'Good morning, children.'

'Good morning, Sir.'

I said, 'Look, we're just going to have a small change to our social studies programme. For your homework tonight I'd like you all to find out something of the history of Geraldton; you know, how it came into being, what industry it was founded on, important dates and events ... and in particular who the current Miss Sunshine is?'

The next day I arrive at school, early. A spring in my step. Hope in my heart. School began. I front the class. The whole twenty-four of them. 'Well, what can you tell me about Geraldton?'

This hand shoots up. It's little Teddy Thompson, the boy I'd punished on my first day at the school. He's got an odd sort of cheeky grin on his face.

I say, 'Yes, Teddy?'

'Well, Sir,' he says, 'my dad said that the name of the current Miss Sunshine is Valma Cope, and he also told me to tell you, Sir, that you may as well give up on her right now because there's no way you'll ever be able to cope with her.'

That was over fifty years ago now, and I'm still managing to cope with her.

My Strength

I came to Australia in 1987. I was from the Philippines, and I married Benjamin Wright, who lived on a cattle station out from Cloncurry, in the west of Queensland. I married Ben when I was a widow. I already had five children previously in the Philippines and I had to leave my children behind because they had to go to school and finish their education there in the Philippines. It was much easier and they were looked after very well by my sister.

When I married Ben we lived on Arrolla Station. Coming from the Philippines I was used to the hard life in the province, working on the farm we had. But in the Philippines at least we had close-by neighbours. At Arrolla Station we didn't have any close-by neighbours. At Arrolla you had to travel very far to see your neighbours. To Oorindimindi Station. To Oorindi Park. To Levuka. But we did not see much of each other because I didn't have the licence for the car so I could not visit easily. We could only talk to each other through the CB radio to see what is the weather and check the waters and see if they are mustering or whatever they are doing. Then once a week we'd come into Cloncurry to do shopping and to see people.

I had my daughter, Maria, two years after I came to Australia. I joined CWA then. The main reason I joined CWA was to be able to get together with the other ladies and also so that our children could all play together. The CWA women and their kids used to sometimes come out to visit us on the weekends and we had fun. We would go on picnics at the billabong, whenever there was water, because most of the time we did not have water.

Then in 1994, Ben died. My daughter and I were now on Arrolla Station all by ourselves and I didn't have the car licence so I could never go into town unless somebody would come and pick me up and take me in there. So I couldn't manage by myself and I got very sad. Then Ben's children from the first marriage said I had to come to live in the town because of the isolation which I couldn't handle.

So Maria and me, we moved to town and Maria, she started preschool at Cloncurry State School. She was very good at adapting herself to our new situation. Much better than me. She coped much better than I coped, with the death of her dad. She was my strength. She was still only four-and-a-half and she was the one who advised me not to worry. 'Do not worry, Mother. Do not cry so much. Things will work out. You will see. Things will work out.' She was my strength. She is a very strong girl. Very strong. Much stronger than me.

Maria was also very popular at the school and all the kids would come and play together. There would be sleepovers, and there was less of the isolation because everybody knows everybody, being in a small town. That's one good thing with a smaller area; everybody looks after everybody else. And Maria, she went all the way from preschool through to matriculation before there were computers. She was a good student. She always tried to do her very best because, without a father, I was now a single mum so I had to do some work to try and keep the ends together, to pay for our food and her schooling.

I got work at the Gidgee Inn and, so that I could always be with her, I got up very early to go cook the breakfast at the inn. After breakfast I came home so that when she was out of school in the afternoon I was always there for her, waiting. When Maria was fourteen she also did some work. She was a waitress at the Gidgee Inn and that supplemented our income because otherwise it was too hard. Just too hard, so we pooled our money to get by.

So Maria went all the way from preschool through to matriculation, here at Cloncurry State School. She finished in 2006. Now she is going to uni. It is a long way away from Cloncurry. She is also working at a job to help pay her way and she does the uni in the evenings. She works with the PCYC over in Beenleigh. PCYC is the Police and Citizens Youth Club. She's involved with the PCYC because she loves children and she doesn't want to sit in an office from eight to five so she does all the outdoor activities. Whatever the programme is, she does it. She goes camping and rock climbing. She teaches judo. She is now twenty-two and she has turned out a success. Her grades are all Distinctions and she's happy with that.

I am also very proud of her because she's a leader, through and through. Right from the start, from preschool to Year 12, she was a born leader. She was the school captain. She has helped me so much. When she was eighteen years old she got awarded Junior Citizen of the Year in Cloncurry. That was given to her on Australia Day 2007. I was so proud.

Not One Word

I first started school at Appila but I was only there for six months before we shifted over to near Murray Town, in the mid-north of South Australia, and that's when I started at Wongyarra School. So you may as well say I went to Wongyarra all me school life. It was a one-teacher school and that feller had what they called a School Monitor to help him out a bit. Her name was Nell Donovan. She was like a teacher's assistant and she looked after the small ones in the lower classes. As for numbers, I'd say that, at one part of the piece, there was sixty-five of us kids.

Wongyarra School is where the story of Mackie and me and the horse and buggy took place. See, Mackie and me were mates. Maxwell Woolford was his real name but us kids just called him Mackie. He's dead now. Anyway there was Mackie and me and I forget the schoolteacher's name but he only had one leg. Just the one leg. Gee he was a big man. He used to get around on one crutch and, I tell you, he could go as fast as we could run, even on that one crutch. Now I don't know how he lost his leg. He came to Wongyarra like that. I mean, his leg wasn't completely gone from right up the top. He had a bit of a stump and he'd pack tons of paper around it then he'd put a little boot on, down where his knee would be. I used to have a photo of him but I gave a lot of me photos away.

Anyhow, I got to Wongyarra when I was just on six years old I reckon, and I stayed at that school all the time except for when I went into Booleroo Centre Hospital. See, I had blood poisoning bone-disease and I remember there was a Doctor Love and a Doctor Last, and I'm not sure which one it was; anyway, either Doctor Love or Doctor Last reckoned I ate some orange peel that'd been sprayed with something and that caused this blood poisoning bone-disease. They call it some other darn thing these days but it started in one leg and so I had an operation and they took a lot of the bone out of the leg and they put it in tight straps and I wasn't allowed to move it because, if I did, I would've lost the leg.

The bone was supposed to grow back and they used to put like a gauze with Vaseline all up and down inside me shin bone to make the poison come out and to stop it from getting infected. While they were putting it in it was all right but, when they were pulling it out, oh it give me hell. Then before they got all the poison out, it closed down again and so they had to open it up again. Not only that but I also had about ... one ... two ... three; I had six other different cuts. I've still got the marks. But the thing was, after I'd had the operation on that leg, the poisoning then went over to the other leg. Anyway, Doctor Which-ever-one-it-was said, he said, 'It's a good job I did that operation or you might've died.'

So I was in the Booleroo Centre Hospital and then I convalesced at home and all that took up twelve months — a whole year — and that's the only time I missed out on going to Wongyarra School. But I don't cry for pity or anything. That's just what happened and I've lived to tell the tale. I'm ninety-four now, so I've done pretty well, ay?

Anyhow, back to the horse and buggy. See, the one-legged schoolteacher boarded with people by the name of Allington and he used to come to school with a horse and buggy. It was a real tame old horse too. Then each day at 3 o'clock, just before school finished, the teacher would get a kid called Jim Curtis to go out and yoke up this horse and buggy and then he'd tie the horse to a tree; you know, so it was all ready for the teacher to head straight off. So Mackie and me, we made this plan up and as soon as Jim Curtis came back in from yoking up the horse and buggy I said, 'Please, Sir, can I leave the room?'

'Yes, Tom, you can leave the room.'

Then I was only outside for a little while and that's when Mackie said, 'Please, Sir, can I leave the room?'

'Yes, Maxwell, you can leave the room.'

So Mackie came out too and we took the horse out of the buggy, then we put the two shafts of the buggy through the fence and then we took the horse around the gate and yoked it back up again. So now the buggy was on one side of the fence, the shafts was right through the fence, and the horse was on the other side of the fence, all ready for the teacher to take off. Now I don't know how the teacher ever got on because Mackie and me, we never stopped around long enough to find out. As soon as school finished we took off. But the thing is that, our one-legged teacher, even though he would've known who done it, he never ever said a word to us. Not one word. Not the next day nor ever. He just let it go. Never said a word. Funny, isn't it?

Which reminds me: see, while we was at school, a bloke from the bank used to come along in his old Ford car every Friday fortnight and take our money. I think it was every Friday fortnight, anyway; but it doesn't matter, the thing is, he'd come along and we'd put a few pennies or thruppence or something into our bank accounts. Anyhow, every time the bank bloke had finished with us, this one-legged teacher would walk back out to the front of the school with him. Like, there was a road outside the school where the banker pulled up in his car. Then this time, just before the banker arrived, the teacher had been marching us around the school. Whenever he done that he'd sit in a chair under a tree and he'd sing out, 'Left, right, left, right, left turn' and all this sort of caper and then he'd blow a whistle for us to stop.

So the bank feller arrived and the teacher blew his whistle. Then we did our banking and we went back and stood in line while the teacher walked with the bank feller back out to his car. Anyhow, while he was out the front with the feller from the bank, Mackie and me, we grabbed the chair that the teacher had been sitting on and we put it up in the tree so when he come back, there's no chair there. And so there he is, he's looking around and he's looking around. All us kids, we're all just standing there in line. But he never asked us about his chair. It's above him, in the tree, see, but he's not looking up, he's looking here and he's looking there, but no chair.

Then there was a girl there by the name of Lydia Someone-or-other. She was twenty years of age and she was still coming to school and, oh, her mother treated her just something terrible. This poor girl, she used to have to get up and milk the cows before she come to school and then she'd have to milk the cows when she got home from school, and that was only part of it. Like I said, her mother treated her terrible. Oh, and that's right, did I mention that this Lydia was twenty years old. Okay, so then when she was about to turn twenty-one the schoolteacher was going to give her a special twenty-first birthday party, but when she found out about the birthday party, she left school. Just like that. Left school, and we didn't ever see her again.

But back to the point of the story: Mackie and me, we'd put the chair up the tree and after the teacher had been looking for it for a fair while, this Lydia Someone-or-other, she said, 'Sir, you'd better be careful or the chair will fall right on your head.'

So he looks up and there it is. Anyhow, Mackie and me, as quick as a flash, we say, 'Oh, we'll get it down for you, Sir,' which we did and then he got us all straight back into the marching again. 'Left, right, left, right, left turn.' But, again, he would've known it was Mackie and me but he never said a word. Not one word. Just let it go. Funny, isn't it?

But the thing of all this is, when that one-legged teacher left Wongyarra School, that was the year I was still at home in convalescence from my leg operation and he came down specially to see me, just to say goodbye. And I was the only kid in the whole school that he done that to. So I must've made some sort of impression on him, ay? But he was a good old feller really. He even helped sort out a special certificate for me. Now, what the hell did they call it? It was some sort of certificate that you can get if you pass the 7th Grade and you want to leave school. And so I got that. Then I never went on to high school. But I often think, Gee, how silly we were back then. And that was the last of me school days because after I'd convalesced I went straight out to work for five bob a week. I was thirteen.

Nothing Else other than Farming

Old Bill, they call me. I grew up on a cattle property near Giligulgul, out in the south-east of Queensland, and that's where I lived for eighty-three years before I come into town. Giligulgul's an Aboriginal word that means 'a big bend of scrub'. Back when the railways first went through the area, because they didn't have any of the equipment like bulldozers and that — it was all man-power in those days — they had to zigzag around the scrub. My father bought the property in 1924 and I was born in 1925. There were two boys in the family. My brother was four years older than me — he's since passed away — then there's me and I still work out on the property. Too right I do. I was up early yesterday and went out mustering for the day, and I'm eighty-six next month.

My childhood was quite good, I guess. We had plenty of country to run around in but, because we didn't have much in the way of new clothes or things like that, I had to wear hand-me-downs from the bigger brother. So I had the short pants that went down over me knees and I had to wear braces to hold them up till I grew out of them. And now you see grown men wearing those sort of pants, that go way down there, and it looks terrible.

With Mum and Dad you never swore or talked about the toilet or anything like that. Then one day, when I was about four, I was having a fight with me brother and so I ran down to hide from him in the toilet. It was one of those old lean-to bush-type things with the pan under it that you had to empty. And so I got into the toilet and I hooked the door with the leather strap so me brother couldn't get in. Then I dropped the braces and pulled down the great big pants I was wearing at the time and I was just about to sit down and, blow me down, there's a snake in there and he's trying to get out of the pan. So I start screaming, 'Snake! Snake!'

Of course, now I'm trying to get out of the toilet to escape the snake and I'm pushing and I'm pushing, but I can't get out because what me brother had done, he'd gone and stuck a post up against the outside of the toilet door so I couldn't get out, and the post had got stuck. And I'll never forget that; 'Snake! Snake!' I'm yelling, and then Mum came down and between the two of them they managed to pull the stuck post out and open the door and I was out of there like a shot and I ran and I ran and I ran, and I tell you, trying to run with those big baggy pants hanging about your ankles is a hard thing to do. But I did it. And no, I don't know what happened to the snake. He was probably just as frightened as I was.

As for our schooling, we did correspondence. Every week the exercise books came out by train. The guard would throw them off in the mailbag, into the small building at the railway siding, and that was our schoolwork. We then had to fill it all in and send it back on the train. I can't remember much of it but what I can remember is that you had to hold the pencil the right way and you had to draw a full page of letters. One time we had to draw something like a 'J', in the alphabet. But the best description of a 'J' I could come up with was the pot hook hanging over the open fire for when we were cooking and so I drew a pretty good 'J'. Then the other subjects we had to do was like they always say, 'readin', 'ritin' 'n' 'rithmetic'. They were the basic ones and some of them old writing books of mine, from way back then, they're now in the town museum and one of them's got 'Well done Billy boy' written in it. That must've been in one of the handwriting books because I was pretty good at that, and if you did real well and everything was right they'd put a blue stamp in it. Though I didn't get too many blue stamps, only the occasional one.

Then when I was ten or so I went to the state school at Guluguba. Guluguba was about seven mile from our property. It was a little one-teacher school with just the one building and it had a set of steps up into it. I don't even think it had a verandah. They just had a bit of a hang-out, that was all, and there was a big bush house down the way a bit where we went and sat and had our lunch and things, and that was made from posts and logs and it had bushes on the top of it so when it rained we got only a little bit wet. But it was nice in the warmer weather.

Back then I rode a pushbike to school a couple of days a week and a couple of days I rode a horse. So we'd either pushbike the seven mile or we'd ride the seven mile. That's fourteen mile each day, all together, so we had to get up pretty early and sometimes we even had to milk the cows before we went to school. Sometimes, yes.

Anyhow I stayed at school at Guluguba for ... gee, you've got me cornered now ... anyhow, after Scholarship I went to Gatton College. Gatton was a boarding school. That's right, I must've been about fourteen or so by then. But Gatton College was all about agriculture, which suited me. At first it was quite a culture shock and they were very strict, which was good. I sort of appreciated it. Well, say, if you didn't have a tie on, you then had to put the collar of your shirt over your coat and if you come to dinner or went to church with it the other way around or your shirt was hanging out, then you were in trouble. And it does make a difference too. So they were pretty strict about dress, and I remember some of them old teachers as being real honest fellers. Good old gentlemen they were.

At Gatton we had to work on the farm. We had to groom the horses every morning and harness them up to go working in the grounds; farming and that with them. Then if you got into trouble you had to groom and tend the horses of a weekend while the other fellers went to sport. That was one of the ways they had to punish you. But I quite enjoyed my time at Gatton. We grew some of our own vegetables and they had a citrus orchard and cows to milk and pigs to feed. That was another penalty too. If you'd done something wrong, instead of playing sport, you had to feed the pigs on the weekend. And they had cattle of course, and also they had goats and sheep on the property.

But all that didn't stop us from getting up to mischief. I remember one night, one of the chappies — a bit of a lad, he was — he caught one of the goats and he tied it onto the rope that rung the school bell. Of course when it tried to run away the bell kept clanging and, because it was in the middle of the night, everyone thought it was for a fire or something, so they were running about in all directions and by the time we got down there, oh, it was a circus trying to catch that goat.

That was back in 1942 when the war was on and at Easter time we had to get out of the buildings because they were going to convert them into a hospital for the American soldiers. So we left school, then about nine months later we went back there into temporary buildings. And boy, didn't we get the bad end of the stick. The Americans had our nice dormitories with the nice hot showers and we got stuck in the bad temporary accommodation with the weatherboard up about a metre, then there were the louvres, in and out, then fibro up to the ceiling. From memory, there were about twenty-four of us to a dormitory and the breeze used to come through and, I tell you, in winter it was as cold as cold could be and there was no hot water so we had to have cold showers. But I'm still alive.

Yes, so the Americans were spoilt. They got all the good stuff. But we used to torment them when they were courting the girls and one night when I was tormenting this big Yank, he took off after me and I could run fairly well in those days and I got back to the dormitory and dived into the bed, boots and all and this Yank comes along with a torch, checking to see who's awake and there I was, pretending to be asleep. It was just lucky he didn't look under the blanket and see that I still had me boots and all on.

Anyhow I survived all that and then after my schooling I just went back on the property. I didn't know about nothing else other than farming. Never even thought of anything else really. My brother had enlisted in the army and so off he went and he left me to it. Then a few years later, when he got discharged because of his health, he come home and bought the property next door and I helped him develop it. We sort of worked together then, right up till he sold out a few years ago. Like I said, he's since passed away now but we ended up breeding some nice cattle before we finished up, and we had a few good horses too.

One Woman and Her Cow

Sorry I wasn't here when you first called. It's just that I've been out shopping and these days I get around in one of those wheelchair things that you drive yourself. You know, the ones you have to plug in and get the battery charged every night. Still I guess I'm not doing too badly for a hundred-and-one-year-old, am I?

So you want to know about my old school days, do you? Well I was four years old when I started at Glamorgan Vale Primary School. That was back in 1913. Glamorgan Vale is about twelve miles out of Ipswich, Queensland, up toward Esk. It was only a little village. Dairy farming, mostly. A dairy farm here, and a dairy farm about half a mile away. That sort of thing. Dad was headmaster there. There were only the two teachers — Dad and a schoolmistress — and the school had about a hundred pupils.

We lived in the school residence. The residence was built low to the ground. It only had one step, and the residence had a verandah right along the front of it. Behind that was my parents' bedroom; behind them there was my bedroom. Then we had a passageway and a front room. The front room just had a piano and some easy chairs in it. It was like a lounge room. Behind that again there was another big room that we used when we were playing with our toys and things, then there was the dining room, which had a fireplace in it. At the back of the residence there was another verandah which had a landing going across to the kitchen. So there was like a breezeway there. I just can't remember now as to where my younger brother slept.

As for the yard: Dad was interested in fowls and so we had three breeding pens of fowls. One was for the Leghorns, another for the Plymouth Rocks and the third had Rhode Island Reds. So we always had plenty of eggs and fowl to eat which was fortunate because the butcher only came once a week. The township of Glamorgan Vale consisted of just the one store and the hotel, and there was a house on the other side of the school and I remember they had their post box on the front verandah. The blacksmith lived further down the road, but his blacksmith's shop, with his forge and everything in it, that was down near the hotel.

But even as a baby I remember how the elder girls from the school used to come and ask Mother, 'Can we have the baby while we're at lunch?' So I got used to playing with the children and as soon as I could walk, if the gate between our residence and the school was open, I'd be over into the school in a shot. Then by the time I was four, Dad said to Mum, 'You might as well let her come to school, she's there most of the time anyway.'

I liked school. I could read by then because Dad had taught me the ABC. Then when I was in Kindergarten I started teaching some of the other children the ABC. But from the time I was five we'd always come down to Burleigh Heads for our Christmas holidays. My grandparents lived in Brisbane and so we'd spend a day or so with them before we got on the train at South Brisbane and headed off on the last leg of our journey. Just before Beenleigh the train would stop and we'd get out and get Mum a cup of tea, then we'd arrive at Burleigh Heads at about lunchtime and we'd stay where the state school is situated now. Burleigh, in those days, was all dairy farming and you could go in with a billycan and get it filled with milk for about sixpence, I think it was.

Then when I was thirteen my father was transferred to Aramac, in central Queensland, but I only attended school there for a year before I went to boarding school at Yeppoon. Yeppoon is on the coast, just north of Rockhampton. It was a new school back then. The Bush Brotherhood had started it up because there were no other schools in the area. Before then there were children who were even having to come right down to Southport to go to high school. So the Bush Brotherhood opened this school at Yeppoon. There were only twenty or so pupils to start with and we had three schoolmistresses beside the headmistress.

If I remember rightly I was sixteen when I left school because I was just going on seventeen in October when I came down to Brisbane to get work. But after I left I tried to keep in touch with some of the girls but then, in 1942, during the war years, I think they were worried that the Japanese might invade Australia and so, with Yeppoon being right on the coast, they packed up everything — all the beds and the desks and the pianos and the boxes of books — and they evacuated out to Barcaldine.

As to any other memories I have of my school days: well, back in those days, I don't know but, people seemed to be different. There was more of a community. Someone would come over and say to Dad, 'Come along on a Sunday and have afternoon tea with us.' Things like that. And one place we used to go to, they grew oranges and mandarins and things and so you'd always come home with a buggy load of fruit.

In those earlier days our main mode of travel was the horse and buggy. We only had the one seat in our buggy, which is where my mother and my father used to sit, and there was a hood over the buggy where you could put all your luggage and everything. Then for my brother and myself, my parents used to put a little stool in the front and I'd sit on that when we were going out and my brother would ride the pony. Then on the way back I'd have to ride the pony because it was usually getting toward dark and my brother wouldn't ride in the dark.

But we never really travelled too far with the horse and buggy. Oh, that's right, yes we did. Sometimes we used to come to Brisbane in the horse and buggy and that was a full day's travel. A whole day in the buggy. I remember we'd come to a little place outside of Ipswich, which was just like a big waterhole, and Mother would have a Thermos of tea and some sandwiches and we'd have something to eat and drink there before we come on to Brisbane. But that was a long journey for the poor old horse. A long, long trip. That's when we used to come down to visit our grandparents in Brisbane. Grandfather was a butcher. I spent a lot of the time in his butcher's shop when I was small and so people nowadays can't fool me about the quality of meat they're trying to sell me. I know exactly what's going on. Oh yes I do.

Then, at Glamorgan Vale, I remember another place we used to go for afternoon tea. It was only about half an hour's drive, or less, in the buggy. We'd visit these people and, in the morning, they'd dig a hole and light a fire in it and fill it with stones and we'd have hot damper from off the stones for afternoon tea. Oh, that was beautiful. I've never tasted damper like it since and, mind you, I am a hundred-and-one years old.

Then I must tell you this one. When peace was signed, Dad decided that we'd have a gala day at the Glamorgan Vale school and so he arranged a big procession. The schoolmistress was the queen of the parade and so she sat up front in a lorry and anyone who had a white frock on was allowed to sit in it with her, and when we arrived at the school we had a picnic. It was a wonderful day and I still remember how Dad always used to laugh, 'Everybody was in the procession except one woman and her cow.'

Yes, one woman and her cow and I could never quite work out why this woman and her cow weren't in the procession. Not even to this day, though I remember very well Dad saying those words, and that was at the end of the First World War. So I go back a long, long time, don't I?

Peggy Eldridge

My father grew up in Scotland. Then just after the First World War he came out here as part of the Dreadnought Scheme which was a scheme that brought older boys out to Australia to teach them to be farmers. He was only seventeen when he arrived and he was sent out to a farm in western New South Wales. But things didn't work out there so he went back to Sydney, where he stayed with some relatives until he got a job in the Public Works Department. Then while he was working there he found out about a three-month course at Sydney University which allowed you to teach in one-teacher schools. After he completed that he was sent to a little school up on top of the Great Dividing Range called Hampton.

He stayed there for about three or four years, teaching between Hampton and another small school called Cheetham Flats. By that time he had a little Ford Tourer; you know, the one with the dicky seat at the back. While he was there he married and they had a baby, but within twelve months his wife died. Of course he couldn't afford to give up work to look after the baby so he decided to keep on teaching and the baby went to live in Sydney with some relatives.

It was in 1931 that he was posted to Clandulla. By then he'd married my mother and I was born in 1933. Clandulla's in central-western New South Wales, between Lithgow and Mudgee, and it was a feeder community for the people who worked at the nearby Kandos Cement Works. Because there wasn't a lot of mechanisation back in those days they had a huge workforce at Kandos and that's why the little community at Clandulla came into being. Kandos was the perfect place for the cement works because there was also coal and limestone nearby: the lime was used in the cement and the coal was used to fire up the furnaces. I believe the cement works had originally been set up after the First World War to provide cement to Sydney as it developed. Then later on, the cement from Kandos was used in the Sydney Harbour Bridge and also in the construction of the underground tunnels, when they ran the electric trains through Sydney.

But oh, there was a lot of poverty in Clandulla. The wages were very low, so low in fact that many people built their own houses; you know, with the dirt floors and the walls made from corrugated iron or just wattle and daub, lined with hessian. Then on top of the hessian, for added insulation and attraction, they made up a basic glue from flour and water and covered the walls with newspapers or magazines. Magazines were the best because they were thicker than just plain old newspaper and, in fact, I remember once going into one of the makeshift houses and reading the *Women's Weekly* stuck up on the walls.

The school residence was comfortable though. Our parents always provided very well for the three of us children. There was no electricity of course and we never used candles. While most people only had hurricane lights, we had Tilley lamps. It was very upmarket if you had a Tilley lamp. We used to carry them around at night time. See that lamp on the corner of the shelf over there, right up at the top — well that was my parents' lamp when they were married.

Then perhaps to get me out of the way of my mother, when I was four, my father started taking me to school. It was a tiny single classroom — just a primary school — and Daddy taught all the six classes. There were a lot of itinerant workers and so sometimes we had up to fifty children. The desks we sat at were big long pieces of timber, about six or seven feet, with ink wells in the front of them and with just the one long solid wooden seat. I'm not sure now if the seats were joined to the desks or not, but there were three desks on one side of the room and four on the other side. Then we had a large blackboard on the front wall and there was the fireplace. In the wintertime my father would go to school and light the fire so the room was a little bit warm for when the children arrived.

But Daddy always used to go to school early to write up the day's work on the blackboard. The junior children were in what was called the 'lower division' and the older students were in the 'upper division'. He religiously followed a teaching programme that he'd written out in big books about A3 size.

We had two tennis courts in the school grounds. They were made by the local community and so, as children, we played a lot of tennis and we also played rounders on the tennis court. Oh, and, I remember, during the Second World War everybody was so terrified that the Japanese were going to invade us that all the men got together and they dug air-raid shelters for us schoolchildren and we had to practise running into the shelters. They weren't covered over like they were in Britain but they were more like a long huge trench, dug into the ground. Actually, during the war a lot of families came up from Sydney to live in the area, not only because of the industry that was needed for the war effort but also because they believed it would be much safer.

My mother came from farming stock and she just loved gardening and, during those war times very little fresh food was available, so we grew our own vegetables in the school gardens. Twice a week the boys had what was called 'manual work', where they were supposed to make little knick-knacks but instead of that they worked in the garden. We grew lots of vegetables. In winter it was potatoes and so forth. Then in summer we'd have peas and beans, and a lot of the produce was taken home to the poorer families.

So my mother was a part of that and also it was expected that the teacher's wife would teach the young girls how to sew. Yes, if you were married to a teacher at one of these one-teacher schools, your job was to teach sewing, even if you couldn't sew. Mum couldn't sew that well but she still taught the girls the basics, like how to do run and fell seams. That's a particular way of making a seam. Then we learnt backstitch and running stitch and hemming. Even now when I go back to Clandulla for reunions some of the women still remember the things my mother taught them. When the Second World War was on, all the girls were in the Junior Red Cross and we knitted big six- or eight-inch plain and pearl squares and my mother sewed them together and they were sent away to be used as blankets. That was when we were about eleven or twelve and the women in the community were involved as well.

So I did my six years of primary schooling at Clandulla; then for high school I went to Kandos. That was an adventure because we had to ride our bikes the five or so miles there to Kandos and the roads were just terrible. They were only tracks really — not sealed at all. Then sometimes we'd get a ride back home on a cement train or in the brake van of a coal train. They'd just let us get on. We never paid any money. But there weren't a lot of boys at high school. You could leave school at fourteen back then so, as soon as the boys were old enough, they usually went to work in the coal mine or they got jobs at the cement works or went timber cutting to help support their families. A lot of local men were employed in the timber industry, cutting support props for the insides of the mines.

But at Clandulla, oh, I remember when the school dentist visited us. He'd come up on the train with all his equipment and he'd set up a dental clinic at the school. It was very, very primitive. I'm not even sure if they had ether back then, and so on the days the dentist came to school a lot of the children would stay away, pretending to be 'sick'.

And the school inspector, he used to come every few months and he was a grumpy old fellow. He'd storm through the tiny classroom, picking holes in everything we did. My father must've been terrified of him.

Then sometimes, when the children were really naughty, Daddy would give them the cane. At the Clandulla school reunions we always have a bit of a laugh about the different things that used to happen, and one fellow, Albert, he was telling me how he burst out laughing one time Daddy gave him the cane. So Daddy gave him the cane again and I forget how many times Albert told me he got the cane on that one day because he just couldn't stop laughing.

We were also talking about the time we found out about diphtheria. Diphtheria causes inflammation in the throat and the throat swells so much that you can't breathe and so then you die. It's one of those horrible diseases that children don't get any more because they have vaccinations. But I can recall one girl — I've forgotten her name just now — but I remember her standing on the school verandah and she was just crying and crying and we didn't know what was wrong. She went into hospital and she died and that's when we found out she'd had diphtheria. Goodness knows how it ever got to Clandulla because it was such an isolated place, but apparently diphtheria's a very infectious disease. So after she died we were all loaded into the back of an old truck and taken to Kandos, where the doctor gave us diphtheria injections. Thankfully no one else died after that. Just one girl got a little bit sick, but she survived. That's right, I think the girl that died, her name was Peggy Eldridge. Yes, Peggy Eldridge, that's it.

Plugger Lockett's Mum

So we're talking about Learmonth, right. Learmonth's a beautiful little town just north of Ballarat, in central Victoria. That's where I grew up in the early years, on a dairy property. Back then Learmonth had just the one main street and a beaut footy ground right by Lake Learmonth. And that lake, I tell you, it was absolutely beautiful. You know, with a nice sandy beach running down into this lovely water. There were five of us children in the family: four boys and a girl. I was the second eldest, and we all learnt to swim there. Many a nice hot summer's afternoon after school we'd go down to Lake Learmonth and take a dip, then we'd sit around and have a nice feed before we drove on home later that night. Whacko. It was really good.

Any rate, just another couple of my memories of Learmonth was when we used to ride about four miles to school on the old pushbikes. Then also, of course, like in most bush towns, sport played a big part in both the community and at school. In summertime it was mainly athletics and cricket and in winter it was footy for us boys and the girls played softball and stuff. Then we used to have the yearly state inter-school sports championships. That was a big muster of all the state schools. My older brother, Mick, he always went well. He was a very good runner. He'd really clean up on the day. I remember one time he came home with five blue ribbons from the inter-school championships. As I recall he won the hundred-yards sprint, the seventy-five-yards sprint, the long jump, the high jump, and if they played marbles he probably would've even won at that as well. But oh, they were great memories and there were some great people down that way.

Talking about great people: one of the local families were the Walkers. They were good at sport as well. They used to live on the other side of the lake. Elizabeth Walker was the daughter. We were around the same age as her and so we all went to Learmonth Primary School together. Elizabeth was exceptional at sport and she had a younger brother, Noel. Noel might've been a year or two younger than Elizabeth. Noel was a good sports person too. A very athletic little feller.

Any case, much later on of course, Elizabeth Walker ended up marrying old 'Plugger' Lockett from up Lexton way. Lexton's sort of just a bit north of Learmonth, and old Plugger's son, Tony, was also known as 'Plugger', and he became a great Aussie Rules player. You do know of Plugger Lockett, don't you? The footballer. Played around two hundred and eighty games for both St Kilda and the Sydney Swans. Holds the all-time goal-kicking record with one thousand three hundred and sixty goals. Brownlow Medal in the late '80s. Yeah, him. A true legend. Well, Elizabeth Walker is his mum, and we went to primary school with her, and even back in those days we reckoned she was one of the greatest looking sorts out there. We all loved her. She was about the same age as us. This was at Learmonth Primary School, and by gee she was a beautiful young woman. Even back then. Yes she was.

Rattling Bones

I'm a little bit chuffed that you've actually taken the time to contact me because of all these stories of the old days; they're just so important for us all to hang on to. But when I heard you having a yarn with Trevor Chappell, on one of those early morning radio shows, and there was a woman on there talking about her school days I thought, Well, perhaps mine has a bit of a twist to the original, too. And so my name is Larry and this was in primary school, back in the '60s. My father was with the Department of the Interior in Canberra and, in those days, it was part of the routine that you went and did a stint in the Northern Territory. So Dad took a turn as a pastoral inspector based in Alice Springs. That's how I ended up in the Alice. It was certainly a different world from Canberra. I suppose for my parents it might've even been a bit of a shock but for me, as a kid, it was more like just one big adventure.

Anyhow, we arrived in Alice and being 'Micks' I went to the local Catholic school, Saint Therese's. Do you know the geography of Alice Springs? Well we lived on the Eastside and, as far as the school goes, if you stood on Anzac Hill and you looked toward the gap, Saint Therese's was directly below you. To get to school we used to walk across the Todd River, through the backyard of Alice Springs High School, then sort of skirt around Anzac Oval, which was at the bottom of Anzac Hill, and Saint Therese's was one street to the west of Todd Street, straight across the road.

I could go on for ages about the experiences we had as kids up there but if you know the Todd River, it's pretty much dry most of the time. Though if you got a lot of rain further up north it'd certainly come down. I distinctly recollect one day;

we were heading home from school, across the river, and out of the blue the water started to flow. It was like, one minute we were standing there in the dried river bed, then the next, the water casually starts wandering its way down and is licking around our feet. So we head off home, all excited, and tell Mum, 'Hey, the river's coming down.'

Of course Mum gets into a bit of a panic. 'What? How deep was it?'

'Oh, it's all right, Mum, it's only a trickle.'

Then the next day, when she went down to take a look, the river's eight foot deep or thereabouts. But then, after a couple of days, it's gone again and it'd run out into the desert down south.

Anyhow, in the river you had all those big river gums and where the water came down it'd scour out holes around the butts of the trees, when the water eddied around them. So once the water had gone south there'd be all these waterholes remaining at the back sides of the river gums. Not huge ones, mind you, but big enough for us young kids to jump in and have a good play. Anyhow we'd swim in those for a week or so before they dried up as well. But we never told Mum what we'd been doing because she wasn't real keen on us swimming in Todd River, especially in the middle of Alice Springs where there were always busted beer bottles and that lying around the place, and so you never really knew what you might end up diving in on. Yeah, so that was our swimming hole every now and then when the water came through, down the Todd.

Now from recollection, in those days, the Alice Springs Swimming Pool was over near Railway Terrace. That's where I taught myself to swim. It was fairly primitive and it was expensive too — something like around 2/6 to get in — and so, with that in mind, in Alice, you mostly played under the sprinkler on the front lawn. That was the best way to cool down up there and that was just another one of those unique Alice Springs' experiences.

Then at the school, we also had the free milk programme. In actual fact, I think the free milk programme was brought in by the Menzies government and that was done to make sure all the kids got a bit of decent nourishment and a good dose of calcium or whatever. It also would've been great for the dairy industry too, of course. With the free milk programme, I suppose the most common story you'd hear is how those little one-third pint bottles would end up being delivered and left out in the sun and by the time the kids got to drink the stuff it'd be hot and not very tasty. That would be your usual story, wouldn't it?

But, no, in Alice Springs it was different because the milk had to come up by rail from Adelaide on the Ghan train. Now in those days, the Ghan ran on the old narrow gauge rail line which made the trip a pretty slow affair. It took something like three days and two nights to get up from Adelaide. So to stop the milk going off it had to be frozen. Now of course, the milk couldn't be frozen in bottles so, before it left Adelaide, they packed it and froze it in those triangular pyramid-shaped cartons; you know, something like what the kids get ice blocks in these days.

So that milk, it would arrive in Alice as frozen milk and, of course, it then had to be defrosted before we could drink it. Now, I don't know if you've ever tasted frozen milk that's been defrosted or not, but it tastes pretty ordinary to say the least. Very ordinary. But then after it had, first, been defrosted and then, secondly, left out in the sun, well, it goes from tasting pretty ordinary to tasting pretty darn terrible. The only way you could drink the stuff was if you got some of those flavoured drinking straws. Back then the straws were made from paper and they had a sliver about halfway down where they inserted the chocolate or strawberry flavouring, and you drank your milk through those in an attempt to make it half-drinkable. Well, almost half-drinkable. So in Alice Springs, in the mid-'60s, you could be guaranteed that you'd never be bowled over in the rush to be the first to get to the free school milk, that's for sure.

As I said, all the milk in Alice Springs arrived in cartons in those days. Us kids got the one-third pint packs; then in town you could get it in the standard one pint triangular cartons, and they were quite expensive. The rule in our family was that we could only afford to buy one, one pint pack of milk per week and that was solely for Mum's use. It wasn't for us kids. We weren't allowed to touch it. It was for Mum, and Mum alone. Oh, there was the Sunshine powdered milk but they still hadn't managed to work out how to get the lumps out of it by then. No matter what you did it still came out lumpy, and watered-down, lumpy milk poured on your Cornflakes made for a pretty ordinary breakfast, I can tell you. So yes, in those days, it was basically either horrible tasting one-third pint packs of milk at school or lumpy powdered milk for breakfast, or nothing. So I think I went without milk for about four or five years.

Of course, after we left Alice Springs and arrived back into civilisation you couldn't get me off the stuff. I don't want to quote quantities but let's say I could've been described as being a very serious milk drinker. But these days, much to my disappointment, I've had to give it away because I've developed a lactose intolerance in my middle age and so milk now doesn't do very nice things to me. Still, I reckon I've drunk that much of the stuff since I left Alice Springs that, with all the calcium that's been stored up in my body, my bones will still be rattling for a long time after they stick me under the ground.

School Days at Mount Mary

My name is Allen Kleinig and I have some memories that I'd like to share of my school days at Mount Mary. To give you some idea: Mount Mary is about ninety miles north-ish of Adelaide and fifteen miles west of Morgan, which is where the old railway line used to transfer goods back and forward to the Murray River township of Port Morgan. The one-teacher school at Mount Mary commenced operations on 8th March 1886 with an enrolment of thirty-four pupils. I wasn't one of those thirty-four. I came along much later than that, of course.

Mount Mary was a tiny settlement, consisting of not much more than a shop, a hotel and the school. The one-room school stood on a low limestone hill, approximately a hundred yards to the south-east of the shop and hotel. The building was constructed from limestone with red-brick corners and an iron roof. The grounds covered one acre, or so we measured, and a few leafy pepper trees and wormwort provided some shelter from the summer heat. They also acted as some sort of camouflage for those couples — who shall remain nameless — who were out to test their sexuality. On one occasion a pair of knickers was seen down around the ankle region. I will offer no more description, other than there was also a couple of sparse tamarisk trees a little north of the shelter shed. They provided almost nil cover and so they weren't much use for anything else, for that matter.

Amenities at the school were primitive. There was a small dilapidated tin shed on the north side. That's where you hung your school bag and, seeing how your school bag usually contained your lunch and your lunch was usually packed in a tin box, it provided the perfect opportunity during the heat of summertime for your lunch to complete its cooking. Fortunately we had a two-thousand-gallon tank of rainwater to quench our thirst; that was until it sprung a leak and then we had to bring our own bottled drinking water. As for our sporting gear, that could only be described as also being 'sparse' as it consisted of just the one cricket bat and a few tennis balls. We were provided with little else apart from a couple of rope-and-wood swings, that had been strung up between some mallee posts, and there was an old seesaw.

Still, we were a lively lot and, after classes had finished for the day, the race was on to see who'd be the first to get to the shop. This was no mere downhill bike ride. Not on your life. To get there we had to negotiate the publican's mob of geese. If we came too close to the goslings, the old gander would get all fired up and it'd be after us with its head down, hissing in threat of attack. Another threat was the publican's wife. She had a voice like a foghorn and if we upset her, or her geese, she'd bellow out a tirade of abuse. But no harm was done. Not usually, anyway. It was all just in a normal school day and somewhere along the line we all received a decent education.

With living a fair distance from town, and my only form of transport being a pushbike, it was decided that I wouldn't start my schooling at Mount Mary until after my seventh birthday. Up until then I was silently hoping that my parents might've forgotten about sending me to school. But the Christmas that I received a raft of presents including a school bag, shoes and other school necessities, I knew my fate was sealed.

The first day still strikes a note in my memory. A new teacher had arrived and the first thing he asked me to do was to make O's all over a piece of paper. Having already been taught the alphabet and numbers at home I soon got sick of that task and began writing different letters and numbers. My scribbled markings seemed to impress the new teacher, as did my progress throughout that first year, so much so that the following year he promoted me straight up into

Grade 3. Though I'm thinking just now that perhaps it was because I would've been the only student in Grade 2 which, of course, would have increased his workload somewhat. Still, it all worked out okay and I did pretty well. The teacher also turned out to be a nice enough person and, fortunately, because of his bad back, he was unable to inflict too much pain with the yardstick. I only came to fully realise that when a replacement teacher arrived three years later and, despite him having one arm smaller and shorter than the other, he was able to use the yardstick with far more painful results. On one occasion, I recall how I had a red mark on my bottom for about a week.

And that wasn't the only occasion I got into strife. For some odd reason I seemed to have an ability to get into trouble. So much so that someone once remarked how they thought that 'Trouble' was born on the same day as I had been. For instance, at school we had a system where we stood all our pushbikes against the south wall of the school, in the afternoon shade, with the youngest children's bikes in the front and the oldest down the back. But one of the younger kids — let's call her Jenny — well Jenny didn't like to be beaten in the chaotic afternoon dash to the shop, did she? She wanted to be first, so she decided to cheat by standing her bike outside the netting fence, where she could be the first away. So I decided to teach her a lesson and tied her bike to the fence with a piece of wire. That afternoon, as we all flew past on our mad dash to the shop, there was Jenny heading back to school howling her eyes out. Next morning — 'WHACK!' — I was in trouble, again.

There was also the time that nail points appeared sticking out of the wooden seat in the girls' toilet. Not my fault ... well, not quite my fault, I must admit. Another occasion my initials mysteriously appeared on the newly installed urinal in the boys' dunny. More trouble. Another time the eggs from a diver duck's nest somehow ended up in another student's egg collection. You just may wonder who got the blame?

Another time a magpie was nesting in the mallee not far from the school and it was swooping upon us as we rode by. The obvious solution was to climb the tree with my school bag over my head as protection and dispose of the newly hatched fledglings. Problem solved. But not so in the teacher's eyes. 'WHACK!' Even more trouble.

In those days there were no student representatives or anything like that, though there was a school council for parents and they held meetings from time to time to plan things like ground maintenance or school picnics. The school picnics were great fun. They were held at the recreational grounds which were partially hidden among the saltbush on the south-west edge of the town. A concrete cricket pitch centred the crude oval. A couple of bush dunnies wobbled in the breeze. There was a small tin shelter shed and the remains of a tennis court. Seating for the onlookers consisted of a long log, nailed upon a couple of short posts. This also proved useful for what we called 'pillow fights' — though if you were the one who got knocked off the log, the landing wasn't too pleasant, I can assure you.

These picnics were held on a Saturday afternoon in the springtime. Events included flat races, egg-and-spoon races, relay races and even a slow bike race. One year we had a 'rooster chase'. My brother won that which, as I recall, made for an excellent Sunday dinner. The bigger teenagers and young men had a flat race of their own. Bowling a ball at just the one cricket stump was also for the older people. Us Mount Mary kids always seemed to win some prize or other; that's apart from the year the kids from Bower School turned up and they won most of the loot. But to make up for any disappointment, a delicious afternoon tea always completed the day, along with the free Amscol Dandy — ice cream in a cardboard cup with a small stick to scoop it out — and there was always plenty of Appelts cool drinks, which were made at Angaston, in the Barossa Valley.

Then, unfortunately, when our numbers had fallen to just seven, we were informed that the Mount Mary school was to close. That happened on 17th May 1956 and those of us who remained were to be crammed like sardines into our teacher's 1948 FX Holden and driven over to Bower School. And believe it or not, out of those remaining seven children, all bar one were either cousins of mine or cousins-once-removed. So we were like one big family. And that was the end of my school days at Mount Mary.

Sneezes

This is 'Summer all Over' with Trevor Chappell. Hello, Richard.

RICHARD — Hello, Trevor. This is just a quick story. In about 1957 I was in a boarding school in Sydney and I was famous for being a big sneezer. Still am. Once I start I just can't stop. I still sneeze at least ten to twelve times just about every day of my life.

So this time I started sneezing in class and when I got to about seven or eight sneezes quite a ruckus was starting up among the other kids. Then by the time I got to ten or twelve sneezes, as you might imagine, the ruckus had turned into pretty much a mayhem. By about the fourteenth or fifteenth sneeze there was pretty much a riot going on in class.

Anyhow, at the end of the lesson period the teacher ordered me up to the staffroom. So up I went and he said, 'Hold your hand out.'

I said, 'What for?'

'Well,' he said, 'no one can sneeze that many times and so I'm going to give you the cane for disrupting the class.'

And so I got the cane for 'disrupting the class'. But I thought it was a bit unfair because I couldn't help it. It's just one of those inexplicable things and, as I said, even now, I sneeze at least ten or twelve times every day. And every time I sneeze I still think of that time, over fifty years ago now, when I got the cane for sneezing.

Swapping Sandwiches

How we got all the way from Victoria to Purlewaugh, in central-northern New South Wales, in our horse-drawn wagon, goodness knows. I was very young when that happened. But I just think there wasn't much work around in those days so Dad just packed us all up and we started travelling. We'd only be in a place for a night or two nights, then we were on the go again. Dad did mainly droving; but anything really. Then when we landed in Purlewaugh he got a job burning off and clearing paddocks so we stayed on the property he was working on.

Now, how many of us was there by then? There was a lot of us anyway. I'd have to count us up. There was Edna; she came on the scene at about that time. So Edna was the youngest. Then there was Elizabeth, then there was Harvey, then James, Henry, me — whose name's Leila — then there was Barbara, William, Toby, Norman, Edward and the oldest, she was called Neroli. So that was us twelve kids — eight boys and four girls — then there was Mum and Dad. So what does that make it: fourteen of us, in all, including our parents.

Yes so, like I said, when we got to Purlewaugh, Dad got this job of burning off and clearing up the paddocks. But we didn't have a house or anything. We still had the wagon of course, but it had other stuff stored in it so we just lived in tents. Mum and Dad had a tent to themselves. Then the boys had a tent and there was also one for us girls. We didn't even have a real kitchen. The cooking was done outside and so we mostly ate around the campfire. If it rained or anything we might've had another tent for that, but I can't remember just now. There was no bathroom. We'd just go to the toilet at a spot behind a tree. We didn't even have a shower or anything, so we'd go and wash ourselves in the dam. You never worried about who was nude and who wasn't. We just all piled into the dam and had a bit of a wash with a block of soap and, after you'd done that, then you'd cart buckets of water home for your cooking and your drinking. So we got a bit of soapy water in our food sometimes.

As for our schooling, when we were travelling we were supposed to be doing our lessons by correspondence. But we didn't learn much. Mum was mostly off doing other things and so she couldn't be bothered much. The oldest sister, Neroli, she used to try and help us the best she could. But she wasn't that well educated either, because she sort of left school very early to help look after all us kids as we came along. Now I'm not sure just how old Neroli was at that time. There's ten years' difference between her and I and, by the time we got to Purlewaugh, I would've been about eight or nine, maybe more. So you can work it out.

But after we got to Purlewaugh, that's when the authorities found out that we were living close to a school and so we were told that we had to go to the Purlewaugh school then. First off there was six of us kids that went off to the school and we rode on three horses — two on each horse. There was Barbara and me and William, and also Toby and Norman and Edward. I think that's how it went, anyway. Like I said, there was that many of us I keep forgetting.

Anyhow, the school only had about twenty or so kids at the most. It was built of timber and it was just one big room with all the classes in together. A little row of the lower grades sat on one side. The next grade sat in a middle row. Then the ones that were in the higher grades, they sat in another row. It was a one-teacher school, and what a horrible old grouch of a teacher he was too. Just horrible. He'd stand out the front of us all, with his cane at the ready to stop us from talking and going on when we were supposed to be learning.

And, I tell you, he was pretty free and easy with that cane. Too right he was. He even used it on me a few times till I swore at him. But Dad soon sorted him out because, one time, after the teacher gave me the cane, Dad cracked up and he went up to the school and said to the teacher, he said, 'If you hit any of my kids again, I'll come up here and flog you with the stock whip.' See, Dad reckoned it was his place to do the flogging on his own kids which, mind you, he did quite often. But anyway that really put the wind up the teacher so he laid off us for a while, then.

So the next time we got into trouble, instead of giving us the cane, the teacher kept us in after school. That didn't go down too well with Dad either. He went back up and told the teacher that he'd also give him a decent flogging with the stock whip if he ever kept us in after school again. Dad was of the opinion that we were already spending far too much time at school because we had all our other jobs to do at home as well. We had to feed the dogs and we had a few pigs that we always got ready for Christmas. Then there was wood to collect for the campfire, and all those other little jobs around the 'house' as we called it. On top of all that we were also supposed to do our homework. Though Dad cracked up on that too and he went and told the teacher that we were supposed to go to school to do our learning there and not after school, because like I said when we came home we had to do all our other work around the place. So after that, if we did anything wrong, we got kept in at either playtime or lunchtime.

But the story I was going to tell you was about when I used to swap my sandwiches with the other kids, because they had nicer ones. They'd have meat on their sandwiches or even sometimes they'd have jam. As for us, we just had Vegemite or we'd have Peck's Paste on our sandwiches, and if you've never tasted Peck's Paste, I tell you, it's as dry as a wooden God. And that's why we used to try and swap our sandwiches. So I'd give the kids a ride on our horse and then I'd say, 'How about you swap your sandwiches for mine and I'll give you an extra ride on the horse for nothing,' and they used to believe it was a pretty good deal to get a ride on the horse for nothing so they'd swap their sandwiches. It was a bit of a con really, but it worked; most times, that is.

Then other times, in return for their sandwiches, I used to tell the kids stories about our travelling days in our horse-drawn wagon and about what we did. I used to tell them about how we lived in tents instead of a house, like they did, and how we washed ourselves in a dam and how we didn't have a real toilet so we did our business behind the trees. And they couldn't believe it. They'd say, 'You go to the toilet behind a tree? What, is there a toilet built there, is there?'

I'd say, 'No you just sit down.'

They'd say, 'You don't.'

'Yes we do,' I'd say, but I never showed them how. I left that up to them to work out.

Then another time when I was real hungry I pinched the teacher's sandwiches. How that came about was that I'd just got into trouble for something or other, I can't exactly remember what. Probably got caught looking up the answers in the back of the textbook because I couldn't work out the answers otherwise. But after Dad had told the teacher he'd flog him with the stock whip if he caned us or if he kept us in after school, the teacher wasn't game enough to give me the cane or keep me in after school, so he said, 'Leila, you get outside.'

I think his aim was to follow me outside and give me a good talking to. But then all the other kids started laughing and going on and so he had to stay in the classroom to try and control them. Anyway as I was walking out, down the hallway, I walked past his briefcase. It was partly open and I just lifted it up a little bit and there was his sandwiches in there and so I took them out of his briefcase and I went out onto the verandah and I sat there and I ate them. So I got two helpings of sandwiches that day and I can tell you, his sandwiches were even better than what I'd swap with the other kids. They were really nice, they were too.

But Friday was a bad day for swapping sandwiches because, back in those days, the Catholic kids didn't eat any meat on a Friday and so they'd only have fish sandwiches, and I wasn't too keen on sandwiches with fish in them. And something else I couldn't understand about the Catholic kids was when the Protestant or Church of England minister come to give us religious lessons the Catholics always went outside and played games and that. I can understand it now of course, with their different teachings and that, but back then we thought they must've had some sort of privilege or other over us to be allowed to go outside when we had to sit inside and listen to a boring old religious lesson. So that's just a little bit about my school days at Purlewaugh. But really, other than the horrible teacher we had, I quite liked school when I was there.

Swearing

After my husband, John, graduated from Graylands Teachers' College, his first appointment was to a one-teacher school out at a tiny mining place called Marvel Loch. I'd never actually heard of the place, and I doubt if John had either. As it turned out, it's in the Eastern Goldfields region of Western Australia, just out from Southern Cross. An interesting point here is that I'm led to believe the actual name of Marvel Loch came from a racehorse that had won the Caulfield Cup back in 1905.

During the early 1960s, when we were at Marvel Loch, the town's population would've been about a hundred and eighty, with a total of around three hundred people in the entire district. In the school itself, John only had about twenty children to start with. I was actually a full-time mother by that stage. We'd already had one little boy before we arrived and another one was born during our time at Marvel Loch. But I was also a qualified teacher and so, later on, when student numbers rose into the thirties, the Department pardoned my married status and allowed me to go and teach the first three grades, though that was just of a morning.

For both John and me, those four years at Marvel Loch were just absolutely wonderful. It was such a lovely place and our experiences were many and varied. I remember when we first arrived and were starting to settle into our tiny little house. Originally it had been a single men's quarters and so we were just sitting there, surrounded by all our goods and chattels, wondering where everything was going to fit. There were packing boxes everywhere and, amid all this chaos, along came a gentleman with a big bunch of grapes and, with his hand outstretched, he said, 'Hello, I'm Alex. Welcome to

Marvel Loch,' and I thought that was the perfect introduction to our time there.

Once we settled into our house, we found the living conditions to be quite good. Marvel Loch was actually on the water line that ran out to Kalgoorlie, which was great because we never ran out of water, unlike some of the other places we lived in. We also had the power laid on. That was also wonderful because, once again, it wasn't laid on in some of the other places John taught, where our only source of power came from the town's generator.

There was a big mine at Marvel Loch called the Navoria mine. With the mine working three shifts, it brought a lot of single men into the town and particularly, at that stage, migrants who were from all over the world. They lived in little dongas that were nowhere near as luxurious as they are nowadays and quite often these men would come up to our place and, even though things were quite tight, we'd all share whatever food we had and they'd bring along their wine or coffee or whatever, and someone had a guitar and we'd all gather around on the floor and we'd have some of the most wonderful sing-alongs. Oh, there were all sorts of nationalities. It was like a mini League of Nations really, and one or two of them had beautiful voices. I think they might've been the Italians because they'd sing 'Arrivederci Roma' and songs like that.

As I said, we'd already had one child and our second child arrived while we were there, and because John was working hard at the school, as well as continuing with furthering his studies, playing sport, and becoming a radio ham, it was a very full-on time in both our lives. John was also responsible for starting the badminton club. Then of course there was the all-important football match on the weekends. During the winter months, the footy was always the big event of the week. John played. Actually he wasn't only just one of the players, he was also the coach and the captain of the side. This was the Australian Rules style of football and so there were only about half a dozen locals in the district who actually knew how to play the game properly. The rest — the 'League of Nations' as I've described them — they were from the mines. Most of them had grown up in various places throughout Europe where soccer was the big game, so hardly any of them knew our rules. Some didn't even have the proper boots. Some didn't even speak, or even understand, the English language that well.

When the football was on, us womenfolk, we'd dress ourselves and our children up to the nines for the big match and we'd go down to watch. Everyone went along. You'd hardly find a living soul in the streets when the footy was on. Of course the ladies did the afternoon teas and our little toddler — the elder one — at half-time and three-quarter time, he used to run out onto the ground with all the other children to listen to his dad's pep talk in trying to gee the team up. Thinking back, it was a funny sort of group of men actually. We might've only won one or two games all season, but it never seemed to matter that much because, with the team we had, everyone was well aware of their limitations. Still that didn't stop our enthusiasm. Everyone pitched in and did their best, and we all had fun.

Another quite special occasion was when the mail arrived in town. That only came twice weekly and when it did, once again, us women, we'd all get dressed up and you'd dress up your baby and go down to the post office to receive the mail, and then we'd stand around, admiring each other's babies and having a chat. Actually the postmaster himself was a bit of a character as well. I could tell you some stories about him but I don't think they'd suit a book like this.

Oh, and there's something else John has just pointed out that I really should make mention of: when we first went to Marvel Loch, our eldest child was about fifteen months. He was the toddler who used to run out onto the ground to listen to John's pep talk to the members of Marvel Loch's footballing

League of Nations. Anyway, the school was adjacent to our house and there was just a bit of wire fence between us and the school grounds. By that stage, as you could do back in those days, our eldest was running about anywhere and everywhere and he was always escaping into the school to play with the children. And the kids just thought he was the greatest fun to have around. They just loved him.

Anyhow, kids being kids, one of John's 'prized' boy students — and I use the term 'prized' with a strong hint of irony — well this lad must've harboured aspirations of becoming a great teacher because he brought it upon himself to conduct our little toddler in the subject of 'swearing'. And those lofty aspirations of this young boy could well have been right too as, not long after these swearing lessons had begun, our little toddler started to arrive home, sprouting all sorts of choice words. Anyway, quite often I used to run into this little chap's mother down the street, and it was, 'Oh, Nancy,' she used to say to me, 'isn't my beautiful son just so kind and considerate when it comes to your little one?' and I'd be thinking, Yes he is, all right. He's taught him how to swear beautifully, that's what he's done.

Telling a Tale out of School

I had no experience of country life whatsoever. I was born in the city. Grew up in the city. Didn't even have any relatives who lived on farms. That was until I met my husband. He came from a station property out of Meekatharra. He'd attended a boarding school in Perth from the age of seven, and so he'd spent quite a bit of time in the city. Anyhow we subsequently met up and married and I went north with him, and we eventually ended up owning a station property in the Gascoyne region of Western Australia, called Dairy Creek, which was just under half a million acres. In those earlier days, Dairy Creek was predominantly sheep, then we did our last shearing in 1999 and after that it became totally a cattle place.

By the time we'd moved onto Dairy Creek we'd had two children — a girl and a boy. Our daughter was three and our son eighteen months. There was no school out there, of course. The nearest one would've been Gascoyne Junction, which was eighty kilometres away and it was only a primary school. The closest town that had both a primary school and a high school was Carnarvon, and Carnarvon was something like two hundred and fifty kilometres away. So that definitely wasn't an option. Our only real option was School of the Air, out of Carnarvon.

With School of the Air, I taught our daughter for her first year, which I must say was sometimes a little fraught. To this day she'll tell you that she's been psychologically scarred by having been taught by her mother. However, she hasn't seemed to have suffered too many ill effects. Then from Year 8 to Year 12 she went to boarding school in Perth. She did well there, then she went on to study naturopathy and has since done Psychology with Honours. So in spite of that first year of School of the Air with Mum, she's done well.

But teaching distance education to your own child was quite stressful and so, after that first year with my daughter, we decided to have governesses. And we had some great governesses. Excellent in fact. In the early part we had a lovely soft, gentle girl which would've been in great contrast to me. She stayed for two years, then we got a sweet girl who'd just finished school. She also stayed for two years. She placed a huge emphasis on art and the creative side of things. The next governess was musical. She played a guitar and composed a song which our children sang over the School of the Air radio. She was fun and light-hearted, so both the children got to experience yet another aspect of life from her. Then our daughter went off to boarding school and, for our son's last year of primary schooling, we got a very academic girl. But because our son wasn't at all academically inclined, they didn't really connect, and that proved to be a little tricky. For the most part he was more interested in being outside, doing something with his dad. Still, she pushed him, which was good because the next year, when he went to boarding school down in Perth, he was probably more prepared for high school than he otherwise might've been.

Of course, with living out on a property, there were always distractions and sometimes the children would run amuck. We had a big creek running past our house and if it rained, the creek would run. When that happened, at any opportunity, the kids would take off down to the creek, shedding clothes and shoes as they went. Never to be seen again. They'd go completely deaf at that point and wouldn't hear us calling them back to the homestead for lessons. So we'd end up having to take off our own shoes and traipse up the creek in search of them, and there they'd be, building dams or playing some sort of game in or around the water. It was all such a great adventure for them. Then when they were older their games involved racing down the creek in tyre tubes, with their mother's heart in her mouth, wondering if she'd ever see them again. And that was more or less the pattern of everyday life while the creek was running. It was far more exciting than having to do schoolwork and, of course, you couldn't stop them from having a bit fun, could you?

In many ways distance education had its ups and downs. On the one hand it was good to have that one-on-one teaching experience with your own children, where you wouldn't leave a subject behind unless they fully understood it. As for the difficulties of distance education: there was always the ever-present anxiety of not knowing where your child was positioned in the scheme of things, and that always left you wondering if you were teaching your child in the right way. But in general, I think the children got a solid basic educational grounding. Though mind you, when both the children were finally in boarding school, I remember thinking, Thank goodness that's over.

Now as for the way they went about their lessons — or 'sets' as they were known — they were sent out in packages from Carnarvon on the mail truck. I can't quite remember the finer details now but I think they came as two-week sets of schooling and the children worked their way through those, under the supervision of either myself or the governess. Then at the end of those two weeks your child did a test on them, which you submitted for marking and any comments or advice the teachers at School of the Air wanted to make were sent out on the following week's mail truck.

That's how it was supposed to work but, in our case, we most probably received several weeks of sets in one go, if not a whole term, because there were always occasions when the road was closed and the mail couldn't get through. Then in addition to having to do your sets of lessons, each day of the school week there was a half-hour School of the Air session over the radio. All the various station children joined in on those. Anyhow, before those half-hour lessons began, while the kids were settling in, they'd be asked if they wanted to share any news they may have and, at times, some of those were quite revealing and funny.

There's just one little classic of a story. Mind you, this may be telling a tale out of school, and it is really only hearsay. But as folklore has it: one time over the School of the Air radio this little boy was asked if he had any news he'd like to share. Now these radio sessions are broadcast throughout the entire region, so everybody for hundreds of miles around was listening in and what's more they were well aware that the boy's mother was away, off visiting relatives or whatever. Anyhow there'd been a thunderstorm out on this little boy's property the night before.

The teacher welcomed the boy on the air. 'And have you any news you'd like to share, Tommy?'

'Yes, Miss.'

'Let's hear it then.'

'Well, Miss, there was a really big thunderstorm out here last night, Miss, and I'm very scared of the thunder.'

'Oh yes, and so what did you do?'

'Well, Miss, I went to get into bed with Daddy, Miss, and guess what, Miss?'

'What, Tommy?'

'Well, Miss, our governess must've been scareder of the thunder than me 'cause she was already in bed with Daddy!'

That was their Education

My grandparents were Scottish pioneers around the Mackay district of northern Queensland and, oh, they were simply the most amazing people. After they arrived in Australia, Granddad worked on a farm in the area. Then, when the authorities-that-be were looking to open up all that bush country around there for sugar cane, Granddad put in for a block about sixty kilometres due west of Mackay, out near a place called Calen. From memory, I think there was already a sugar mill about twenty kilometres west of Mackay, at Mirani, and there might've also been one at Finch Hatton.

Anyhow Granddad got his block of land. But then to even get out there, they had to follow a blazed trail out from Mirani. A blazed trail is where a surveyor goes through the bush on horseback and marks the trees with coloured ribbon or rope. So you get given a colour and you follow those trees that had been marked in your colour and they eventually led to your particular block. There were no roads whatsoever. Just thick bush. There wasn't even a track, so they couldn't get a buggy through.

So Granddad and the eldest child, Aunty Agnes, they went out on horseback to settle on their block of land. Aunty Agnes would've only been about fifteen at that time and she worked like a man beside Granddad, clearing the land and setting up just enough camp that it would be okay for Granny and the remaining children to come out to live. So basically Granddad and Aunty Agnes more or less survived off the land and they slept in a tent with a swag, and they only came back into Mirani every now and then to visit the rest of the family and to get supplies.

Granny didn't go out at first. By then she'd already had seven of their eight children. There was no such thing as contraception in those days, other than the word 'No' and, of course, that didn't always work. People just accepted the fact that they might have seven or eight children. Granny and the rest of the children stayed behind on a property at Benholme, which was about six k's out of Mirani, until Granddad and Aunty Agnes had set things up for them.

When Granny eventually took the children out to live on the block, there was no house — just a great big canvas extension to a tent that was rigged up between trees. And because they had pretty big wet seasons, to stop it getting all muddy inside, they had a basin and a towel at the opening where you washed your feet. Then for flooring they had laid pine boxes down over the dirt floor and to try and make the place a bit cosier, Granny put old sugar bags over the boxes to act as a bit of a carpet. Also, by then, Granddad had rigged up all these beds, made from chicken wire so they had some sort of spring to them. And it was two kids to a bed. So it was all very basic and primitive to start with.

In those days there was a great community spirit. I mean you might not see your neighbours from one week to the next but, if you ever needed help, everyone would come and pitch in. Anyhow back in Scotland, Granddad had worked for the railways, up north, near Peterhead, and he really knew how to work draughthorses. One story goes that, when Granddad first brought draughthorses out to the block, he took them out to one of the paddocks he'd cleared and some of the men from the nearby farms came over to see him work them. And, apparently, these men just stood there with their eyes popping out because they'd never seen such a straight drill in their lives. After that, whenever they saw Granddad out in the paddock with his horses it was, 'Let's go 'n' watch the old Jock plough with his horses.' So yes, Granddad knew his horses.

Also, one of the first things Granny did when she came out to live on the block was to get Granddad to work up some ground for a garden. So it wasn't long before they had some veggies and they'd catch a lot of their own game in the bush too. Oh, that's right, they'd also taken out a couple of milking cows but, because of the ticks, that proved to be a bit of a struggle. Mind you, these weren't just your ordinary old cattle ticks. These were the shell-back scrub ticks; the ones that really can kill.

Of course there was no school out there. With the block being so isolated, there wasn't even any way you could get correspondence lessons sent out. So Granny did it all herself. She sorted out the lessons and, being very deeply Presbyterian, she taught the children how to read, mainly from the Bible, and she taught them how to write. She also taught them maths. History was taught through the telling of their own stories. I guess that's why my family have always been storytellers. Then, when they eventually got a small hut and some money, Granny got a little pedal organ and through the singing of hymns, that was their musical education. And it must have worked because I know that three of the girls also learnt to play the organ. And that was about it really. That was their education. But I must say, my grandmother had a wonderful soprano voice and, years later, when they came to live in Mackay, she led the singing at church each Sunday.

Then later on, Granddad built Granny a lovely, lovely four-bedroom Queenslander-style home; you know, with the big wide verandah and the stairs coming down the front and dividing and going out either side at the bottom. Oh, he was so clever. He never learnt building as a trade but he still carved all this lovely curved woodwork along the front of the house. Just beautiful it was.

Oh, and I remember when my sister and I went there as little girls, after lunch Granddad used to go out on the front verandah and he'd have a nap on a sort of divan thing. Anyhow he had this great big bushy moustache and when he'd go to give us a kiss, we'd go, 'Oh no, Granddad, it tickles,' and all that carry on. Then one time he was out there on the verandah and he was supposed to be sleeping and we snuck up on him and my sister gently lifted his moustache and said, 'Come on, Bev, quick, kiss him.' And we took it in turns at giving him a little kiss while he pretended he was asleep.

But even to his dying day Granddad retained his thick Scottish accent. I remember how we would always complain about having freckles and he'd reply in his Scottish brogue, 'Ach if you were at 'ome in Scot'lan' you wouldn't have an-ay freckles,' and we used to think how Scotland must've been almost near to heaven because it was a place where no one had freckles. Oh, they were wonderful days and with so many, many lovely memories.

Anyway I've gotten off the track a bit, haven't I? But that's how those children were educated. Granny taught them all by herself, and so none of them went to primary school and none of them went to high school, but they all grew up to hold down good solid jobs and the two boys, they both became very successful sugar cane farmers. And of course they were as honest as the day is long. That was the code you lived by in those days. You know; 'your word is your bond' sort of thing.

That's Art

My mate and I were in a town near Winton this time, working in schools. So we rocked up to this place and, as like a lot of schools in outback Queensland, this one was set up high off the ground, on pillars. These pillars, they'd be about fifty centimetres in diameter and they're quite tall so the area under the school building is like a place where the kids can go when it's raining or where they can eat their lunch and stuff like that. So at this school, the kids would just sit there and they'd stare at these ugly pillars. Anyhow the principal wanted us to do an artwork with the kids, to make the pillars look more attractive.

'I'd like a mural depicting the history of transport in the area,' she said.

Well, I just thought: number one, what an absolutely boring topic and number two, all the transport around the place was like semi-trailers and trains and stuff like that and you can't paint a semi-trailer or a train going vertically, upwards. It just wouldn't work. It'd look stupid. To make any sense at all, you'd have to paint them going horizontally and, on something that was only fifty centimetres in diameter, a semi-trailer would end up having to be so small that no one would really be able to see them. They'd lack impact.

Anyhow we said, 'Yeah, yeah,' and then the principal said she had to nick off and go to a conference for a couple of days. So in her mind all the pillars were going to have trucks and trains and things painted on them.

Now this was around World Environment Day and being an environmentalist, when we sat the kids down, I said, 'Right, we're here to help you do a mural, so how's about, to celebrate

World Environment Day, we do pictures of insects and plants all up the pillars?'

'Yeah, wow,' they said.

I said, 'Now we don't want to paint boring old things like daisy flowers, do we?'

'No, no,' they said.

I said, 'What we want are some really Australian-type things like banksias and grevilleas and interesting insects and things like that. So how about we go and look up how to draw native plants and insects?'

'Yeah, wow.'

So the kids did all this research and they got the draft drawings done and we started painting, and the mural turned out absolutely fantastic. We even painted a little dedication: 'This mural was painted in celebration of World Environment Day.' And everyone thought it was great.

Everyone except the principal, that is. When she came back from the conference she wasn't impressed at all. Not one little bit. We tried to explain but, 'No, no.' Anyway it was already painted so we couldn't do anything about it. So that's just a little story about how one small school in the outback of Queensland got an environmental mural they never wanted.

But I tell you, there's some funny ways of thinking out in places like that because, what I was going to say was, in the process of doing the painting I had this little kid come up to me. He would've only been about ten and he said, 'Are you a Greenie?'

I said, 'Yes I am and I'm proud of it.'

And he looked straight at me and he said, 'We don't like Greenies around here.' Yes, this is a little kid of about ten, even less. He said, 'We don't like Greenies around here.'

'Well,' I said, 'why is that?'

And without even hesitating, he said, ''Cause they get in the way.'

From the mouths of babes, ay? So where did that come from, I wonder? My first thought was, Hey, kid, don't introduce me to your parents.

But, as I said, a lot of people around that way think differently. Or perhaps it's just us Greenies. I mean, they're good souls — great souls, many of them — but it totally confused me because there are these Creationists living out there and even though they're surrounded by heaps and heaps of dinosaur bones and fossils, they still maintain that dinosaurs were never a part of the scheme of life — that they never existed. Hughenden's even got the Muttaburrasaurus in its museum. So, what, did someone plant these things there? God, maybe. Yes, perhaps that's it. God created the dinosaur and just planted their bones there for people to come along and dig up and put in their museums ... durr?

I remember another time we went out to a place called Lark Quarry. Lark Quarry's between Winton and Longreach, and there's lots of dinosaur fossils there. I actually got chills all through me when I got there. It's like a moment frozen in time, because the ground is all fossilised and you can see the footprints of small dinosaurs, like raptors, actually running away from the larger dinosaurs. It's all there in the footprints: the big dinosaurs chasing the smaller ones. It's an amazing place. It's like Jurassic Park.

But, oh, I've got to tell you this. Talk about art replicating life. One of the local councils has even tried to recreate that exact same thing down the main street. They have a little sculpture of a raptor down one end of the street and spaced out behind the raptor are these eight or ten big dinosaur footsteps made into fibreglass rubbish bin covers. You wouldn't believe it, would you? Yes, they're like a dinosaur's foot that's been chopped off at the ankle and they've got green scales and big yellow toe nails and they cover the rubbish bins. And they paid someone like a zillion dollars to come up with that concept. And over time these bins have had cars reversing into them and everything, so they're all squashed and dented. Yes, there's about eight or ten of these feet laid out down the main street looking as though this big dinosaur's chasing the little guy. You've got to see it to believe it.

I said to my mate, 'Now, that's art ... NOT.'

The Best Means of Defence

I grew up on a little farm about seventeen miles out of Wingham, at a place called Caparra. Wingham's in the mid-north coast region of New South Wales, near Taree and Gloucester; those sorts of places. There were five children in the family: one sister and four of us boys. It was a dairy farm and though it was only small as far as acreage went, back in those days, fifty cows was a reasonable-sized herd to manage. When I was younger it was all hand milking, then as time went by, we went to machine milking. So the whole family lived off the fifty cows — that was seven of us, if you include Mum and Dad. But, of course, as us children grew older we started to move away.

My brother Alex was the third eldest. He was about four years older than me. Alex was a keen boxer. Better than average, I'd say. Actually, later on, when he went into the Air Force he had quite a few fairly important bouts where he did very well. But back then, in those old Caparra days, when he was first starting out, there used to be a boxing circuit in the area. Say one week they'd hold a tournament in one particular town then a couple of weeks later they'd hold another one in a different town, and so Alex used to follow the boxing circuit around. As to just how far he travelled: the circuit most probably covered a couple of hundred kilometre radius out from Gloucester. I can't recall just who ran it, but I do know there were some very capable boxers at the time, and Alex more than held his own.

Alex was a middleweight. He wasn't professional of course. He just took it up as a sport. He'd even set up a bit of a gymnasium in one of our old barns out at the farm and, of an afternoon, after we'd finished school and then completed our farming chores he'd take me down to the barn and do a bit of training. The gym was a pretty rough and ready affair. It consisted of not much more than a punching bag, with a speed bag and a heavy bag. We had those heavy old gloves back then. Then after he'd done a bit of a workout Alex would practise his technique on me. As you might be able to imagine, being four years younger and nowhere near as capable as Alex was, I soon learnt how to defend myself quite well. Though that wasn't Alex's theory. Alex always reckoned that the best means of defence was attack … and so I was attacked quite a lot. Actually, being his sparring partner, you could say that he played me, pretty much, as his punching bag.

Anyhow Caparra was where I started my schooling. It was a one-teacher place. Quite isolated. The teacher was a male. There would've been around fifteen or so of us children and the teacher taught all six classes, all in the one room. From memory, the school was a weatherboard structure, with a tin roof. Just one room, as I said. It most certainly wasn't air-conditioned. Though we did have a couple of windows, of course. Actually I can't even recall us having any heating, so when it was hot we sweltered and when it was cold we froze. Any rate I went right through there, at Caparra, until sixth class, which was the last year of primary school.

From Caparra I went to high school at Wingham, where I boarded with a little old lady. She was a widow who was about forty though, to me, she seemed very old. It was quite interesting; she had a cottage down near a creek that ran into a large marshy area. Of course, given conditions like that, you had your usual abundance of frogs and snakes, but along with the frogs and snakes there were thousands and thousands of mosquitoes. So many in fact, that each night before I went to bed I had to spray my bedroom thoroughly and shut it up for about half an hour to try and get rid of the mozzies. Then just before I went to bed, I'd shake the mosquitoes off the blanket and sweep them up off the floor. And not only were there lots and lots of these mozzies, but they were big too. So huge in fact that I swear, one night I was woken up by two of them having a heated discussion as to whether they were going to pick me up and take me back home to the swamp to eat me, or just eat me right there on the spot. Yes, dine in or takeaway. So they were pretty big. And there were lots of them.

Any rate, other than my trials and tribulations with the mosquitoes on the home front, I had to face an even bigger problem at school. With having been so isolated out on the farm at Caparra, we'd had an extremely limited social life. So when I arrived at Wingham High School, where there was up to a couple of hundred students, I found it very difficult to make friends. I was particularly shy and so I didn't mix in that well. To make matters worse, I was only average at sport. Yes, I did a bit of running, but I wasn't fast enough to be noted for that. Didn't like football. Didn't even really know how to play the game properly, anyway. I played a little bit of tennis but, once again, I didn't shine at that. Same with cricket. Really I didn't shine at too much to be honest. Even at school I could only be described as an average student. Maybe even a bit below average.

So I guess with being as shy as I was and as average as I was I became a pretty easy target for bullying. There was this one feller. He was in the class above. Well he got a real set on me. I don't know why, but he did. I'm sure I wouldn't have instigated it but anyway this feller took a real disliking to me. Every chance he got he'd be at me. It was relentless. It got so bad that even the teachers picked up on it. And I only mention this because I'm dead sure it would never happen today, but a couple of teachers got together and they said, 'We've got to put a stop to this.'

So they organised a set of boxing gloves. They got us together; me and this feller. We stripped down to our underclothing. Everyone gathered — pupils and teachers alike

— and they formed a circle around us. One of the teachers took on the refereeing duties and off we went, to settle our differences. And that's when my brother Alex's words came back to me — 'The best means of defence is attack'. So that's exactly what I did. I attacked, and it worked. I finished him off in the first round. They had to stop the fight. And that's what ended my problem because after that, not only wasn't I bullied any more but my standing at school shot up, as did my social life.

The Bush Classroom

My name is Bernard Arrantash and I was a primary schoolteacher. Between 1973 and 2005 I conducted annual camping safaris for my Perth state-school kids, out into the outback of Western Australia — particularly through the Murchison Goldfields region — where I shared with them some of the pioneering history of the places we explored. By the time I'd retired in 2005 I had conducted thirty-six of these camping safaris and had taken a total of eight hundred students out to visit the Murchison.

One key location we frequented was the township of Cue. The prospector Tom Cue discovered gold near there in 1892. Consequently the town was named after him. I'd also take my students fifteen or so kilometres north of Cue to a place known as Milly Soak. The Aborigines had told Tom Cue about a place between two flat-topped hills where there were lumps of 'that sunrise-coloured shiny stuff' lying around everywhere. And that's where Tom Cue first discovered gold and that discovery led to a rush and some early punters collected a good retainer. But then, as happened with many gold finds in such remote places in Australia, the prospectors were faced with a fearful dilemma. The area may have offered a potential fortune in alluvial gold but, due to the total absence of drinking water, mining at that location was virtually impossible. In the end many prospectors were forced to abandon their patch for fear of perishing from thirst.

In the case of Tom Cue's find, it was discovered that a well had been dug in an ancient river bed about three hours' walk north of the gold find. That well is now known as Milly Soak. But even at the well, life was tough. Food supplies still had to come all the way from the coastal port of Geraldton, which was far to the west. And even though the bullock and camel teams would set out for Cue and Milly Soak, more often than not, long before they arrived, they'd find eager markets for their goods at closer places like Mullewa, Pindar, Wurarga and Yalgoo. So those orders that had been placed by the Cue and Milly Soak prospectors were often not fulfilled. Without a balanced diet, and with poor sanitation, the heat and drought, and disease and fevers being ever present, sadly some of the pioneers at Milly Soak were forced to move elsewhere.

But when the students arrived at Milly Soak, what I did was, I had composed some verses of bush poetry about three prospectors who perished there. Then after we'd looked at the well, I'd sit my city students down under a nearby ghost gum and read my piece to them:

> It was a lonely path they trod
> Those pioneers of old
> For mile on mile they'd tramp and plod
> In search of elusive gold.
>
> The Murchison's harsh and dusty clime
> Brought flies and thirst and sweat
> Fresh water, at least for much of the time
> Was the hardest of all to get.
>
> In eighteen hundred and ninety-two
> A rumour began a new rush
> There was word of a find by Mister Tom Cue
> On the 'mulga wire' of the bush.
>
> George Hammersley's speed was rewarded
> He owned an athletic frame
> Of Harris, not so much was recorded
> Not even the man's first name.

George Hardy was the third of these wiry males
A writer, aged twenty-three
He'd left his job in New South Wales
For his gold prospecting spree.

But drought had served a mighty blow
Supplies weren't getting through
Fresh meat was scarce as driven snow
And the fever struck at Cue.

Hammersley, Hardy and Harris were struck
To Milly Soak they fled
But the fever drained the last of their luck
In that ancient river bed.

They breathed their last in 'ninety-three
Each a wretched, lonely bloke
'Neath a leafy white-trunked river gum tree
At whispering Milly Soak.

And now on a slope nearby they lie
Three graves, alone and stark
But surely this was a fine place to die
In God's own natural park.

Yes, it was a lonely path they trod
Those pioneers of old
For mile on mile they'd tramp and plod
In search of elusive gold.

Then after I'd read them that poem we'd walk up the hillside to visit the bush graves of those three prospectors. For me, that sort of practical exercise has to be the very best kind of classroom.

Every one of those annual safaris was self-funded by the participants. We maintained our own bank account and even though the majority of the money went into paying for food and fuel, over time we built up an impressive inventory of our own tents, catering and camping equipment. And even then, our trips still usually left us a little in the black.

So then, when we'd accumulated sufficient funds, we'd organise for some overseas guests to come out to Australia and share in our outback adventure. Over the years we had five pairs of such overseas guests and for each pair we paid their return airfares and covered their expenses. In each case they were a boy and a girl, aged about twelve. Our first two guests were from the United Kingdom. That was in 1979. Then in 1991 we had two guests from Malaysia. That was followed by two guests from the Solomon Islands in 1997, two from Mauritius in 2002 and two from Kenya in 2004.

This is a story about the Kenyan boy, Dogal Mwabili, who was one of our guests from Kenya. On that particular trip we had a convoy of eight four-wheel drives, carrying sixteen adults and twenty-four students. Dogal was one of those twenty-four. He'd suddenly found himself in such a foreign place, with a different language and culture. Even our values were in sharp contrast. As an example: Dogal's village home near Voi in Kenya was a place of relative hardship and poverty, where the few goats his family owned were their most prized asset. So in the West Australian outback he thought it was such a waste at seeing so many mobs of feral goats just roaming wild.

Dogal was actually quite an extrovert. He was, by nature, not only precocious at times but also highly motivated by any opportunity to acquire something for himself, even of minimal material value. What's more he was keen to show off that gain to as many people as he possibly could. In his mind this would raise his standing within the group.

One mid-afternoon during that 2004 safari, our convoy of four-wheel drives was driving through the bush, heading toward the monolith of Walloo Hill. Our plan was to camp at the base of Walloo Hill for that night. However, when we were about half a kilometre north of our destination, our convoy was forced to stop while a staked tyre was changed. While we were delayed I gathered the kids around and talked about the gnamma hole we'd seen a couple of days earlier at Walga Rock. Now a gnamma hole is an Aboriginal waterhole. In ancient times, wherever rainwater and dew was seen to run off down a rock slope, the Aborigines would form or deepen a hole, by whatever means possible, in the lower slope of the rock face to catch that water. Some of these gnamma holes can be a metre or more deep, and a metre or so in diameter.

Anyhow I mentioned that Walloo Hill also had a gnamma hole and I told the children that, after the tyre had been fixed and we'd made camp, there'd be a small prize for whoever found the gnamma hole first. A few minutes later, with the tyre changing still not completed, some of the kids told me that young Dogal had been seen running off through the bush, toward Walloo Hill. I wasn't too concerned. As a precaution, while on safari, our students always wore a whistle on a cord around their necks so that they could summon help if it was required. What's more, I knew Dogal had a good sense of direction and the great monolith of Walloo was a fail-safe landmark.

Of course I knew what Dogal's mission was too and, sure enough, just as the convoy was about to start up and move on, back came Dogal, running toward me and shouting triumphantly, 'I've found it! I've found it, Mister A. Please can I have my prize?' Well, I think he said 'please'.

'No, Dogal, you cannot have your prize.'

'Oh, why not? You said ...'

'But Dogal, I don't know if you have found the gnamma hole. You'll need to show it to me first and then you may have the prize.'

'All right, I'll take you there now. Come on.'

'No, Dogal, first we must move the convoy around to where we're going to camp at the south face of Walloo Hill.'

At this point, a somewhat deflated Dogal resumed his seat in his particular vehicle and off we moved. Some twenty minutes later we pulled up at our chosen spot. Then, with the campfire location designated and the vehicles and their trailers suitably deployed in the surrounding bush, Dogal came bounding over. 'Now, Mister A, can I show you the gnamma hole and get my prize?'

'No, Dogal. When all the tents have been erected and the bush toilets are dug and set up and enough firewood is collected, then you can come and ask me.'

Off he scampered. Rarely have I seen such an energetic and willing little camper as Dogal was that afternoon. After I'd sent him back twice to gather even more firewood, I was ready to relent. I secretly placed the prize — a packet of lollies — in my pocket. 'Okay, Dogal, now you may show me where you think the gnamma hole is.'

Now Walloo Hill would be about a kilometre around its base, perhaps more. In this case the gnamma hole was on the north face while, as I said, our camp was off the south face. But Dogal's sense of direction wasn't going to fail him in his mission. Unerringly he set off, straight up and over the crest of the giant outcrop, and he led me directly down the opposite face, and straight to the gnamma hole.

Dogal was as proud as punch.

'Well done, Dogal,' I said. 'Yes, that's indeed the gnamma hole. So here is your prize. Now I want to take a photo of you here, holding the prize.'

So Dogal balanced himself on the edge of the gnamma hole and the photo was taken. Then when I turned to head back to camp, Dogal hesitated.

'What's up, Dogal?' I asked.

'Mister A,' he said, 'can I give this prize back to you?'

'But why, Dogal? You were so keen to win it and you certainly deserve it.'

'But Mister A, if I give it back to you now, you will then have to present it to me again at tea time, back at camp, in front of everyone else, won't you?'

It didn't take me long to understand what he was thinking. And of course I duly obliged him by doing as he asked.

Recalling this event as I am now, these many years later, I'm thinking that Dogal might've gone a long way back in his home country of Kenya. He certainly had the wits and the will about him.

The Most Important Thing

My name is Ethel Priestly. I'm eighty-eight years of age. I was born on a washing day in 1924 and, as I say, I've been washing ever since. In my family I had four sisters and a brother. Joan was the eldest. Then there was Wilfred, Muriel, me, Beryl and Joyce, the youngest. We lived out on a two and a half thousand acre cattle-grazing property called Green View, which is near Woleebee, a small town about three hundred miles north-west of Brisbane. Dad also leased another property of a similar size nearby which he later purchased outright. When I was born there was no doctor or anything out there so my father's mother helped deliver me. She wasn't trained or anything. She was just an ordinary girl who'd come onto the land and had learnt most of her bush skills from the black people who lived in their gunyahs on the property, and they used to deliver their own babies.

Dad and his family were the first white people in the area. When he bought the property it was just trees and scrub so he had to blaze a lot of it to get it suitable for grazing. By blazing I mean he cleared the land by cutting down the trees and the scrub and burning it all. Dad and his brother built our first home. It was the one that Mum came from the city to live in, when they got married. It was quite a big house, built on a hill with four steps at the back and eleven steps at the front. It had a kitchen, a dining room, four bedrooms and a verandah.

There wasn't really a house yard as such, just all this scrub, and I remember when I was little how the dingoes would come in near the house at night and howl and howl. So we were right among nature. Mum said that when Joan was a baby, she was feeding her on the back steps one time and an old emu came up and pecked her on the breast. And I'd say, for a city girl, new to the bush like Mum was, something like that would've been quite frightening. But women had to be strong and brave back then because those were the pioneering days, and a lot of the time the women were left very much on their own while their husbands went out mustering for weeks on end and so forth. And there were no cars back then. It was horse and buggy or sulky or you rode a horse or just walked.

Our mother always maintained that education was the most important thing in anyone's life and, of course, out there, there was no school. Anyhow the property owners around the area were mostly our relations. They also had children so, when one of the uncles donated some land, they wrote to the Education Department about setting up a school. The Education Department said that if the locals built the school themselves and could guarantee a certain number of students, the Department would be willing to provide a teacher. I can't remember now just how many students they had to have; I think it was twelve or something. In fact I think we might've ended up with more than the required number. Hang on, I'll add them up: there was one, two, three, four ... six ... eight. Yes, we had about twelve or fourteen. So anyway, everyone got together and they built the school which was named the Sundown Provisional School. It was just a one-room building with a bare wooden floor. There was a window at each end and a door at each side and on one side there was a verandah with some steps and there was a rainwater tank off the verandah, facing south. The school was built up off the ground, about this high, and that's where we'd crawl to when we were playing hide-and-seek.

Then after they'd built the school building, and we said we had the required number of pupils, the Department gave us a teacher; a Mister Skinner. He boarded at our place because no one else would take him. Mum was so keen on seeing we had a decent education that she not only took in Mister Skinner but she took in all our future teachers as well. But this Mister Skinner was a greenhorn — very much new to the game — and he was also very new to country life. Oh and I remember he was very much in love with a lass called Peggy that he had to leave behind in the city, and by this time we had a telephone. It was one of those old wall-mounted receiver ones; you know, the ones with the handle that you had to turn around to connect with the telephone exchange, then they'd put you through. Anyhow Mister Skinner had a very broad accent. Scottish maybe, or perhaps it was Irish because he was Roman Catholic. I don't know. But he was madly in love with this Peggy and he'd ring her every night and after one of their conversations I remember he took his ukulele and he walked the three miles from our place, all the way back to the school building, singing love songs to his Peggy. Such a strange man he was.

So Mister Skinner was our first teacher, then we had Mister Tyson, then Mister Shields. Mister Tyson came from Kingaroy. And now here's an interesting story. See, sometimes my father would kill one of our bullocks for meat and with the topside beef he made bacon out of it. I wish I'd found out exactly how he did it but our stove was in a recess that jutted out from the house in a tin enclosure, and there was a shelf on the stove where Dad used to smoke the meats. With this topside beef he would soak it in brine, then he'd spice it and he'd smoke it and when he thought it was ready to eat he would slice strips from it. Those days bacon was very salty and you had to boil it before you fried it. I mean, you don't do it now because they pump all sorts of odd things into it. But oh it was beautiful. Anyhow, as I said, this Mister Tyson came from Kingaroy and he just loved Dad's topside bacon and I still think he must've somehow got Dad's recipe because as time went on, over in Kingaroy, they started making almost exactly the same thing. From memory they called them swizzle-sticks or something.

Oh we ate lots of different things back in those days. You had to, to stay alive. We ate whatever our father ate and we were brought up to enjoy everything that was put on our plate. As I said, times were very tough. I was born in 1924 and in the 1930s there was the Depression and we also had a terrible drought and our cattle were so poor that we quite often ate kangaroo and wallaby and scrub turkeys. We also ate witchetty grubs. They were nice. When they're cooked they taste like corn. We even ate porcupine. Yes we did. There's nothing wrong with a porcupine, just as long as you get a young one. The older ones tasted like ants but the young ones were just like fresh pork. We also had chooks and they're very useful because you can eat their eggs and you can eat them as well.

We also had poddy calves and, I tell you, this time we had a white one. Tibberly we called him. He became like a pet. Anyhow, one time after he'd grown into a bullock, Mum asked us to go and collect some firewood. We thought, Right-o we'll get Tibberly to help. So we harnessed him into the sulky and away we go up the paddock and we loaded up all this big long wood into the sulky, to bring back home, to be chopped up with the axe. Oh we were so proud of our efforts because we had this huge load of wood. So then it's back home with it and, just as we get near the house, all of a sudden, Tibberly did the scamp. He started kicking and buck-jumping and the sulky was shooting up and down and the wood was flying here, there and everywhere. Then he took off, hell for leather, straight into our new chicken-wired house yard and he got the shafts of the sulky all caught up in the wire fence, and that was the only thing that stopped him. But oh, what a mess it was.

Anyhow, as I said, when I was young we had a big drought and so, as soon as we got home from school, Mum would have something prepared for us to eat then we'd have to go up to a well, about half a mile from the house, to fill the cattle troughs with water. What we had done was, we'd cut the top off a four-gallon kerosene tin and put a wire handle in it, just like a billycan. Then we'd attach a rope to the handle and we'd throw the tin down into the well, bring up the water, then tip it into the trough for the cattle to drink. Anyhow, some of the cattle that came in to drink were wild unbranded scrubbers; very dangerous they were too, particularly the wild mickies — the wild bulls. When they came in we'd have to hide and wait for them to leave. Then when they'd gone, we'd go for our lives, back down across the creek, and over the hill before they charged us. One time we had to hide right down inside the well so they couldn't get to us. Then of course after we got home we still had our homework to do and many a night, after we'd done our written work, we'd go to bed and read our school books until our teacher came in to blow our lamp out.

But those big mickies, they'd go you all right. Occasionally we had to walk the three miles to school and if ever we came across thc big mickics we had to creep along the creek bed and, when we thought we were clear enough of them, we'd jump up and run for our lives to the school building. But usually we rode to school. We had two horses. Muriel, me and Joyce were on a mare — a female horse. Muriel sat in the saddle and we tied a pillow behind the saddle which was where me and Joyce sat. My brother, Wilfred, had the saddle on his horse with Merle sitting on a pillow behind him.

Wild horses were another danger. One time we were riding to school and Wilfred had made one of his many cricket bats. Just beautiful it was. Made out of sandalwood. But the mare must have been in season because, when we were about half a mile from the school, down from off the hill galloped this wild stallion and, as he got nearer, he started rearing up on his hind legs and whinnying. Oh he was a savage beast.

As I said there were the three of us girls on the mare and Wilfred shouted, 'Go for your life. Get to school as fast as you can.' So we took off on this mare, and Wilfred — who still had Merle on behind him — well he just took to this huge stallion with his new cricket bat. Oh dear, I can still hear that stallion whinnying like he was roaring and he was rearing up on his hind legs, then he'd come crashing down on his front hooves. And there was Wilfred going smash, smash, smash with his new cricket bat, right between the stallion's ears.

Anyway we got into the school grounds and we'd just got off and unsaddled the mare; next thing, here comes this stallion and it cleared the fence into the schoolyard. So we took off and hid in the school building and all day that stallion was in the schoolyard, rearing and whinnying and going on. Then when it was time for us to go home all the boys chased the stallion around and around until we managed to saddle up the mare and away we three girls went for home, and praise God the stallion never caught up to us. What those boys did to it I don't know, but we managed to get home.

Yes, so there were many scary experiences. Another time we were coming home from school and there was this huge storm heading our way. Anyhow we had to ride over this ironstone ridge that had lots of ironbark trees on it and we'd just got down off the ridge and onto the flat when the lightning started striking all around us. And the horses stopped, dead still, and they just wouldn't move no matter how much we switched them, and there were electric flames flickering around the bridles and the stirrup irons and we just sat there in fear, on our horses. See, a horse knows to stay still when there's danger. Then when the danger is over they move off. My father always said that if things got too bad what you should do is to take your saddle off and put it over your head and lie flat.

Another thing I remember was how we learnt the multiplication tables so we'd never forget them. What we did was to gather a heap of small stones off the hill and if you wanted to work out, say, what three times eight is, you'd put three stones down and you did that eight times, then you'd count them all up and, what have you got? Twenty-four stones. And we did it like that, right up to our twelve times tables. And when you do it that way, you'll always remember it, I can tell you. So then we'd write the answers down on the slate. A slate's a greyish coloured piece of slate, the size of an A4 writing pad, and its got a border all round. The pencils we used were also slate and because they broke so easily, they came wrapped in paper and when you wrote with it on the slate it would come out white. But oh, those slates were marvellous. When you'd finished, you just wiped it off with a wet cloth, then you'd dry the slate with a dry cloth and it'd be ready to use again. Pity they don't have slates today. It'd save a lot of expensive paper. It'd save a lot of trees.

Yes, so our mother was very keen on us having a good education. Dad was too but he was more of the mind that a woman's place was in the home, looking after her family. I remember when one of the teachers said that Muriel and I were bright enough to go and do our higher education in Kingaroy and that would enable us to go out into the world and get good jobs. Mum thought it was a good idea, but Dad wouldn't have a bar of it. He told us that the day his daughters had to go out to work to make a living was the day he was broke. He thought that it was his responsibility to look after us all. Funny, isn't it? I guess it was just a pride thing really, and if my father had stayed alive, none of us girls would ever have gone out to work.

Then after Dad died I went governessing. That was a great experience even though the people used me a bit. Well, a lot actually. Other than being the governess I became more or less their housekeeper as well. And I was good at it. Like any of the girls in our family we'd learnt to turn our hands to anything. We could cook. We could clean. We could teach. Do the accounts books. Anything, really. At first I was governessing just the one child. Then when the war broke out, two young evacuees came out to stay on the property. So that was three. It was schooling by correspondence by then and they all got good marks. Too right they did, and that was because I'd been so well educated myself.

The Sentence

Oh dear, outback school stories. Well I've been going back through my diaries and I've got one, though it's not really set in the outback. The setting's more along a very isolated part of our wind-swept southern coastline, at a small village, which will remain nameless for obvious reasons. Now I've forgotten how it all came about but I'd say the school must've received some sort of grant to get a writer — an author — to go down there and spend a week with the children. Though heaven knows why. For starters it was in the middle of winter. To make matters worse I was obviously the first author they'd hosted.

Anyhow this happened quite a few years ago and it's only now that I can see some sort of humour in it. If you don't mind I'll read pretty much straight from the diary and you can make of it what you will.

The first entry is from the day of my arrival.

Day One — Monday

Having been stuck on a tiny bus for more hours than I can cope with, I eventually arrive at the small village on the southern coast. Worst trip ever. Rain. Hail. Wind. Thunderstorms. Even the bus was blown all over the road. Feeling claustrophobic. Feeling crook. In need of fresh air and a good lie down.

Get off the bus, wind so wild it almost rips my hair out. This air is not only fresh, it's freezing. Icy. Rain stings my skin. Ouch. Even though it's already midday, the whole town seems to be in darkness. Am met by the host teacher. As we push our way through the wind to her car I'm told there's a power blackout. 'Happens all the time. A lot of the time we live in the dark. You'll get used to it,' she says. I'm a summer person. I like the sunlight. Warning bells go off in my brain.

Her car looks as battered as I feel. It also rattles and blows smoke, though it's still seemingly in better nick than most vehicles I see around town, not that I can see that much anyway. Pass through town centre. Most of the shops are shut or have been closed down, with boards across their windows. Bank is open, though host teacher says, 'It only opens occasionally.' Go in to get out money for accommodation etc. as am told that everything here is pretty much 'cash only'. It's a very small village. Much smaller than I'd imagined. Very isolated. To find pen pals, host teacher tells me how the school kids write letters and give them to the men who work at the local abattoirs. They're then wrapped in plastic and placed in with the packs of beef that are headed for export.

'Have they found many pen pals?' I ask.

'No,' she says.

I ask about the wind.

'It's usual. Umbrellas are useless. You'll get used to it,' she says. 'Stick a poker up the chimney. If it doesn't blow away, it's safe to go outside.'

The wind still blows.

Host teacher takes me sightseeing. We pull up in the middle of nowhere.

'Look,' she says.

Can hardly see through the sheeting rain, occasional hail and fogged-up car windows. I ask, 'What at?'

She says, 'The abattoirs. We're world famous for our export beef.'

I think I can almost make out a couple of dull lights in the foggy distance. I say it looks impressive.

She agrees.

The wind blows us back to the school. Arrive at the school and set up a display of my books. Looks impressive until a male teacher says how it would've been better if I'd brought a load of KFC instead. It'd be more appreciated, or so it seems.

Wait for kids to arrive. None turn up. Am told it's vaccination day and the kids have taken off in all directions. Teachers in hot pursuit to round them up. Wait in staffroom. Read noticeboard. Message 1: 'Jean won't be in her school uniform this week as her brother has gone on a school camp and he has taken the only clean ones we have.' Message 2: 'Tom won't be able to see today. He's lost his glasses, again.'

A teacher's aide arrives. She's in her mid-thirties. Cold sores bursting from her swollen lips. It's ugly. I can't look at her. She starts complaining about how she'd recently been 'wrongfully dismissed' from her other part-time job at the pub. 'I've tried ter change me ways since I settled down,' she says. Then adds, 'I mean, yer don't know what yer likely ter catch these days, do yer?' I don't want to know about it. 'Oh, 'n' watch out for the Year 8s,' she warns me.

Host teacher returns. 'First up is Year 8s.'

Go to Year 8 classroom. Empty seats. No one's there. Breathe a sigh of relief. Short-lived. Male teacher has rounded up a wild bunch of half-drowned students. It's obvious they would've preferred to have had the vaccination than sit through an author talk. The teacher's forgotten my name. He introduces me by saying, 'Not sure who she is but she's supposed to be a writer and so she's rich.' He asks the kids if they've read any of my books. No one moves. 'How about some questions?' the teacher says, then settles in at his desk to do his footy tips. A hand shoots up. Relief.

'Are you staying at the pub? My aunty just got the sack from there.'

'Yes, I am staying at the pub and I'm sorry to hear about your aunty.' I put two and two together and surmise that the aunty and the teacher's aide, the one with the cold sores, are one and the same.

A second hand rises. 'The tadpole in our classroom is floating upside down in its tank. Dead as a maggot.'

'I'm sorry about that,' I say.

Another hand lifts. 'Did you write *The Gizmo*?'

'No. Sorry. That was Paul Jennings.'

'Well that's the only book I've ever read all the way through,' he grumbles.

I apologise again.

Not off to a good start but I have to somehow find a way to connect with these kids. Okay, it's vaccination day. I have a thought. I say, 'Well at least the needle you'll have today will stop you from getting tetanus.'

'Why?'

Good, there's some sort of interest so, to keep hold of their attention, I go for the shock value.

'Well if you get tetanus, your jaw locks shut and sometimes they have to smash out your front teeth so you can be fed through a straw.'

Five kids burst out crying. Three pull their sodden beanies over their faces. Two fling themselves into hiding under their desks. The teacher has to stop doing his footy tips to go and restrain a couple of others from escaping the classroom and running away, again.

A change of tack is needed. I ask what they would put in a time capsule that's going to be opened in a hundred years' time. Answer 1: 'Undies 'cause me mum don't like washin' 'em.'

Another escapee is dragged into the classroom. Wet as a shag. Grotty trackpants and top. Looks like he hasn't had a wash in months. His head is shaved — nits? Lice? Worse? 'Hello,' I say, trying to sound pleasant. No reply. Slumps into an empty chair. Slams his face on the desk. There he stays. Sulking. I don't ask why.

I stand in silence, wondering what I should do. I look at them. They look at me. The teacher continues doing his footy tips. I wonder if they could even write a sentence.

End of lesson. End of day. Host teacher takes me to my accommodation — the pub. It's old. Run-down. Get my key from reception. The receptionist turns out to be the same thin, dark-haired woman who works at the bank I went to earlier on in the day. 'But only when it's open,' she says.

Too tired to inquire why a bank only opens occasionally. Too tired to eat. Find my room. Go straight to bed. Can't sleep. The heating's broken down. It's freezing. It's blowing a gale. Perhaps tomorrow things may improve.

Day Two — Tuesday

As tired as hell. Wind still blowing. Staffroom chat.

'Don't drink the water. Don't even clean your teeth in it.'

'Why?'

'There's some sort of health warning. Water must be boiled before use.'

'Why?'

'They've found dead animals and faeces in it.'

I suddenly feel sick.

'Don't go ter the local doctor.' It's the teacher's aide, the one with the cold sores; they're worse than yesterday.

'Why?'

'The doctor's a vet.' I'm told that she went to see him about her cold sores. ''N' look what's 'appened.' I don't look. She goes on to say how the doctor's given a few of the local blokes vasectomies and now some are impotent and others have fathered children. A couple of the women have had their tubes done and have since had babies. A local footballer once broke his leg in two places and by the time the doctor had finished with it, it'd been broken in four places. 'But 'e's a great vet. 'E's real good wiff animals. 'E can whip the nuts out of a bull before it can say moo.' Apparently the doctor-cum-vet also works at the abattoirs.

Another class. Hoping for better than yesterday's Year 8s. It's not. The teacher forgot I was coming. Said he'd spent hours preparing the day's lesson and now, with my arrival, it's all been a complete waste of his time. Try to act bright, but nobody's read any of my books. Again. Nobody's interested. I survive by getting them to write down their favourite joke. At least I've got them writing and they're engaged and they're quiet. That's until one kid raises his hand and says, 'Miss, how do yer spell "fart"?' and all hell breaks loose.

That night there's only two of us in the hotel dining room. Me and an elderly gentleman who says he's from the Gold Coast. He's in his eighties. He looks sad. I ask what he's doing so far from home, and in the middle of winter. He says that his wife threatened to leave him so he decided to leave her first, before she left him. I mention how it seems like an odd thing to do, to leave someone who's going to leave you. He agrees and asks for some womanly advice. I tell him I'm a writer, not a relationship counsellor, though I do offer him one suggestion — 'Don't drink the water.'

'Too late,' he says, and he rushes out of the dining room.

The waitress appears. It's the thin, dark-haired woman who's also the receptionist at the pub and who works at the bank, but only when it's open. I ask if there's any of their world-famous beef on the menu. She says there isn't because it all gets exported overseas.

Day Three — Wednesday
Wind still blowing. It's threatening to snow. I've broken a tooth. Staffroom discussion about the matter. Advice: 'Don't go to the local dentist.' Am told that he spends most of his time down in his piggery and he only turns up to work when necessary and when he does, he wears gumboots, dirty trackpants and an old lumberjack shirt, doesn't wear a mask or gloves, and uses a car battery to run his drill. Known to all as 'Jab-'n'-stab'.

Suggestion 1: 'Stick your tooth back in with glue.'
Suggestion 2: 'Try and fill the gap with Polyfilla.'
I decide to suffer.

Day Four — Thursday

Wind still blowing. Rain buckets down. Thunderstorms, and hail hits like shards of glass. Still crook but won't go and see the doctor. Am still in pain with broken tooth but won't go and see the dentist. Also coming down with a headache and the dreaded lurgy.

Assigned to the Kindergarten class. Kids all scratching — lice? Nits? Worse? Squash into a chair built for four-year-olds. Knees scraping my chin. Hips ache. Bum goes numb.

Problem: how can I run a writing workshop for kids too young to read or write? Brain wave: exercise their imaginations by drawing pictures. Subject — every kid's favourite — aliens.

Question 1: 'Where would aliens live?'

Answer: 'Mars.' So far so good.

Question 2: 'What would they eat?'

Answer: 'Mars Bars.' I ignore that one and plug on.

Question 3: 'What would an alien look like?'

One boy with a big itch under the front of his trousers comes up and draws a circle on the blackboard — yes, good, the head. A girl with an itchy bottom comes up and draws a circle under the first circle — yes, good, the body. Another girl with an itchy head then draws two circles on either side of the body.

'Oh,' I say, 'what are those?'

'Muscles,' she says, and I breathe a sigh of relief. Then she adds, 'Just like me mum's got.'

Another boy comes up and draws two lines protruding from the head. Yes, good, the antennas.

'No,' he says, with an itch. 'They're his "test-ikles".'

'Oh,' I say.

'Yeah,' he adds, 'just like me dad's got.'

Aliens that eat Mars Bars, have muscles on their chests and 'test-ikles' on their heads. These kids have got me rattled.

The school day comes to its end. I've started to itch. I need a strong hit of scotch to settle my stomach and numb the pain from the broken tooth and kill off the headache and the pending lurgy and try and forget about the itch.

The barmaid — the same thin, dark-haired woman who's also the waitress and the receptionist and who also works at the bank, but only when it's open — pours me a scotch and tells me that lots of people here have more than one job. Some have two. Some more than two. She has lots.

Two men enter the pub. The barmaid tells me that one is the husband of the ex-town bike and the other is one of the ex-boyfriends of the ex-town bike. They both work at the abattoirs. In the boning room. She says that the ex-town bike is her best friend. She says the ex-town bike used to work in the pub but she recently got the sack. I imagine cold sores. The two men settle in at the bar. One to my right, one to my left. They don't talk to each other.

While having a drink to settle my stomach and numb my tooth and kill off the headache I'm getting with the onset of the dreaded lurgy and to dull a strange itch that's coming on, I see a donation jar on the bar with the words 'Funeral Parlour Fundraiser' written on it. The thin, dark-haired woman says that, at present, if you die, your body is held in one of the freezers at the abattoirs, along with the export beef, until they can get a funeral director to come and sort you out.

I drop two dollars into the jar.

The husband of the ex-town bike tells me that not long ago a man and a woman died at around the same time and they had trouble fitting them both into the freezers along with all the export beef. The ex-boyfriend of the ex-town bike says, 'They was neighbours anyway, so they wouldn't'a minded.'

I have visions of corpses and beef carcasses being squashed in together. I slip another couple of dollars in the jar and thank God that the export beef wasn't on the menu last night.

We're interrupted by someone coming out from the kitchen. A man. He's wearing green gumboots, a red trench coat and a battered old trilby hat. He's got a banana in his hand and he's talking to it. I'm told by the bloke drinking next to me — the husband of the ex-town bike — that the man in the green gumboots, red trench coat and battered old trilby hat had stopped talking when he was five, after he'd been kicked in the head by a Poll Hereford. 'Didn't say "boo" for years, till he saw his first banana and hasn't stopped talking to bananas since.'

The other man — the one who's one of the ex-boyfriends of the ex-town bike — tells me that the other bloke — the husband of the ex-town bike — is only pulling my leg and that the man in the gumboots, trench coat and battered hat had been mistreated by his parents. He said the parents had too many children and there was nowhere else for him to fit into the house and so they made him live in the chook shed and they fed him the leftover dog food and wheat and pollen-mix, and that's why he is like he is. 'A bit mixed up.'

The thin, dark-haired woman — the best friend of the ex-town bike — adds that the madman also likes oranges but because his parents used to give him a thrashing whenever he dropped any of the orange peel, he now eats the orange peel as well. I ask what he does at the pub and am told by the barmaid — the best friend of the ex-town bike — that the man wearing the gumboots and the battered old hat and the trench coat, chops the wood for the pub's fires but gets stroppy when he sees any of the pub's fires going. I'm told that he also washes the dishes — 'poorly' — and wanders around the dining room, talking to bananas, picking up the dirty plates and dribbling.

The husband of the ex-town bike says that oranges are the best cure for cold sores. He says he's been eating a lot of them lately. The bloke who's one of the ex-boyfriends of the ex-town bike orders an orange juice.

I've had enough. I can't take much more of this. Not only am I feeling crook and my broken tooth's still aching and my headache is turning into a migraine and I'm coming down with the flu and my itch is getting itchier, I'm now also thinking that I could be going mad. I pile all my loose change into the donations jar for the Funeral Parlour Fundraiser, say goodnight and hope I don't die in my sleep.

Day Five — Friday

Last day. I'm feeling as crook as a dog. My broken tooth is giving me hell. My migraine's killing me. The lurgy is ripping at my throat. I'm itching all over and I had nightmares about bananas. Wind still blowing a force-nine gale. Rain. Hail. Sleet. Host teacher takes me on an early morning farewell sightseeing tour before I'm due at school. Her car is blowing more smoke than before. It rattles even worse than before.

Host teacher almost runs over a flock of large birds walking across the road. I'm told they're muttonbirds. I ask if you can eat them. Host teacher says they're protected animals so you can only eat them if they've been run over, or something. She says they don't taste too bad. Apparently the dark-haired woman, the one who works at the bank, but only when it's open, and who's the receptionist and the waitress and the barmaid at the pub and is best friends with the ex-town bike, well, she practises taxidermy on the muttonbirds that have been run over and keeps the results in the freezers at the abattoirs so they won't go off.

I dread to think.

Arrive at school. No one thought I was coming today. Nothing's prepared for me. I go and sit in the staffroom and wonder why I was even asked to come here in the first place. I just want this to end. To make matters worse, as I'm about to leave, I'm asked if my literary agent could possibly organise for a 'footy star' to visit next time as it would be more 'appropriate' for the kids.

I add depression to my list of woes.

Am taken back to the pub, then to the bus terminal. Host teacher asks if I've had a good time. I lie through my broken tooth and mumble, 'Beaut.'

I then get onto the bus. There's only one other passenger: the old man from the Gold Coast. He looks like he's won the lottery. He tells me he's going back to his wife. She's decided not to leave him. She wants to give it another go. Said she couldn't live without him.

I look out the fogged-up bus window. There seems to be some sort of trouble or other. People are in animated discussion. The thin, dark-haired woman, the one who works at the bank, but only when it's open, and who's the receptionist and the waitress and the barmaid at the pub and is best friends with the ex-town bike and who practises taxidermy on the muttonbirds that have been run over and keeps the results in the freezers at the abattoirs, along with the export beef and the dead bodies so they won't go off, well, she jumps into the driver's seat of the bus.

'The driver's crook,' she says and starts the engine.

The Stawell Gift

My name's Bill Cole — as in Nat King Cole — and during the mid-1960s I grew up as a teenager on a historic farming property called Warranooke North. For those that may not know, Warranooke North's situated in the Wimmera region of Victoria, some thirty or so miles north of Stawell, which is where they run the famous sprint footrace every Easter — the Stawell Gift. And that's where I did my education: at Stawell Technical School.

Now, I couldn't sprint for nuts. My forte was more our school's annual cross-country race. I always did quite well in that. Basically it was a run of around four and a half to five miles and not just on roads but off-road as well and at times in quite steep terrain.

Anyhow at Stawell Tech all the pupils were divided into different house groups. I was in Mariners House and, at the time of this story, we had a nutty house master-cum-maths teacher by the name of Mister Sinclair, or 'Sinkers' as he was more commonly known among the students. But as always, there were plenty of house points up for grabs with the annual cross-country race and so this particular year Sinkers decided that, just to get us in good nick for the event proper, he'd send us kids in Mariners House off on a practice run. We had to head off from the school, then the course took us down a road. From there we went down another road that was running down the side of Big Hill. Then, when we reached the bottom of Big Hill, we had to turn around and run back up to the finish.

So off we go and I'm running along calmly in about fourth spot — well positioned — when suddenly, out of nowhere, I hear this voice yelling, 'Get a move on, Bill.'

Well blowed if I know where it's come from. I stop. Have a look around. No, there's no one to be seen. Not a soul. Must be going mad. But then I hear the voice again. 'Move it, Bill.'

That sort of put the wind up me a bit so I took off and I eventually ended up coming home in quite an easy second place. But after I'd finished I was still a bit bamboozled about the phantom voice so I mentioned it to another lad who'd also been taking part in the race. 'Oh,' he said, 'that was Sinkers. He was sitting ten feet up a bloody gumtree.'

Like I said, Sinkers was a bit of a nutter.

But the fun and games didn't end there. A couple of weeks later the main event took place where all the kids in the school were involved. After having done the practice run, I was feeling pretty confident. Now, what used to happen was that they'd send us off in groups of twenty or thirty, at various intervals. Okay, so off I go with my group and I adopted my normal tactic, which was to stay within the pack, but in a position where I could still keep an eye on the leaders.

About a mile and a half into the race I was comfortably placed. I think I was coming about tenth or eleventh. Then when we came across a hessian bag that was hung over a barbed-wire fence, we had to hop over that and run through the paddock. Easy, right? So I get to the bag and I hop over the fence and I'm into the paddock. The paddock's full of stubble so running's not that easy. It's also pretty steep so I can't see clearly down to the bottom of the paddock. But I keep going. I'm doing well. So far so good.

About a hundred yards or so into the paddock I get a better look and I can see this dam ahead of me. The dam's all fenced off with red flags around the outside of it. Good idea because you don't want to end up running around in a muddy mess where all the cattle and sheep have been traipsing in for a drink, right? Wrong. When I get to the dam the bloody teacher who's down there says, 'You've got to do a counterclockwise lap of the dam and you must run inside the flags.'

Now the flags had been set so close to the edge of the water that, on the upper side, I'm running on the hard, sharp edges of the dried cattle and sheep hoofprints. Then on the lower side, the other foot's virtually in the water where there's all this thick, unforgiving clayey-mud sort of stuff. And that's where I made a tactical error because most of the other fellers took their sandshoes off and they ran straight through the water, which, in hindsight, is what I should've done. But I didn't. I headed off around this damn dam with my left sandshoe in the water and the right sandshoe outside of the water.

After the lap I'm stuffed. My right foot's fine but my left sandshoe's caked in an inch and a half of this horrible, sticky, loamy mud. Anyhow, from the bottom of the hill, where the dam was, I then had to run up to the top of the hill. Off I go, but the further I run the more the mud dries out, and the more it dries out, the more my left sandshoe starts to feel like I've stuck my foot into a bucket of wet concrete and it's beginning to set hard.

Still, I plugged on. Then when I got to the top of the hill there was this small track which had been washed away to such an extent that it was little more than just a strip of half-baked clay and, with my left sandshoe already being caked in clay, I just can't get any traction. I'm going like the clappers and I'm getting nowhere fast. To make matters worse there's blokes passing me left, right and centre.

Anyhow I finally managed to run out of the paddock and get to the top of the hill. That's where I scrape some of the mud off before I headed back to Stawell Tech via North Park. When I arrived, there's no one in sight. I had no idea where the bloody hell I'd finished. Though something was for sure, it certainly wasn't anywhere near first place.

The Volunteer Air Observer Corps

Between 1930 and 1935 I attended Clybucca Public School. Clybucca is beside the old Pacific Highway. It's about twenty kilometres north of Kempsey, on the New South Wales north coast. Slim Dusty country. Back then the Clybucca School ranged between twenty-five to thirty students. It was your typical one-teacher country school. Just a single room, with a brick fireplace. There was a small verandah around two sides of the building. A rainwater tank. About thirty or forty yards down the back was a girls' and a boys' toilet. Pit toilets. It also had a tennis court, which was made by the local community. A clay court. In fact, to scrape the tennis court level, I can remember we used to drag along an old iron tyre, which had come off an old sulky wheel.

Everyday school life was pretty much the usual, I guess. Though one unusual facet of school life, at least along the coastal regions during the war years, was the establishment of the Volunteer Air Observer Corps, or the VAOC as it was more commonly known. I can give you a bit of detail on that because I've got a history of RAAF units here and it says how RAAF intelligence devised the VAOC in the latter months of 1941 with the express purpose of sighting and recording enemy aircraft over Australian territory. At that time it was felt that there was the distinct possibility of a Japanese invasion. The VAOC covered a one hundred and fifty mile inland band, from Port Douglas, Queensland, to Port Lincoln, South Australia, and in Western Australia, from Albany to Northampton. Tasmania had observation posts set up around its major industrial areas and the VAOC was later extended to Daru Island, which is south of New Guinea, and then also to Darwin, in the Northern Territory, and to Geraldton, in Western Australia.

VAOC personnel were recruited from the local areas. They had to be persons who weren't required for military service. They also had to be British subjects by birth, of good repute and able to pass a basic hearing and eyesight test. Though the 'British subjects by birth' was waived on occasions because Aborigines were recruited in northern Australia. Members were entitled to wear a special armband and they were also issued with 'Air Observer' and 'Chief Air Observer' badges.

In many cases these observation posts were established at schools where, during school hours, the more senior students, say from between ten to fourteen, would be placed on a roster system. As soon as they heard an approaching aircraft — and remember the aircraft were pretty slow in those days so you'd hear them for a good while — but whenever that happened the observer would leave class and go out to see if it was visible. If it was, they were then required to describe the characteristics of the aeroplane by using a specially drawn chart; like whether it was a single wing or a bi-plane, the shape of its wings, number of tail fins, if it had one or two engines, plus its general direction from the observation point. The observer would then send an 'Airflash' message to a control centre and pass on this information. In our case the township of Taree was the nearest control centre.

As with many schools in those days, Clybucca School didn't have its own telephone so, being a classified reporting centre, a special line was put into the school. It was an official phone and it got priority through the exchange as an Airflash message. As I said, in the case of Clybucca School, students did the observing during school hours. Following that the teacher then took over until the local farmers had finished their milking and so forth. My father was the co-ordinator of that community roster. He was known as a Chief Air Observer.

Now, even though the VAOC was devised with the purpose of sighting and recording *enemy* aircraft, it actually ended up recording *all* aircraft. As there were no sophisticated navigation aids on most aircraft back in those days — perhaps apart from a direction-finding loop aerial to get a fix on a known radio station — many pilots or crew could easily become lost, particularly when the weather had 'socked in'. By 'socked in' I mean when the visibility becomes so poor that not even the seagulls were flying. When the visibility was that bad, it prevented the pilots from using the coastline or the railway lines — the 'iron beam', as it was known — as a guide. In a situation like that, these volunteer air observers could then track their whereabouts and, perhaps, via radio tell the pilot or whoever where the nearest airfield was.

The history of it says, 'The Corps peaked in manpower in 1944 with approximately 24,000 members, manning 2656 observation posts and thirty-nine control posts.' And that, 'between January 1943 and August 1945 the organisation had "definitely" saved seventy-eight aircraft, had "substantially" aided another 710, and "assisted" a further 1098. Assistance given ranged from supplying tea and biscuits to a downed airman to advising their bases of their whereabouts and guarding the aircraft.'

So, yes, the school students were definitely involved. Most certainly my two younger sisters, my younger brother and some of my cousins were among the school observers at Clybucca. In fact, one of my younger cousins once showed me a photograph where he was wearing the 'Air Observer' badge and I remember my father being very proud of his 'Chief Air Observer' badge. I even have a letter here from my brother, who was about twelve at the time, in which, among other things, he says, 'I remember the air observers while I was at school at Clybucca in 1941–42. You used the old "ring the handle" type telephone on the wall with a priority through the exchange to the Taree Control Centre. Airflash Taree Control. And then you conveyed the information using the identification code.'

Then at the end of the war all of the volunteer Air Observers got a special certificate from the government thanking them for their contribution to the war effort. That included the school students as well. Anyhow, that's where the VOAC comes in and I thought it might just be a bit of a different take on one of your usual school days stories.

(Quotations in this story are from *Units of the Royal Australian Air Force: a concise history*, vol. 1, compiled by the RAAF Historical Section, and published by AGPS Press in 1995.)

Their Home-patch of Dirt

All our working lives we'd been schoolies with the Victorian Education Department; my wife in Secondary Libraries and me in Special Education where I worked with kids with difficulties and the disadvantaged plus, on the other side of the spectrum, the gifted and talented. From one pole to the other. And that's what maintained the balance for me, working with both. Then when early retirement packages were all the go we decided to bail out. We were both in our mid-fifties back then. Just spring chickens really.

During the early days of our retirement we did some of the things we'd always thought we'd like to do. We built a mud-brick cottage on our property. We also went overseas. Then after, oh, I don't know, three or four years of dithering about I still didn't feel ready to put the slippers on and settle down, and for a long time I'd been saying to my wife, 'You know, I really should go north and look at something different.'

Why the north? I don't really know. There wasn't any particular affinity that I could identify with other than having had, and enjoyed, a couple of holidays in central Australia. Anyhow I must've been going on about it quite a lot because one day my wife turned around and said, 'Well why don't you stop talking about it and just go and do it.'

So I did. I lobbed into Alice Springs and when I'd had a bit of a look around I came to the realisation that if I was going to gain any sort of true insight into how things really were, the best way would be for me to find some work around the place. I was thinking that perhaps a bit of relief teaching might satisfy whatever was niggling away inside me. Then after I'd done a stint of that, I'd pack up and go home. So I went to the Education Department in the Alice and I told them who I was and where I'd come from and what I wanted to do and two days later I was handed the keys to a troop carrier and a map, giving me directions to an Aboriginal community a few hundred kilometres north-west of Alice. 'And you start Monday. Off you go.'

So off I went. It was the full bit: the old unlined troopie, the dirt road leading onto a sand track. And so I arrived in this remote community. No television, of course. There were the usual dumped cars and tractors etcetera. Lots of dogs. Generator electricity only; and so one of the first things I had to learn was that, before you opened up the school for the students, you had to go and start the generator. Then once that was done you'd maybe have to jump in the troopie and have a bit of a whip around the community to collect the kids who hadn't turned up. After doing that you'd have to get them all settled in at the school and then, by about 10 o'clock, you might just be ready to start getting onto what you were supposed to be getting into.

I wasn't the only teacher at that first school. Luckily there was also a lovely lady there who introduced me to the idiosyncrasies of the area. And there were many of them. So there were just the two of us 'whities'. Though, later on, when I came back and did another stint by myself, I did happen to be the only 'whitie' in the community.

Now, as to just how many kids attended the school: well, like in a lot of those remote communities they try to cater for Kindergarten right through to secondary and, as anybody who's worked in those communities would know, attendance depends on many factors. Still, I thought I was doing pretty well if I managed to maintain about eighteen to twenty kids. Mind you that included a bit of babysitting for some of the parents and also a few of the older teenagers might drop in to the school because they didn't have anything else to do. But, yes, I'd say it would've been around the eighteen to twenty mark.

As for the school itself: due to the millions and millions of dollars that have been pumped into those remote communities, the school was basically well-equipped. I mean it was just a portable/demountable or whatever they're called, depending on whatever state in Australia you're from. But, yes, that was all fine. As for the teacher's accommodation, unlike some of the schools I worked in later on, the building was in pretty good nick. After I got the generator going and the water pumped up into the tank and that sort of thing, it certainly wasn't too difficult. So basically, although it was a remote area, the buildings were in good order.

Then after I'd been out there for about six weeks or so I got in touch with my wife and I said, 'This is fantastic. You've just got to come up and have a look.'

'Okay,' she said and so she came up and, being a schoolie as well, she was signed up on the dotted line equally as fast as I had been. Of course, now that there were the two of us, it meant I had to get out of the particular community I was already teaching in and move to a larger one that would accommodate both of us. And we loved the experience. We also felt that we made some sort of a difference. We tried to get the kids to wear school uniforms. We made them have showers before school, and we made sure they had some breakfast. And so that's how the day started.

As for the kids themselves, be they around Kindergarten age through to the teenagers, they were an absolute delight to work with. Of course, as with any children in those particular age groups, they were as beguiling, cunning and as shifty as any kid can be. But, no, they were great.

As for the parents: now I must make it clear that this is a very rough generalisation of the communities we worked in but, of those parents who came in to help out at the school or were appointed as teacher's aides or were paid for this or paid to do that, I'd say that nearly ninety per cent were the women from the particular community. And they were fine. Then as for the blokes: when they appeared, they were okay. But the huge bugbears that beset those communities were always in evidence, especially with the blokes. That's with the grog and that sort of thing, and when that happened that's when things really started to go astray.

But on the whole, they were usually quite solid communities, actually. For want of a better term, the people in those communities were quite territorial. They had their own place name and, although it didn't look like it, there was a fairly rigid system of hierarchy and control over who lived there and who did not.

It was one of those unfortunate facts of life really, that back then they were quite desperate to get people like us out into those Aboriginal communities. And so, with a bit of coming and going, we ended up working in quite a few communities over a period of about three years. We did a few stints on the western side of the Stuart Highway and some on the eastern side. Though, these days, since we've both well and truly left teaching behind, I still always wonder how the kids are going out there and what they're doing, particularly the beaut little Kindergarten kids.

My next biggest concern is about all my beaut Year 5 and Year 6 girls, and what's happened to them. I mean, we've all read the statistics so I don't need to spell them out to you, but we all know what it's like for some of those adolescent girls out in a few of those communities. Yes, so I do think a lot about those beaut kids and about what's become of them and how much of it has actually been their choice, and that's because they're all pretty much locked into the system.

I mean, it's quite clear that both the Northern Territory Government and the Federal Government have provided lots of excellent support. Some say, perhaps too much. So numerous opportunities have been made available. Secondary education in the Alice has been provided for them. But of course, the ever-present problem is of the kids being so locked into the ways of many of those communities. And that's pretty sad because, when those students of mine were younger, they weren't into the grog or the dope or the petrol sniffing or anything like that. There was that wonderful, wonderful innocence.

But then for any of them to break that cycle and to leave their community is a very difficult thing for them to do. For example, just take a couple of teenagers who might go into Alice Springs to start secondary college. The chances of them remaining there would be pretty slim, really. Usually they'd get homesick and be back in the community within three or four months, and that's even with the excellent support services and back-up, second to none. Unfortunately, none of that seems to matter because the call of their community and of their home-patch of dirt is just so overriding.

There's a Redback on the ...

Yes, well my name's Anne. I'm currently living in the Brisbane area but, back in the early 1970s, I went over to the Northern Territory where I took up a position as a schoolteacher on Brunette Downs Station. A very young and naive teacher too, I may add. Now to give you some idea, Brunette Downs is in the Barkly Tablelands area, about four hundred and fifty kilometres north-west of Mount Isa. At that stage it also happened to be one of the biggest cattle stations in Australia, being something like just over twelve thousand square miles. So it's pretty big.

I'm not sure just who runs Brunette Downs these days but back then it was owned by King Ranch Australia and while I was there it was my job to teach all the Aboriginal kids on the property. And I can tell you, being more or less a city girl, I had to very rapidly learn as much as I could about the Aboriginal people, their ways and their culture. And they certainly don't teach you that sort of stuff at teachers' college. So I went through a very steep learning curve. Almost perpendicular. But once I'd settled into it I really enjoyed the experience and I learnt a lot during my time out there and, to this day, I really believe that we, as white people, could learn a hell of a lot from the Aboriginal people; for instance, as far as caring for family goes.

Anyhow, all that aside, there I was on Brunette Downs and one day I was teaching these kids in the school room when I felt this thing crawling on my neck. Must be a fly, I thought, so I tried to wave it away, you know, like you do. But it just wouldn't budge. So I gave it a slap and as I squashed it, it felt just like someone had placed some burning tongs on my neck.

This's not good, I thought, and when I took a look at what I'd squashed, I realised I'd been bitten by a redback spider.

By then it was almost lunchtime so I said to the kids, 'Look, how about you go out for lunch a bit early today,' and when they'd gone I went up to the clinic to see the nursing sister up there. A funny sort of person she was, too, I might add.

'I've just been bitten on the neck by a redback spider,' I said.

'Oh,' she said, and she gave me a vacant sort of look. 'Are they poisonous?'

'Yes, of course they are,' I said, astounded that she didn't seem to know the first thing about spider bites.

'Oh,' she replied, 'then I'd better get in touch with the Flying Doctor to see what we can do about it.'

'Thanks for all your help,' I replied, with just a little more than a hint of sarcasm.

So while she was trying to get in touch with the Royal Flying Doctor Service I went to my room where I had a first-aid book from teachers' college — an ancient old thing it was — and I had a look in that. It said that if you're bitten by a spider, the first thing you should do is to put a tourniquet on. Well that seemed a bit ridiculous, especially with me having been bitten on the neck. Anyhow, by that time I was feeling quite sick. I was also starting to get quite a fever so I decided to go to bed which, as it turned out, was the best thing for me to do.

In the meantime the nurse had been on the radio to the Royal Flying Doctor Service and explained my situation to the doctor. Apparently she was told to treat the situation just like I was in shock and to keep a close watch for any further developments.

Now, what you've got to realise here is that, out there, when anyone's talking over the radio to the RFDS or to School of the Air or whoever, every Tom, Dick and Mary within cooee is able to listen in on the conversation. And mind you, they do, and all the time. So unbeknown to me, my being bitten on the neck by this wretched redback spider ended up being broadcast throughout the Northern Territory and over into western Queensland.

Anyhow I survived.

Then a couple of months later a few of us went to this picnic race meeting up at Borroloola, which is up on the Gulf of Carpentaria, on the McArthur River. That was quite an extraordinary place, too. And oh dear, didn't we have a time and a half up there. It was an absolute hoot. I tell you, my life-education kept expanding non-stop and at a rapid rate while I was teaching in the Territory.

Anyhow, there I was at Borroloola and I ran into this guy from Mallapunyah Station. Mallapunyah is something like three hundred and fifty kilometres north-west of Tennant Creek. And, well, this bloke was a sort of a legend around the area. So anyhow he came up to me and he said, 'Oh, gee,' he said, in his real droll, laconic bush voice, 'so you're the teacher from Brunette Downs, are yer? The one what got bit on the neck by the redback spider.'

'Yes,' I said, 'that was me. Why?'

And he just stood there for I don't know how long, ogling at me; you know, eyeing me up and down from tip to toe. Quite embarrassing it was really. Then after he'd had a good hard look he shook his head from side to side and he said, 'Jeez,' he said. 'I would'a liked to 'a been that redback spider.'

They Wouldn't Do That These Days

I now live in Launceston, Tasmania, but back when I was eight years old my father decided to bring our whole family — my mother, myself and my younger sister — out from England. Ostensibly that was because I was a fairly bad asthmatic and Dad thought that the Australian air would be better for me. When we arrived, of course, he discovered that Australia has just as high an incidence as everywhere else. Though having said that, oddly enough, after I got here I didn't have any asthma attacks. In fact, just to go a bit further down the line, when I was twenty-eight I went to Europe in the high-harvest month of August and I did have an asthma attack. I wasn't prepared for it either so there I was with no medication and in a country where I couldn't speak the language, although my husband did. So that was quite curious and frightening.

Anyhow we arrived in Melbourne at the beginning of October 1948. It was Show Day and the stevedores were on strike and so we had to carry all our own luggage off the ship. Our hotel was at the top of Swanson Street, nearly opposite the Royal Melbourne Hospital. From memory the Royal Children's is further along Flemington Road. I forget the name of the hotel, though, with my father being a teetotaller, he was absolutely horrified because, at every meal, these Australians automatically placed jugs of beer on the table. But we were only there for about four days before we headed out by train to Dunkeld, in the western district of Victoria.

We went to Dunkeld because my mother had a pen friend, Kitty Funk, who lived there and, when my father decided to immigrate, Kitty and her husband, Walter, were our sponsors. So that's why we went out there. I don't know what it's like now but, back then, Dunkeld had just the one general store and only a few shops on the main street. Not much at all. Unfortunately Kitty died just before Christmas 2010, a month after her hundredth birthday. It was quite sad. She was a very good person, and we owed her a lot.

Our father didn't stay with us in Dunkeld because he got work back in Melbourne, pretty much straight away. He was a halftone colour etcher. He would use acid to etch a black plate, a yellow plate, a blue plate and a red plate and each of those images would then be superimposed to get the full colour picture. Apparently he was very good at his job, and very talented, because he was given the task of reproducing a lot of the artworks in the Victorian Museum. He was very skilled with his hands because during the war he manufactured gun sights for the bombers — the aeroplanes. Anyhow that's why he left us there on the farm with Kitty and Walter and he went back to Melbourne to start his job and also to look for a house for us.

As for my schooling, I was born in Bromley, England. Then during the last year before we came out to Australia, we moved to Catford. In Catford we lived in a two-storey house and I went to a very old-fashioned school where all the boys played in one playground and all the girls played in another playground and between the boys' and girls' playgrounds there were high brick walls with broken glass on the top. That was to keep the girls and the boys apart.

Dunkeld was very different to Catford. The Dunkeld school consisted of just two small classrooms: one for the infants and one for the older students. We had two teachers plus a headmaster. In the room that I was in there were two rows of Grade 3s, then I think there was a full row of Grade 4s. I was in Grade 4. Then there was a full row of Grade 5s and then there was only about four children in Grade 6. The desks were the old-fashioned double-desks that were slightly sloped toward you. They had the ink wells at the top-centre and two children to each seat.

As for my English accent, I think with us being in the country area, the people were a lot more accepting and a lot more friendly than they may have been in the city. Though, I must add that, some of the Australian terms were confusing to me. At times it was almost like a different language. It was no good me saying how I had a 'vest' on because the other children called a vest a singlet. I called my footwear 'Wellingtons' while they called them gumboots. I called them 'sweets'. They called them lollies. Then, with the actual schoolwork, I'd never come across mental arithmetic or factors before. They were the things I had to learn from scratch. I also heard frightening stories about how people would have driven over a snake and it got flipped up underneath and somehow found its way inside the car with the family.

The farm house that we were staying in at Dunkeld was about two miles from the school. It sat above the Wannon River, at the foot of Mount Sturgeon. After Mount Sturgeon came Mount Piccaninny and at the end of the Grampian chain was Mount Abrupt. These mountains were named by the explorer Major Sir Thomas Mitchell.

I do remember the emus running free and you'd often see a pair with their chicks wandering through the farmland. That was a big surprise for a young girl from England. Well, everything was sort of a big surprise for a young girl from England: the chickens, the cattle dogs, the snakes, the emus, the kangaroos. We even tried our hand at milking the cows and churning the milk to make cream and butter. Then there were all the different sorts of flowers. And we'd been on strict rations when we were back in England and the very first Christmas we were there, at Dunkeld, we went up to Corack, in north-west Victoria, for the Christmas Day meal and we just couldn't get over the amount of food on the table. There was hardly room for the plates, and I remember Dad saying to someone, 'Oh, the table just groaned under the amount of food.'

And also at Corack: Corack is wheat country, so it's very flat and, as far as the eye could see, there was just nothing, and I remember my mother saying how the huge open spaces made her feel very small and quite afraid. I mean, to give you an idea, they were harvesting wheat in what they called the 'two-mile paddock'. So she found that wide open space very daunting.

Anyhow in Dunkeld, to get to school, we'd start off from the homestead and we'd walk down the lane until we got to the main gate at the road. Beyond the road gate there was the common and in this common there was a pair of magpies and, in nesting season, they'd swoop down and have a go at you. That was also a new experience for a young English girl I can tell you, and not a very nice one either.

Oh, and I remember at one stage there were horses on the common and one day me and my sister and my mother and a local woman were crossing the common and these horses decided to have some fun with us. What they did was, they'd come charging up at us then, right at the last split second, they'd stop and wheel away. And that was very frightening too. I don't know if that's what affected me so much because another time there were cows grazing on the common and I became too scared to walk through there. I mean they were the pretty docile sort of milking cows but anyway what I did was, I sort of skirted around them and went through fences and then through some pretty rough country and come in to school through the back scrub.

Then just one other thing: when we were first at Dunkeld, Kitty's husband, Walter, had a Model T Ford. It didn't have proper windows. It was one of those with the curtains that you could take in or out, and one evening Walter said, 'I'm going to shoot some rabbits. Do you want to come along?'

So we all hopped in this Model T Ford. Mum, my sister and I were in the back and Dad was in the front with Walter, who was driving. So we were going along the road and suddenly

Walter sees a rabbit and so he put the car into low gear to leave it idling along and he said to Dad, 'Here, hang on to the steering wheel,' then he popped out and off he went to shoot this rabbit. Now Dad had never driven a car in his life before. So there he is, hanging onto this steering wheel for grim life, steering us down this road and hoping like heck that Walter would come back before we came to a turn. Which he did, luckily.

But we only stayed at Dunkeld for a short while because, in early 1949, we moved to West Bentleigh, which then was an outer suburb of Melbourne, on the border with Brighton. So I started going to West Bentleigh Primary School. That was a lot different than Dunkeld, I can tell you. It was a big double-storey blue-stone building with about eight hundred pupils and every teacher had about sixty-plus children in their class.

And just a little quick story: at Dunkeld school I can't ever remember the teachers shouting at the students. Everybody seemed so well behaved. But in my class at West Bentleigh, the teacher in the room above us, well, he had such a bad temper. When he got going you could hear him yelling at his children and when that didn't work he'd start throwing the ink wells. Yes, he used to throw ink wells at the students. You could hear it. I mean they wouldn't do that these days, would they?

Things that Us Kids Know

My name's Courtney. I'm eleven years old and I come from a little town in the middle of Queensland called Yaraka. There were only eighteen people living in Yaraka before I was born, and so I became the nineteenth. I have a younger brother, Zac. My mum and my dad love to travel and so about three years ago we left Queensland. We had a caravan that we lived in and we also had a horse truck where we kept all our motorbikes and surfboards and toys and Dad's work tools. We've been to lots of places in New South Wales and Victoria and we travelled through South Australia on our way here to Western Australia.

Before we left Queensland, Mum and Dad organised Zac and me into doing our schooling through Mount Isa School of the Air. There's probably about six or eight other kids when we have our on-air lessons. Mostly they're from around Mount Isa, but there's also some from other places like Wave Hill Station, in the Northern Territory, and also from down near Birdsville and around Cameron's Corner. Cameron's Corner is on the border of the Northern Territory, Queensland and South Australia. So there'll be kids from all those areas and then there's me from Western Australia and we're all calling the teacher in at Mount Isa, on the computer, at the same time, though because of the two-hour time difference between Western Australia and Queensland it can still be dark when I start my lessons.

I'm in my first year of high school now. We were going to go back to live in Queensland so that I could go to a normal school but Dad was offered a job on a cattle, sheep and goat station. When that happened, Mum and Dad decided that I should stay with School of the Air in Mount Isa and do my first year of high school with them, then after that we'll see what happens. Over here, most of the kids who live on station properties and leave School of the Air in Grade 7 go to boarding school in Perth. But because I was born in Queensland I think I'd like it if we went back to live in Queensland because I really miss my cousins and all my old friends.

With doing high school on School of the Air, it can get pretty intense. We have to do art and science and studies of society and environment and English and maths. On top of all that I do Indonesian as well. I also did French for two years but I didn't like it. For four days of the week I have two on-air lessons each day. Mondays and Wednesdays it's English and science, and Tuesdays and Thursdays it's maths and studies of society and environment. Then, like I said, I'll have my art lesson at six-thirty in the morning and Indonesian right after that. So tomorrow morning I'll have, like, almost two hours straight on the phone and computer.

They also have set booklets for our schoolwork. They send them out in the post and you do that work then you post it back to Mount Isa where it gets marked. The booklets used to be sent out in two-week units but, because we travel so much, they now give us more lessons in the one go; like up to a whole term or something. So you just tell the School of the Air people in at Mount Isa where you'll be and they send you out a big box of gear that we store in the caravan, and every time we finish a unit it goes back to Mount Isa.

By doing my high school with School of the Air, I don't know but, there seems to be, like, heaps more work, and there's no public holidays or student-free days. But the good thing is, if you do have some days off, like if you do the mustering, then you can catch up on your lessons later on. Mustering always comes first, and I love doing that. So in that way it's really good because you can have as many breaks as you want, just as long as you catch up later, yeah, and so you're the boss of your own time and Mum can have a break and go surfing while you're on air and doing your schoolwork. But there's also the bad things, like, how you don't really get to play with too many other kids at all. You can talk to each other on the phone and that, but that's all.

For School of the Air we now use a computer programme called iConnect. So these days you just make phone calls and they do it over the telephone, on a computer link-up, that's got like a web-cam on it, so when the teacher draws something and holds it up on the screen, everybody in the class can see it. They stopped doing the lessons on the HF Radio about five or six years ago now, and some funny things used to happen on those. Like, if one kid's got his hand on the speaker button then the teacher can't turn them off and you could have the mum going crook in the background while the kid's talking away and that goes out over the radio, everywhere, all over the place. I remember one time when we were at our uncle's house, Zac was on air. The teacher was a woman from the city so she didn't know anything about what we did in the country. It was a Monday morning and she says to one of the kids, 'And so what did you do over the weekend?'

The kid goes, 'Well the Preg Tester came out and we did some preg testing.'

The teacher goes, 'What's preg testing?'

And the kid said, 'It's when the vet sticks his hand right up the cow's butt to feel if there's any babies inside.'

And the teacher got really embarrassed. She didn't know what to say, so she goes, 'Oh well okay. Moving right along. Now, who's next?'

Yes, usually the teachers are from the city so they don't know anything about how it is for us kids in the country. Like, you're not allowed to talk about guns and killing things or anything like that. But one time we had this real fun teacher who was from the country and so he knew all about it and, like, he said to one of the kids, 'What did you do over the weekend?'

And the kid said, 'I went over to my friend's place and we went cane toad hunting.'

'Oh,' said the teacher, 'did you use a croquet club to kill them or did you kill them with a golf club?' and that was funny because usually we're not allowed to talk about things like that; you know, things that us kids in the outback areas know about, but the teachers don't.

Dad also tells a pretty funny story about one of the on-air lessons, but what you've got to understand is that if you're on the radio, sure as eggs the people from the next-door station are listening in as well. Like, everyone listens in on everything that everyone says. So, you know how that, when you're on a cattle station, you cut your station's mark in the cow's ear so that everyone knows that it's one of yours? It's like your own station's identification mark. Then another thing you might not know is that a 'killer' is an animal you kill for your own food. Do you understand that?

Good. So anyway the teacher was talking to this kid over the HF radio this time and she said, 'So what did you do on the weekend?'

The kid said, 'Oh we went out and we did a killer and Dad cut its ears off and he shoved its ears right up the cow's bum and then he said to me, he said, "Those bastards from next door will never find them up there, son."'

And all the neighbours were listening in.

Those First Few Weeks

My early childhood was spent on a sheep property at Kojonup — Kojonup being, predominantly, a farming community in the south-west of Western Australia, about two and a half hours from Perth. It's near Katanning and Wagin: little towns like that. Dad and Mum were leasing a place there — Amber Downs — that was owned by a big farming family. There were just the two of us girls in our family and when we were old enough we went to Kojonup District School. But our parents always had a great love of the north and one year we did a family trip up to the Kimberleys then, when we got back home, Dad said, 'We're buying Nallan Station, ten miles out of the goldmining town of Cue.'

At that stage I was eleven and my sister was ten and, in our minds, Cue was a sort of blink-and-you'll-miss-it little place on the Great Northern Highway, south of Meekatharra and Newman. So when Dad said that that's where we were now going to move to, my sister and I, we took one look at each other and went, 'What are we going to do? How are we going to cope? There's probably not even a Bets and Bets shoe store there.'

This was in late 1985 and so we packed up all our things, said goodbye to our school friends and off we went. By the time we arrived at Nallan, it was pretty dark. We were a bit on edge about the whole thing to start with but when we saw a snake, that was it, we certainly didn't sleep too well that first night, I can tell you.

Nallan was a Merino sheep station of about a quarter of a million acres. Dad was already familiar with sheep farming, so that was all right. Then along with the sheep, a small tourist business had been set up. During the winter months a lot of people from down south headed towards the sun, to places like the Karijini National Park, and some of the smaller tourist operators would stop over at Nallan and the people would either stay in the shearers' quarters or they'd camp. Also, at that time of the year, the wild flowers were pretty spectacular and, with the gold prices being reasonably high, Cue was still quite buoyant. It's a pretty little town really, with all its historical old buildings.

Of course we had to go to school and those first few weeks at Cue Primary were a real eye-opener for me. On the teaching staff there were probably only about three people, and that included administration. My teacher was also the principal and, after having come from a classroom of around thirty children, it was quite a shock to suddenly find myself as the only female in my Year 5 class of three. Then on my first day at the school the teacher–principal arrived and the first words he said were, 'Well, okay, open up your books and I'll be back in a sec.'

Off he went and we opened our books, and we just sat there. And we sat there. And we sat there. Then around lunchtime I asked the kid next to me, 'Well, where do we go from here?'

'Oh,' he said, 'he's got lots of other things to do as well.'

In the end he didn't come back until the end of the day, and that proved to be pretty much the daily pattern. In the morning it was, 'Open your books,' then he'd shoot off to teach other groups and also, being the principal, he had all the office work and lots of other things to do as well. I actually felt a little sorry for him really, with so few on the staff and a whole school to run; but he'd occasionally breeze back in just to see how we were getting on.

Anyhow, between the three of us in our class we soon worked out that I was good at English. The boy next to me was good at maths and the other boy, Tony, he was good at science. So we all helped each other out, and that was basically our education through the remainder of Year 5 and then through Years 6 and 7 as well. I was probably the most studious of the three of us because sometimes the boys would say, 'See you later,' and they'd jump on their pushbikes and ride the kilometre or so into town, to spend their time in the video shop or wherever. Then when the teacher returned, he'd see that I was the only one sitting there and he'd have to go down the main street to round them up. 'I think you'd better come back to school, boys.'

'Yeah, okay,' and they'd wander back while he rushed back to school and got on with all the other things he had to do.

Another funny thing happened during those first few weeks when I was at Cue Primary School: one day we were all having our morning tea and an Aboriginal girl came over and she said, 'Would you like to swap smoko?'

'Okay,' I said, so I opened up my bit of orange cake and some apple. I gave that to her and she passed me her morning tea, which was all wrapped up in Alfoil. 'Thanks,' I said and when I unwrapped it, there was this cooked lizard leg, claws and all. I couldn't believe it. My eyes just about popped out of their sockets. 'Oh, no thank you,' I said and passed it back. Then when I got home that afternoon I said to Mum, 'I'm not going back to that school, it's terrible.'

Of course, we did continue going to school and being fourteen kilometres out of town, and with no school bus coming past our place, we had to drive there. By 'we' I mean my sister and I. That's how we learnt to drive. I remember our first driving lessons. It was in the ute, and we'd take it in turns to drive most of the way into Cue before either Mum or Dad would take over and take us the last couple of kilometres to the school. I probably shouldn't have said that, should I? Because we were both well underage and there we were, we were driving on a highway. Anyway, that's what happened.

There's another incident that sticks in my mind about those school days at Cue, and this is not a nice one; but because of its remoteness most teachers didn't want to be posted there.

And when they were, they were always looking forward to their holiday break so they could go back to Perth or wherever — back to civilisation. Then I remember on the last school day before one of our holidays, a student threw a rock through the windscreen of a younger female teacher's car. I don't know why he did it but, because it would've taken ten days or so just to get a new windscreen sent up, it meant she was forced to stay in Cue for her holidays. She was devastated. That was just awful, but things like that did happen occasionally and I guess not only at Cue.

Anyhow, as you may have gathered, those weren't the best years of my educational life. Then when my sister got to Year 7, Mum decided to put her on School of the Air through Meekatharra and I went away to boarding school from Year 8. That was in Perth, at St Hilda's Girls' School. Having to adjust to going back into a mainstream school was a real shock to the system too, especially for the first few weeks. But I soon got to love it because some of my old friends from Kojonup were at St Hilda's as well and I got to catch up with them. It was like a reunion I guess, and that was lovely.

To Find a Better Life

I went to Melbourne University for five years where I first studied music, then went into teaching. I'd always wanted to teach because I thought it would be a good way of mixing my life's passions of music and art with my love of teaching and of children. I decided to focus on primary education, mainly because it just seemed to be like a bit more fun, and, of course, I do enjoy working with the little ones. Though as I've since found out, teaching the littlies may even be a bit more challenging in some ways.

After I finished uni I took a year off to do some overseas travel and, during those travels, I worked in Switzerland as a nanny. That was a great experience. I was living with a family who had four young girls, aged two, five, eight and ten. French was their first language but with their parents wanting them to have a stronger knowledge of the English language, I mainly spoke English with them. I also taught piano to the older two girls and we all did a lot of other music and singing as well, which was fun. The family had previously spent a year in Australia where they'd lived in Melbourne and some of the children's memories of their Australian adventures were quite funny. At one time their parents had taken them out to Ayers Rock and, as you do, they'd taken them to see Ayers Rock at sunrise, Ayers Rock at midday, Ayers Rock at sunset. So if Ayers Rock was ever mentioned they'd roll their eyes as if to say, 'Oh, not the big rock again.'

When I got back from my big world trip, I spent three years teaching at an independent school in Melbourne. That was good training for me, as well as it being another great experience. But I really think that the year I'd had overseas was a very significant one. It was like a turning point in my life. I just loved it, and by the time I arrived home I'd not only developed a great love of travel but I'd also developed a strong interest in teaching ESL — English as a Second Language — and, in particular, I'd become very passionate about teaching disadvantaged children. Now, perhaps all those interests had always been there within me, I don't know, but they certainly came to the fore after I'd seen first-hand how people lived in different parts of the world.

Around that time I had a friend who'd gone to teach in an Indigenous community in the north-west of the Northern Territory, near Port Keats. In the middle of that year, 2010, another girlfriend of mine from university and I, we caught up with this teacher from Port Keats and she told us all these fantastic stories about the experiences she'd had up there. And it wasn't all just one-sided either. She also told us the truth as well; you know, about all the many difficulties she'd faced and just how challenging it all was.

My girlfriend from uni hadn't really done any sort of travel. I doubt if she'd even lived anywhere other than Victoria really. So I guess she was up for a new experience because, after hearing these stories, we just looked at each other and said, 'Are you keen?'

'Yep, I'm keen, if you're keen. So why not? Let's do it.' With that decided, our only stipulation was that we both wanted to be near the water.

We then had to go through the application process. That took the remainder of 2010, and right up to just before Christmas we still didn't even know if we had a job up there. Then we finally got notification that we'd got a placement with the Top End group of schools, out on Croker Island. Croker Island is in the Arafura Sea, about two hundred and fifty kilometres north-east of Darwin, in the west Arnhem Land region. It's just off the coast from Gurig National Park really; Gurig being at the northern end of Kakadu National Park. So at the beginning of 2011 off we went to Croker and then we worked together, we lived together and did everything together for that year. There were about sixty children enrolled in the school — not that they'd all turn up, mind you — and there were five of us teachers. I taught Transition, Year 1, Year 2 and, well, you basically had to teach everything really.

The community we worked in was called Minjilang. It was very small, with a population of only around three hundred people. On the island there's just the one main community of Minjilang, and then I think there's about nine small outstations. I can't actually give you the dimensions of the island because a lot of it is sacred land, which meant us white fellers couldn't venture too far. Actually, Croker Island has quite a sad history. In the early 1940s it was one of the places where a lot of Aboriginal children were sent to as part of the 'Stolen Generation'.

Then later on, during the Second World War, when they were afraid that the Japanese were going to take over the island, there's this amazing story where a missionary lady, Margaret Somerville, took nearly a hundred of the Aboriginal children off the island and she led them across thousands of kilometres by boat, foot, truck and train, until they reached safety in Sydney. What a journey that must have been.

But it's a beautiful island really, and it's still quite culturally in tune with its people, the Yarmirr people. You'd fall asleep some nights to the sound of clap sticks and the sound of the waves. Most of the time the people from the community would just sit out on the beach and try and catch their dinner, and if they didn't catch anything they went without. When that happened, you'd have some extremely hungry children turn up at school the next morning. Then sometimes they'd go out and hunt dugong in the traditional way. They also hunted different types of turtles. I can tell you, there were certainly some interesting smells in the classroom during long-necked turtle season.

It was a good year really, with lots of fun. The children were amazing. Very excitable. Vibrant. It was difficult to get them to sit still for any length of time. They were always fidgety, and for some reason they had a great attraction to our white skin. They were fascinated by how smooth my legs were to touch, after I'd shaved, and then there's a small mole on my arm that they were forever trying to pick off. But it was also a very difficult year in many ways because the community was quite tough to live in. In some situations I guess they would still be considered to be living in third world conditions. So I think for both of us, we needed a change and we decided that it would be a good thing to also experience teaching in another Indigenous community.

So this year, my friend and I, we're at Daly River and we're teaching at Woolianna School. We've kind of moved from a coastal region to more inland, and I must say that I do miss the beach. But every community has its strengths and its weaknesses and at Daly River it's a different experience again. On Croker Island we shared a house within the actual community itself whereas at Daly River, for security reasons, we live outside the community, in a caravan park. But I do love the challenge of working with Indigenous children. It adds another dimension to teaching. You're always having to be thinking ahead to the next project, or a tricky question might come out of the blue and you have to come up with an immediate answer for that. Plus, in communities like where we are now, you've also got kids coming in from different areas who have different cultures and so they may well speak a different dialect or even a different language for that matter. But it's great. It keeps you on your toes and so now, I don't really know how I'd go with teaching back in the mainstream.

Really, I guess that, with my cumulative experiences of travelling overseas, along with those of working on Croker Island and at Woolianna School, I've come to realise that 'education' is the real key to helping a lot of these children get out of poverty. That's one of my personal beliefs. So one day, perhaps I'll go and teach in somewhere like South America. Actually I'd like to go to Brazil. I'd like to go into the *favelas* of Rio de Janeiro where the ruling drug-lord system has caused so many people to live in such poor conditions. I'd like to go in there and help educate the disadvantaged children so that they could at least then have the opportunity to escape their poverty and their suffering, and to go and find a better life.

To Pine Creek, whenever

Back in the late 1960s to the early 1970s my husband and I were doing a big trip around Australia and by the time we got to Darwin we needed to earn some money, so we got work out on Douglas Daly Station. Douglas Daly's south of Darwin, on the way to Katherine. It was a cattle station, basically. My husband got a job there as one of the managers and, other than doing yard work, I got involved in weather recording for the Bureau of Meteorology and during the dry season I also worked for the CSIRO where we did experiments into which grasses and pastures were best for that particular climate.

And that's where we were living when Cyclone Tracy hit Darwin, Christmas Day, 1974. Though, I was actually staying up in Darwin itself, at the time. That's because my daughter was due to be born on Christmas Day 1974 and so I'd gone up to Darwin to prepare for that and I was staying in a caravan. Of course, when Cyclone Tracy came through, I lost the lot, caravan, clothing and all, didn't I? But we survived and I was flown in an air force Hercules down to Adelaide, where Jules was born in early 1975.

So between 1971 and 1980 we had three children. Pete was the eldest. Then there was a year and a half between Pete and Jules. As I said, Jules ended up being born in early-1975, after Cyclone Tracy. The youngest, Shaun, was born in 1976. So by 1980, Jules would've been five, Pete nearly seven and Shaun would've been about four. But there was no school or anything out on Douglas Daly Station. They didn't even get School of the Air. I mean, apart from the two-way radio, we didn't really have any other real means of communication. Also, we were the only family living out there. It was all single men. So seeing that there were no other kids around the place, my lot pretty much used to run wild and, because it was always so hot, most of the time they didn't even wear clothes which, mind you, saved washing.

So it was a pretty free and easy sort of life really, though it did have its moments. One I remember very clearly: see, there were wild buffaloes roaming around the place everywhere and sometimes they'd come in, near to where we were living. Then this time I just happened to go outside to check where the kids were and there was little Jules standing there, patting this wild buffalo. I stopped dead. I mean, there's this little kid — she was only about two at that stage — standing there, stroking this massive buffalo on the nose. Of course, I didn't want to scream out and upset the buffalo in any way, so I just took a deep breath, raised my voice ever so slightly then, struggling not to sound panicked, I said, 'Turn around, Jules. Just turn around and come slowly back to Mummy.'

Anyhow, when Jules heard me, she just sort of nonchalantly turned around and wandered back over to me, and the buffalo didn't do anything. It just stood there. But I think it was because the buffalo didn't sense any danger from Jules, and that's why it didn't react. In actual fact it looked like it was enjoying being stroked on the nose.

For the kids' early education, they went to Pine Creek; that's whenever they went, of course. Pine Creek was the nearest town to Douglas Daly to have a school. But it was a fair effort. I mean, to get there — I don't know — I guess it would've been about fifty miles along the dirt track from where we lived, out onto the Stuart Highway, then another fifty miles to Pine Creek. That's the old Stuart Highway of course; not the one you see today. Back then it was really windy, with just a narrow strip of bitumen down the middle. So if you came across another car or, worse still, a truck, you had to pull off the bitumen, into the rough, so you could pass each other. So then, as to how long it took? I mean, that depended on the condition of the road and I suppose I was a little bit naughty really. I did sort of go pretty fast. I mean, there wasn't a lot of traffic. You virtually had the road to yourself and of course on the crests and that, you pulled over to the side a bit, just in case there was an oncoming vehicle. Anyhow, in the end, when it was the dry season and the road had been graded, I'd say I got the trip down to about two hours each way.

Yes, so I'd pack up all the kids and we'd bounce our way down the track then out along the highway, off to Pine Creek. Sometimes we couldn't go, of course. Say if one of the kids was sick or something then it wasn't worth packing them all into the car, just to take one kid to school. Other times, if I got too busy ... well, look, to be honest, they really didn't get to school that much, I'm a bit ashamed to say. In the wet season they rarely went because there were three waterways between us and the highway and they were usually flooded. And that could cause a few problems.

I'm not really trying to make excuses but, what you've got to realise is that, I was the only woman out on Douglas Daly, and I was young, so I didn't know any of the motherly stuff like I do now. I remember one time, during the wet season, all the men had gone fishing and so I was there on my own, just me and the kids. Anyhow I heard Jules going 'Yuck. Yuck'. And when I turned around I saw that she'd drunk some disinfectant. It had been on the bench and Jules must have pulled one of the chairs up to sit on the bench and when she saw the stuff she drank some of it.

As I said, in the wet, when the waterways were up, you were pretty much isolated, so I thought, Oh no, and so I read the label on the bottle to see what I was supposed to do. It said to give her milk. I did that but nothing really happened other than she started to get a bad temperature. By near on dark and with her temperature still rising, I was in a real panic. Then I saw the vehicle lights coming back. Anyhow the men arrived and they said, 'All right we'll get the station truck and see if we can get through the flooded waterways to the highway.'

When they said that I thought, Well, I'd better go and put some clothes on her. And it was only when I actually picked her up that she projectile-vomited. Then straight away her temperature started to drop and so we were saved from taking the trip because really, the chances of getting through were pretty slim, with the water being right up.

The main waterways we had to deal with were Middle Creek, the Douglas River and Hayes Creek. Oh that's right, another story about the wet. See the little settlement of Hayes Creek had a pub and one Easter weekend, not long after Jules had been born, we decided to go into Hayes Creek for a few drinks. We headed off early one morning and we managed to get through a couple of the creeks but, as we were trying to get through the next one, the short wheelbase Toyota got stuck and, when we tried to turn it around, it stopped, and then it started to sink. That was pretty scary because with the water rushing by so fast I couldn't even stand up and so my husband and the feller who was in with us, they had to help me get out of the vehicle. Anyhow, they got me over onto the bank. Then they went back and they carried the bassinet, with Jules in it, over.

'Right,' they said, 'you stay here while we walk back to the station and get help to try and pull the vehicle out of the water.'

'Okay.' And so I sat there, and I sat there and I ended up sitting there the whole day, waiting for them to return. I remember I had my tobacco and papers lying out so they'd dry and I had Jules' milk bottles in the creek, to keep them cool. And even though I was in the shade and I had wet nappies over the bassinet, Jules still got sunburnt and she came out in blisters. Anyhow the men didn't get back till about 5 o'clock. But the bit I didn't hear about — not until much later anyway — was that when the men got over to Douglas they got on the grog, didn't they? They just told me it took them that long to get there and back and I was silly enough to believe them.

But I can't really go into too much detail about the Pine Creek school because, like I said, the children only got there 'whenever' and when they did I only came in and dropped them off and drove back out to Douglas Daly, then returned in the afternoon to pick them up again. But they had students coming in from everywhere to go to that school. I've still got some class photos and only about half of them were white kids. A lot of them were Indigenous or part-Aboriginal, then there were also a few Asian kids. Elaine Gano, she was one of the teachers. She spent many years at the school, then after she retired she stayed on and got on the council and both her and her husband were very involved in tourism.

Oh, now I do remember one sort of funny thing: I didn't normally buy my kids treats, but I did this one day. I bought them some chewy; you know, chewing gum. So we were driving home from school and the kids had their windows open and they were having a great time of it. Anyway, Jules had very fine hair and of course with the window down and her hair flying everywhere, all the chewy got stuck in her hair, didn't it? And I just could not get the stuff out. Oh, it was stuck everywhere. I just about had to shave her head.

Anyway, by about 1981 I thought, No, this is not good. They're hardly getting to school, and my marriage wasn't going too well either. Then some people who lived out on a tin mine near Pine Creek, they decided to move down to Tennant Creek so that their kids could get a better education. So yeah, I guess that helped make up my mind and so I came down to Tennant, and the kids all ended up learning how to read and write and do their arithmetic and all that. And they've all grown up well and with good jobs, and they're happy. So I guess everything worked out okay. But we've still got a lot of ties with Pine Creek; Jules especially. Only just the other day she went to a big wake that they had up there.

Welcome to Marble Bar
In memory of John Cox

In the 1970s I went up to teach in the Pilbara region, up in the north-west of Western Australia, at a place called Marble Bar. You may already be aware that Marble Bar has the reputation of being one of the hottest places in Australia, if not the world. In fact, back the early 1920s, Marble Bar set a world record of having something like a hundred and sixty consecutive days where the maximum temperatures reached a hundred degrees Fahrenheit or more. That equates to it being thirty-eight degrees Celsius or greater.

By that stage of our lives Nancy and I had three sons — the eldest being at boarding school — and I can still recall the day of our arrival at Marble Bar. In fact, it's etched in my memory. To start with Nancy, myself and the two boys that we still had living with us caught a 6 a.m. flight from Perth up to Port Hedland. At Port Hedland we changed into a smaller plane and we flew the remaining hundred and fifty miles or so out to Marble Bar. It was hot — stinking hot, actually. The place was certainly living up to its reputation.

After we landed, most of the other people that had been on the same flight were met by friends and so forth. Then a taxi came along and picked up two young lady teachers who'd also flown in from Port Hedland with us. 'See you later,' we said, then we waited for the taxi to come back out. And we waited, and we waited, but still no sign. So there's the four of us, standing out under the shade of the wing of this small aeroplane, trying to escape the blazing heat, waiting for a taxi that didn't turn up.

Anyhow, finally we managed to get in contact with somebody in town and they came out and gave us a lift into Marble Bar.

So we got into town and we'd been told that the key to the school residence would be waiting for us at the store. We went to the store. No one was there. The store was shut. At that stage we hadn't realised that most of Marble Bar had a siesta time from one until three of an afternoon, so we were once more left to stand around in the heat. Anyhow the storekeeper finally turns up and we get the key and we go over to the school residence.

As with all school housing, the place was only partly furnished. It had a couple of beds, a fridge, a table and chairs and a lounge — just the basics — then you had to provide the more personal items, like your bedding and your linen, the crockery and things like that. Now, we'd previously sent all that stuff up by ship, from Perth; it was to be unloaded at Port Hedland and brought out to Marble Bar. The only trouble was, when we arrived at the school residence none of our personal gear was there. Not a skerrick, and we only found out later that, with it being the wet season, the cyclones out along the coastline had slowed the shipping down. Actually, now I think about it, I think our gear had already arrived in Port Hedland but it hadn't been brought out as yet.

When we opened up the school residence it was in a mess. It was filthy. It definitely needed a decent clean before anyone could have slept in the place. It fact the whole design of the house was wrong. I can only surmise that someone from down south must've just taken a look on a map, drawn a latitudinal line across Australia, and decided that Marble Bar was in a cyclone zone. So that's how they designed it. The residence was built up on stilts. There was no air-conditioning. There were no glass windows, just timber shutters that you had to push out and clip into place with an iron bar. Of course, these types of shutters were not only dangerously hard to manoeuvre but they also allowed all the red dust and the insects to infiltrate the place.

Time was getting on by that stage so I decided the best option was to go down to the local hotel — the Ironclad — to buy the family a much-needed drink and while I was there I'd have a look around at what the accommodation was like. My thinking was that perhaps we might be able to stay the night at the pub then tackle the rest of our problems the following day. Off I went, only to arrive outside the Ironclad to find an enthusiastic group of barrackers, cheering on a couple of brawling Aboriginal women. Definitely not the family atmosphere I'd been hoping for.

Next option was the staffroom in the school building. Perhaps that would provide a safer refuge for the night, and a place where we might be able to get a drink of water and have a cup of tea. Back to the school I went. At least the staffroom was a bit cleaner but, of course, we were still without mattresses or linen. Actually, I wasn't worried too much about bedding. It was still far too hot for sheets anyway. By now we just wanted to have something comfortable to lie on. After the day we'd had, sleep would be no problem.

And that's when our luck changed. I just happened to run into a chap. I think he was the local plumber or something. He was all smiles and cheer and when I introduced myself as being the 'newly arrived headmaster of the school' the first thing he said was, 'Welcome to Marble Bar. You're lucky that you arrived while we're having a cool change.'

'What do you mean by a cool change?' I said.

'Well,' he said, 'it's only a hundred and six degrees Fahrenheit.'

That's over forty degrees Celsius.

Great, I thought.

But anyway this chap had a ute and when I told him of our situation he said, 'Look I might be able to find some mattresses for you.'

'Good.'

So he very kindly drove off and I think he managed to borrow a couple of mattresses from the local hostel or wherever, and so we ended up sleeping the first night on the floor at the school; and that was our introduction to Marble Bar.

Back in the 1970s Marble Bar had a population of around three hundred and fifty. At that time there was a great move to explore the country around the Pilbara region for possible gold deposits. A tin mine was already well established, plus there were a couple of other mines around the place. The main gold mine was quite an historic old mine known as the Comet Mine. The Comet Mine was about twenty miles out of town. Now as it turned out, once a month, these mining companies would take it in turns to put on a meal for the community. That was a wonderful treat for everyone because it became quite competitive as to which mining company could lay on the best meal.

Oh, and just one little story about an occasion I had at one of these meals: it was being held out at one of the camps and the mining company had put in an improvised swimming pool. As you may imagine, the gathering was largely male. As usual it was hot and so a fair bit of grog was being consumed. But there was this slim, smallish young lady there. A geologist she was, with one of the mining companies. As it happened I was standing next to this young lady just as one of these big burly blokes boasted to his mates, 'I reckon it'd be a good idea if we threw that geologist sheila in ter the swimming pool, ay?'

The young geologist must've also heard the comment because she turned around and said very quietly to the chap, 'Look before you do that, I just need to let you know a couple of things: firstly, I wouldn't like to be thrown into the pool, thank you very much, and secondly, I am a black-belt holder in jujitsu.'

And that defused the situation pretty quick, I can tell you.

'Sorry, Miss,' replied the bloke. 'Only jokin'.'

But we had many wonderful times there, at Marble Bar. The school buildings weren't up on stilts, like the residence was. They were built more along city lines. There was a line of three classrooms, with a breezeway in between. We had water tanks at each end for drinking water. Then separate from the main schoolrooms was a prefabricated pavilion that had been, as we used the term, 'sent up from the coast'. I'd say there were about a hundred and thirty children at the school. They were aged between six and fifteen, and the interesting thing about that was, there was such an accumulation of kids from all different sorts of backgrounds. Only about twenty per cent were white children. They were the sons and daughters of the service people to the town; people like the postmaster, the clerk of courts, the shire clerk and so forth. It was expected that, when they were old enough, they'd leave Marble Bar and go off to one of the boarding schools in Perth where they'd attain a higher standard of education before going on to university or wherever.

So that was the white kids. Now I'll use just the ordinary, common-day terms here because that was how we described them back in those days. Other than the white kids there was also a group of children who were known as being 'half-castes'. They were half-white and half-black. Then there was another small group of Aboriginal kiddies who had oriental features. Rounding out the school population was a group of full-blooded Aboriginal kids who'd been brought in from the bush to attend the school. They came in from as far away as Jigalong Community and other such places over that way, and they stayed in a government hostel that was run by an elderly couple in their sixties. This couple had been missionary people before coming to live in Marble Bar so they knew the Aboriginal kids very well. They had the kids' trust, which was very important because you never got anywhere with Aboriginal children until they trusted you. But the thing that really did surprise me was that some of these full-blooded Aborigines had never been in a room of any type before, let alone a classroom. So it was our job to make sure that they became comfortable within these new surroundings and that the curriculum was varied enough in order make education meaningful for them. Sometimes it even had to be unorthodox.

I'll give you an instance of that: there was one young full-blooded Aboriginal girl who was about twelve. Her name was Katerina. She came in from the bush. Actually, I first saw her arriving in town with her father. I just happened to be down the street for some reason or other and there she was, this very slight girl, carrying a billycan of water and walking along with her dad. Before arriving in Marble Bar, Katerina had lived out in the open spaces, on the bare ground and, like all of these Aboriginal kiddies, she would speak in such a shy whisper that you'd have difficulty hearing what she was saying. And she never looked you in the eye. None of the Aboriginal kiddies did. But oh, when this Katerina got upset, she was a very fiery girl at times. I'd heard she'd once bitten a chunk out of a welfare officer. Then she had a glass eye which she'd take out and throw at anyone who annoyed her.

The story with the missing eye came about after she'd apparently copped a stone or something during a family dispute, and that's how she lost it. But, like so many, Katerina had never been in any sort of room or classroom before. She didn't know her numbers. She didn't know her colours. I mean, I could show her a blue pencil or whatever and say, 'This is the colour blue,' but it wouldn't have meant anything to her. Maybe she would have her own Aboriginal word for it, but she didn't understand it in the English language.

Anyhow the previous headmaster at Marble Bar had set up one of the walls in the staffroom/kitchen area with a small library and he'd arranged it according to the Dewey Decimal System. As you may well know, the Dewey Decimal System uses both numbers and coloured dots to categorise books. So I'd mix all the books up before class then I'd show Katerina a book and I'd say, 'This little dot is blue. Look at the colour.' She'd look at the coloured dot. Then she might have also had a bit of blue on her dress, so I'd point to the blue on her dress and I'd say, 'That's also the colour blue.' She'd give a slight nod as if to say she understood what I was saying, then I'd say, 'Okay, Katerina, I would now like you to put all the books that have blue dots together.'

And eventually she could do that. So she learnt her colours more in a visual sense, rather than just by name. Then because the Dewey Decimal System depended on numbers from 1 to 10, I did the same with the numbers, and that also worked. It took time, yes, but it worked.

But once you got their trust, those Aboriginal kids were just absolutely delightful and, I must say, they were also extremely insightful. I remember the time we were going off to Goldsworthy for a sports day. Goldsworthy was about seventy miles away. We were in the school bus, and halfway there we had a comfort stop and the bus driver said, 'Right-o, boys off to the right. Girls off to the left.'

Off they went and I said to the driver, 'God, we'll never see them again.'

'Don't worry,' he said. 'When I blow the horn, they'll come back.'

And they did. And the magic of it was; here we were out in the centre of this barren, dry, dusty landscape and nearly all of them brought back something to show us. I remember one young fellow, he showed me a string bean looking sort of thing. Actually it looked pretty much like the beans you buy in a shop. He'd picked it off a bush and he said to me, he said, 'My people use this to clean their hands,' and he rubbed it into his hands and it foamed up just like soap.

Then another kiddie came up and she was holding out a different plant. She said, 'My people use this if they get sick stomachs.'

It was wonderful. Miles out in the middle of nowhere and here were these Aboriginal children teaching me, their teacher, about all these amazing things. Actually, Nancy and I were only saying the other night just how privileged we've been to have gone to some of these places like Marble Bar because, in doing so, our lives have been so enriched by the experience. Absolutely.

So that was Marble Bar. It was another wonderful time for both of us, though I might just add that we did have a couple of close shaves. For instance, one particular afternoon a load of sand arrived. It was going to be used in the jumping pit for our Marble Bar school sports day. Then that evening I'd been working late up at the school and as I was about to walk back home, there in the dim light, I saw this fat, squat, reptile-looking thing laying on the door stop. Initially I thought it might be just some sort of lizard or what have you. I was just about to move it out of my way with a flick of my foot when I saw a builder fellow who was down at the end of the building. Anyhow I called out to the chap, 'Hey, come and have a look at this.'

So he came up to take a look. Now he must've somehow had a shovel with him because, next thing it's — 'THWACK — THWACK — THWACK' — and he's killed it.

'You have no idea how fortunate you are,' he said.

'Why's that?' I asked.

'Because that was a death adder.'

We'll Send for Clarry

Over the couple of years that I was at my first one-teacher school, student numbers fell from fifteen down to about nine, and it had to average nine to exist. So I don't know whether it was foolish of me or not but, when the school inspector came through, I said, 'Would you suggest that I might benefit from being in a place with more children?' Anyhow he wrote that in the report and so perhaps that was the basis of me being dispatched to another one-teacher school where the student numbers were well above nine and the wintertime temperatures used to fall so low that they boasted about how the ink in the ink wells froze.

That school was Hazelgrove, about five miles out of Oberon, in New South Wales.

When I first arrived, I boarded out on a property. It was basically a sheep stud along with annual crops of spuds and peas. Mind you, they also had a beautiful setting for their outside toilet. It was the usual pit type, but the husband wasn't the keenest of handymen so the toilet door was perpetually left hanging in an open position. This dunny faced the west and by gee there was a delightful view of the valley. Great sunsets. In summer it was fantastic but in winter you had to scrape the snow off the seat before you sat down. And that was a very sobering experience I can tell you.

Anyhow, their house was at the bottom of a steep hill and to get out of the property you had to drive up a pretty rugged track that was full of ruts and gutters and so forth. At that time I had a little Hillman Minx and from a cold start, off I'd go and the car would skid and slip and it would cough and on quite a few occasions it would cut out and I'd end up down the bottom again. Consequently I'd end up having to walk the four or five miles to school. So after a few months I said to the people I was boarding with, 'Thank you very much but I think I'd be better off if I move into town, closer to the school.'

As it happened, on the day I was to move, it snowed and, of course, the little Hillman just would not make it to the top. I then worked out a system where I sort of zigzagged sideways up the hill. What I'd do was, I'd go up a little way, then I'd reverse sideways across the hill in the opposite direction, go up a little way further, repeat the process, and so on and so forth. In doing so I found that, if I also stood beside the Hillman, with the driver's door open and my left foot on the accelerator pedal, and pushed with my right leg and my shoulder, virtually scooter-style, I could make some progress. So I zigzagged and I zigzagged and I pushed and I pushed the thing and I suppose it took me twenty minutes or more to go the mile out to the front gate. But I eventually got there, and I found that in town, after I'd finished school, it was a different world. I played a bit of tennis, that sort of thing, and joined in on more community-based activities.

Hazelgrove occasionally had up to forty-two children on the roll. In those days if you averaged over thirty-five it then became a two-teacher school. With me being trained to teach only at one-teacher schools I would normally have been moved on and Hazelgrove would've become a two-teacher school. But I was sort of lucky in that there were a number of itinerant workers in the area, potato and pea picking, so I averaged a bit less than thirty-five; and they were tough little kids. Difficult at times, though excellent at sport. If you dared leave your crease during a game of cricket, they'd throw the stumps down in a flash, and all from thirty metres. So you had to be on your toes. But it was a lovely community, very friendly, and on many a long winter's night I would be invited into one of the homes on a Friday and we'd sit around the wireless and listen to the Test match in England.

Summertime also had its experiences. I recall a time with a couple of these little 'toughies' at the school. One particular summer a fellow from Oberon said to me, 'Why don't you bring the children in for swimming lessons at our local council pool?'

That was a good idea and so I did it all officially and at 2 o'clock every weekday I shut the school and we all went into Oberon. Some of the students travelled in the school bus — a panel van with two long stool-seats in it — and a few of the parents ferried the rest into town. Now to describe Oberon pool as it was back then, I'd say it had a certain green tinge to it that most probably would've kept tadpoles alive. Anyhow, this day, I lined all these little kids up along the edge and I said, 'Right, in the water,' and into the pool they went, and I with them.

Now among all these tough little nuts there were two twelve-year-olds; oh, and they were the toughest of the bunch. Real little troublemakers at times, they were. Unbeknown to me, they'd never been in water above their heads before and so, all of a sudden, there was this frantic thrashing of limbs and so forth. At first I thought they were going to drown but then, in sheer panic, they grabbed onto me. At that moment I'm sure they felt that their lives were in my hands, and for the briefest flash I felt like saying to them, 'So, are you sorry for being nasty to me, or not?'

Another thing about Hazelgrove was that, as well as having your usual Protestants and Catholics and so on, there were also families of Seventh Day Adventists. That caused a slight problem in as much as, whenever we had a working bee, the working bee had to be done twice: once on the Saturday because the Protestants and the Catholics went to church on the Sunday; then you'd have to have another working bee on the Sunday because the Seventh Day Adventists couldn't make it on the Saturday. Actually, I think we built the tennis court twice.

But as in most of those small bush towns you had your real characters. One such fellow ran the local post office and each afternoon, when I went down there to pick up the mail, I'd stay and have a chat with him. I imagined him to be a bit like Mark Twain; you know, with a large walrus moustache and he was also a heavy smoker. This was back in the days of the party line. Are you familiar with the party-line system? That's where the one telephone line is strung out and used by a number of people. You know, the call would come in to the telephone exchange and the post office and it would be patched through along the party line where one ring was the signal for the Smiths, two for the Browns and so on. The downside there was that everyone along that one telephone line — including the person at the telephone exchange — could listen in on everyone else's conversations. Anyhow we'd be talking away and if the phone rang this fellow would say, 'Come on inside, John, and warm yourself by the fire.'

In essence that offer was done so that he could listen in on the party line. And he didn't miss a beat; though, with being such a heavy smoker, he had this hacking smoker's cough and many were the times he missed turning the phone off before he could cover his cough. So everybody knew he was listening in, anyway.

A couple of other great characters at Hazelgrove were the people I boarded with in town, Clarry and his wife. Clarry was the local undertaker and he drove an ancient hearse. Other than being the local undertaker, Clarry also ran a small property down the hill. Anyhow, Clarry and his wife were devout Catholics and whenever I found myself at the kitchen table having a cuppa while the Catholic priest had dropped by, Clarry's wife would always say, 'Come on, Father, try to convert him.'

But the thing I was going to tell you was: my room was out on the enclosed verandah section of the house and one morning I was woken by this 'BUMP ... BUMP ... BUMP'. So I looked out the window and there's Clarry carrying an empty coffin under the verandah.

'What are you doing?' I asked.

'Oh, this is where I keep all my coffins,' was Clarry's reply, and so that's when I found out that I was sleeping just above Clarry's empty coffins, which I must say was a touch unnerving.

Then there was the time when the local council engineer — Barry — was also boarding in the house and when Clarry saw us this day he said, 'Can any of you blokes write signs? I've got to put this bloke's name on a coffin.' We must've looked quite shocked at this suggestion because before we could answer he said, 'Oh, don't worry, I'll just scratch it out with a nail.'

So that was Clarry. A real character. I remember when Barry hadn't been feeling too well. Well, to be honest, he was as crook as a dog. Now I don't know what was wrong with him but he'd been sick in bed for a couple of days and one morning Clarry's wife said to me, 'Oh, John, would you mind going in and waking up Barry for breakfast?' Then she gave it some thought and added, 'But, John, if you see that he's looking a little pale and peaceful, just tiptoe out and we'll send for Clarry.'